# THE PARK SYNAGOGUE

3300 MAYFIELD ROAD | CLEVELAND HEIGHTS, OHIO 44118

Presented By ~~DR. & MRS. HAROLD KLEIN~~

In Memory of ~~MINNIE KLEIN~~

KRAVITZ
MEMORIAL LIBRARY

MARCH
1996

# TURNING
## — *to* —
# TORAH

# TURNING

## — *to* —

# TORAH

## The Emerging
## Noachide Movement

Kimberly E. Hanke

JASON ARONSON INC.
*Northvale, New Jersey*
**London**

**Library of Congress Cataloging-in-Publication Data**

Hanke, Kimberly E.
    Turning to Torah : the emerging Noachide movement / Kimberly E. Hanke
        p.  cm.
      ISBN 1-56821-500-2 (softcover : alk. paper)
      1. Hanke, Kimberly E.  2. Noahides—United States—Biography.
    3. Spiritual biography—United States.  4. Noahides.  5. Noahide
    Laws.  6. Christianity—Controversial literature.  7. Christianity
    and antisemitism.  I. Title.
    BP605.N63F46   1995
    299'.93—dc20                       95-18664

Manufactured in the United States of America. Jason Aronson Inc. offers books and cassettes. For information and catalog write to Jason Aronson Inc., 230 Livingston Street, Northvale, New Jersey 07647.

To my daughter
Alecia

whose love and encouragement
has sustained me

and whose generation
I hope this work will benefit

# CONTENTS

## PART II
## ONE NOACHIDE'S JOURNEY

# PREFACE

In 1989 I set out to write a book for Gentiles who were searching for the truths of Torah. At that point, I was overwhelmed by how misinformed and therefore easily misguided most of the Gentile world was regarding the Bible. However, it has only been in the past year that my study of Torah has made it apparent how little I know. One year from now I may be even more humbled.

But as a dear friend of mine has repeatedly cautioned me, "You must talk to people where they are." And a Noachide leader told me that there is a great need for books to aid the ex-Christian and new Noachide as they begin on this Torah path. Part II of this book, "One Noachide's Journey," was written for this purpose. Please keep in mind that my understanding of Torah as expressed throughout this narrative is that of a Gentile just starting on the path, not that of a learned rabbi.

Part I was written to inform anyone interested in the Noachide movement. The Noachide Laws date to Noah's ark and before, but a dynamic, widespread movement did not begin until recently. Most Noachide groups were not even aware that like-minded groups existed until 1991 when the *Wall Street Journal* published an article on the subject.

This book will not tell you exactly what the Noachide movement is all about, because the movement has not yet developed to such a point of clarity. Rabbis are struggling to meet the needs of thousands of new Noachides. We are witnessing the true emergence of a movement, not a new religion, but rather an existing Torah religion that is newly practiced. This is an unfolding of God's plan in the fullest sense.

This movement is a tandem hang glider shared by Jews and Gentiles. We may enjoy each thermal that allows us to soar together. But we must also be constantly wary of every shift in heat and wind that threatens to thrust us downward.

I invite you to take hold; the winds are right today.

# INTRODUCTION

In the early 1980s, Rabbi Menachem Schneerson, Rebbe of the Lubavitch chasidic Jewish community, announced that Jews must study the ancient Noadic Covenant and so prepare themselves. Rabbi Israel Chait, dean of B'nai Torah Yeshiva in Far Rockaway, New York, began teaching his students in the mid-1970s to study the Noachide Laws because Gentiles would soon be coming to them for teaching. Rabbi Chait had learned this from his teacher, Rabbi Joseph Soloveitchik. A prophecy was about to be fulfilled.

> Thus said the LORD of Hosts: In those days, ten men from nations of every tongue will take hold—they will take hold of every Jew by a corner of his cloak and say, "Let us go with you, for we have heard that God is with you." (Zechariah 8:23)[1]

Many Orthodox Jews took this message to heart and began to study the Seven Laws of Noah. In 1981, Z. Berman Books of Brooklyn, New York, published a book by Aaron Lichtenstein entitled *The Seven Laws of Noah*. In 1983, the Edwin Mellen Press published David Novak's

*The Image of the Non-Jew in Judaism.* In 1987, Targum Press published *The Path of the Righteous Gentile—An Introduction to the Seven Laws of the Children of Noah* by Chaim Clorfene and Yakov Rogalsky. The Jewish community had begun preparations.

In 1988, I called a rabbi at the local Orthodox synagogue and asked, "What can you tell me about the Noadic Covenant?" "Where did you hear of this obscure text?" was the reply.

From every corner of the world—Europe, the Philippines, Nigeria, the United States—Gentiles began contacting rabbis. They had the following three things in common:

1. a love for the God of Israel
2. a desire to follow instructions God gave Gentiles
3. a certainty that they were alone in their beliefs

For nearly two thousand years Christian doctrine has been defined as being diametrically opposed to the doctrines of Judaism. Yet today, thousands of Christians have left the Christian faith to embrace a Torah faith taught by Orthodox rabbis. Such a radical transformation is an enigma and a curiosity to the secular media[2], the Jewish community, Christians, and oddly enough, even to these new Noachides (pronounced No-a-kides).

> The LORD said to Abram, "Go forth from your native land and from your father's house to the land that I will show you." (Genesis 12:1)[3]

To follow God, Abram had to go out of Ur. Like Abram, these Gentiles had to leave the faith of their fathers, friends, and co-workers. They had studied Jesus and their Christian Bibles and yet came away with a pure monotheism that was new to them—and frightening. This new-found perspective on God radically altered how they read their Bibles. Their Christian friends, pastors, and priests did not share this enlightened view. The ex-Christian found him- or herself alone just as Abram must have felt as he came out of Ur.

As these non-Jews continued their studies, they stumbled onto Judaism and found the perspective of Orthodox Judaism to be in keeping with their new beliefs. Finally, they had found a community of religious people who viewed God as they did. Yet, rather than reaching the end of a quest for spiritual truth, their meeting with the rabbis began a journey in tandem with the Jewish community.

Israel was instructed to be a light unto the nations. The nations, one individual at a time, have begun to recognize that light and cling to it. The prophecy in Zechariah 8:23 is indeed being fulfilled today.

While interviewing Noachides at the Seventh Annual B'nai Noach Conference, I discovered that they were not simply disgruntled Christians angry with a few hypocritical leaders. Nor had they intentionally rebelled from their Christian faith. Most had been raised in the church: their families, friends, and social life all had centered on the Christian community. Families were torn apart as spouses could not accept these new beliefs. I found that Noachides are not Gentiles in childish rebellion against Christianity but rather individuals who have grasped pure monotheism in a sea of idolatry and then cried because this new revelation separated them from the people and culture they had always known and loved.

Rabbis and other Orthodox Jews study God's ancient instructions to Gentiles, scrambling at times for answers to the myriad of questions posed by B'nai Noach. Though excited to fulfill God's instruction to be a "light unto the nations," they remain fearful. Gentiles have a long history of approaching the Jewish community and eventually attacking them spiritually, physically, or both. This conflict became apparent during a session at the B'nai Noach Conference.

A large bearded man boomed from the pulpit, "I could not thank you enough for the tremendous amount of time and energy you have expended on our behalf. You have probably invested more time with us (Noachides) than any other rabbi. But I get angry, as do many who heard you, when you make statements such as 'I don't want my children to play with your children.'"

The Orthodox Jewish man to whom these words were directed sat in a pew a dozen rows from the podium. His eyes were sad as he responded, "I'm just being honest about my feelings. Of all the rabbis here, perhaps I have been the most open about my true feelings."

Seven years of study and experience including two trips to Israel enabled me to empathize with both viewpoints. Until this point in the conference, I had emotionally kept my distance as though the movement was not mine.

A woman seated in the pew directly behind me warned, "The rabbis won't be back next year, not if we keep making it so difficult for them."

The mere possibility of that happening compelled me to quickly walk to the front of the assembly hall after the speaker had finished. I joined the group of rabbis who stood close together discussing the heated confrontation we had all just witnessed. I waited for a lull in the conversation.

"I want to thank you for hanging in here through these difficulties." Suddenly, I felt my impartial writer shell fall away, and my voice break as I appealed to them, "We need you. These are only birth pains."

The rabbis fell silent and stared at me for a moment. Then they quickly reassured me of their commitment to the Noachides.

Shortly thereafter, the eldest rabbi spoke from the pulpit. He was deeply moved, he said, that like Abraham we each possessed the strength of character to come out from an idolatrous culture. He was in awe of the personal sacrifices each of us had made, and he felt that the rabbis' sacrifices made in support of the movement paled in comparison. This man was well respected by his fellow rabbis and by local Gentile leaders of the Noachide movement. His wealth of knowledge and his compassion for each person involved became obvious to me as I heard him speak and later as I watched him interact with individuals at the conference. I breathed a sigh of relief to realize our movement was being guided by such leaders.

J. David Davis, leader of the largest known B'nai Noach congregation, recently said to me, "There is no such thing as pure B'nai Noach."

The movement today has not developed to such a point of purity. And I also relate this statement to our Jewish partners on this tandem hang glider called Torah faith: is there such a thing as pure Judaism? We are all growing.

*Turning to Torah* is the story of the Noachide movement and the people who have committed themselves to it, both Jews and Gentiles, past and present. Together we study the Bible and obey as we learn. And together we unravel and at the same time fulfill the mysteries of the Torah God gave us.

# I

# THE NOACHIDE MOVEMENT

# 1

# MODERN-DAY JEWISH ORIGINS

Although the Noachide Laws have been in existence since the days of Noah, their study has been neglected among most Jewish people since their inception. The reason is simple: the Seven Laws do not apply to Jewish people. They apply only to non-Jews. In an age of mass assimilation, the need for Jewish people to study Torah for application to their own lives is great and Torah scholars are few. Therefore, the question of the day is not why the Noachide Laws have been neglected but rather why rabbinic leaders are suddenly focusing attention on them.

First, Torah instructs Israel to be "a light unto the nations"—to Gentiles. Some have tried to perform this *mitzvah* by living a Torah-based life. And indeed we Gentiles have witnessed loving families and close Jewish communities. But we have seen this Torah-based life as a separation, as a culture and a religion not only different from us but a people not interested in including us in their world. Their light seemed only to be for their benefit, not ours.

I have come to realize that this separation is not Jewish initiated, but rather is observance of God's Torah instructions. I appreciate the fact that if there were no observant Jewish people, the light of Torah would not be available to me today. For this reason, all Noachides encourage Jewish people to be Torah observant. After all, who will teach us the Seven Laws if Torah has been abandoned?

Being a light in this way—observing Torah—has not previously been interpreted, at least not in practice, to include reaching out to Gentiles with Torah teachings. The de-emphasis on outreach to Gentiles is understandable, however. Jews have always been persecuted for being different. Merely being Jewish, let alone living an obviously observant lifestyle, has consistently provoked Gentiles to act against Jewish people. Reaching out to teach Torah laws that pertain to the non-Jewish populace has simply been too dangerous to consider.

Some rabbis see this danger as having substantially subsided today, especially in the United States. The lack of persecution gives many rabbis a reason to feel safe in offering to teach the Seven Laws. But this new safety cannot fully explain the modern willingness to teach Torah to Gentiles. After all, the Golden Age of Judaism directly preceded the Spanish Inquisition.

Renewed messianic fervor is another theory offered to explain some rabbis' current willingness to teach the Seven Laws. Many Orthodox Jews believe that before *Moshiach* (Messiah) can come, not only must Jews be observing Torah but Gentiles must also be observing their portion of Torah: the Seven Laws. Perhaps the atmosphere of messianic fervor in the first century was the compelling factor causing Jews to reach out to Gentiles in Jesus' time. Recognizing that this outreach spawned nearly two thousand years of intense Jewish persecution, however, messianic fervor alone could not serve as sufficient reason to reach out to Gentiles at this time.

There is yet another reason for rabbis to fear teaching Gentiles. Though society is more tolerant of the Jewish people today, most Jewish people are not tolerant of rabbis who perform this *mitzvah* of teaching Gentiles. The pressure imposed on these rabbis is considerable and the many reasons for this lack of tolerance are discussed later.

No reason mentioned here is sufficient to explain the timing of the current outreach of Torah teaching to Gentiles. Motivations for fearing and avoiding the non-Jewish world remain as compelling as ever. I cannot explain why modern rabbis urged their students to begin studying the Noachide Laws in preparation for Gentiles who would be coming to them. I only know that they were correct to do so. The time has come. In unprecedented numbers Gentiles have begun to seek out rabbis, asking them, "What does the God of Israel have for us?" And thankfully, some Torah-observant Jews have summoned the courage to overcome their fears and begin teaching us.

Current rabbinic involvement has even reached the level of the Chief Rabbi of Israel, HaRav Mordechai Eliahu. He has endorsed a booklet written by two rabbis entitled *Suggested Prayers for B'Nai Noah.* Encouragement from this rabbinic level has been crucial to both Jews and Gentiles in the Noachide movement.

Bar-Ilan Center in Jerusalem has begun to offer Noachide studies for Gentiles. To be admitted, prospective students must come with letters of recommendation from an Orthodox rabbi and a recognized leader in the Noachide movement. Studies include classes on the Hebrew language, Bible, selected talmudic passages, the Land of Israel, the Principles of Faith, history, and archaeology. This is a wonderful new door open to Noachides.

Annual U.S. Noachide conferences include rabbis as well as Jewish lay people from Orthodox *yeshivahs* and even chasidic rabbis. These teachers come from many areas in the United States and Israel to teach as much as they can in the limited time they can offer. In addition, the first worldwide Noachide conference was held in Jerusalem in the fall of 1993.

Scattered around the country, small groups of Noachides meet in homes. Some groups, like my own, are fortunate enough to have a local Orthodox rabbi who teaches on a weekly basis. Other groups gather around a telephone each week to receive their rabbinic teaching via long distance. The majority of Noachides, however, rely on the mail to bring them whatever reading material they can find. This material includes articles appearing in *The Gap*, a monthly newsletter published by Emmanuel, a large Noachide group in Athens, Tennessee, which serves as a clearinghouse for information.

*The Root and Branch Noahide Guide* is a book published in Jerusalem by an organization of the same name. This resource explains the Seven Laws and lists organizations, people to contact, books, and cassettes. It also contains reprints of articles written about the movement and transcripts of radio and television coverage of the movement.

### DEVELOPMENT OF THE NOACHIDE MOVEMENT

The movement was conceived, by God, in Noah's time. The incubation period began to intensify approximately fifty years ago when rabbis and their students emphasized the study of the Seven Laws. After Israel's Six-Day War in 1967, Christians began to see Israel as a powerful modern reality, in contrast to their past view of a people who were hanging on to pre-Jesus times. Israel opened up to Christians, who came in droves to see the land, archaeology, and Christian shrines. As a result of all this activity, Christians read their Bibles in a new light. All the elements were in place for the birth of the modern-day Noachide movement.

One of these Christians was a Baptist preacher from Tennessee by the name of J. David Davis. When he studied his Bible with an open mind about Jewish people and their place in God's plan, his beliefs began to change. He shared his views with his congregation and eventually removed the word *church* and the cross from the church building. These actions, occurring in the Bible Belt, were scandalous and highly publicized, starting with an article in the *Wall Street Journal* in March 1991. Although individuals had approached rabbis before this time, the Emmanuel congregation was the largest ex-Christian group known to be making such dramatic changes.

The rabbis who had been making preparations for decades had been waiting for just such an event. Several rabbis called Mr. Davis the day after the article was published. Other articles quickly followed in the *Herald Tribune* (Europe), *Kol Israel*, the *Jerusalem Post* and others, as well as television coverage on *CNN*, *CBS Nightwatch*, and *Larry King Live*. The birth of the modern Noachide movement had finally taken place.

The prophecy of Zechariah 8:23 has begun to be fulfilled in our time. Rabbis, some reluctantly, feel the pulling on the corners of their cloaks. And now that we Gentiles have taken hold, we will not let go.

# 2

# THE SEVEN LAWS

As an unlearned Noachide, the faith of Noah is a bit of a mystery to me—a mystery to study and to live. When I was a Christian, I learned that the Oral Law was a work of fiction by the rabbis of old. Because the Seven Laws are detailed only in this Oral Law (*Sanhedrin* 56a), examining its validity was necessary. As a woman who had experienced the love of God firsthand, I knew He must have loved us Gentiles enough to give us instructions on how to live.

An Orthodox rabbi explained to me how he knew the Oral Law not only to be valid but also that it was given at Sinai simultaneously with the Written Torah. A just God simply would not have given the Torah commandments such as "observe the Sabbath" without telling Israel how to do so. The rabbi gave a thought-provoking example from Moses' time.

When Aaron's sons offered a "strange fire" not commanded in service to God, they were killed by God (Leviticus, chapter 10). Then Moses became angry at Aaron and his remaining sons for not eating of the sin offering as Moses commanded them as priests. But Aaron knew it would not be pleasing to God to obey this command. How

did he know? Aaron was aware of instructions beyond those that
Moses commanded, which would prohibit Aaron and his sons from
eating of this offering: these instructions were in the Oral Torah. Moses
conceded to Aaron's argument.

Many questions about Gentiles must have arisen in Moses's time,
including what to do with them, what they must observe, and how
they must live to be pleasing in God's sight. The Seven Laws of Noah
emerged between the lines of the Written Torah and more fully in
the Oral Law.

The Talmud is rarely studied by Gentiles. Though that is chang-
ing, we Noachides still rely heavily on rabbis to draw the Seven Laws
out of the Talmud and explain them to us. In Aaron Lichtenstein's
work *The Seven Laws of Noah*, he lists the Seven Laws as follows:

1. a prohibition against theft
2. a prohibition against homicide
3. a prohibition against illicit intercourse
4. a prohibition against idolatry
5. a prohibition against blasphemy
6. a prohibition against eating the limb cut from a living creature
7. a positive command to observe justice

It is readily apparent that these laws are merely headings, broad cate-
gories that require explanation and expounding in order to incorporate
them into a Torah-based lifestyle.

The purpose of my book is not to provide talmudic references for
each law. Nor is it to tell one how to obey each commandment. This
work I leave to able rabbis. However, each person must study these
seven areas and apply them to his or her life just as Israel must do
with all 613 instructions God gave specifically to them.

To avoid idolatry, for instance, we must first define idolatry from
the Orthodox view of Torah. Our Christian backgrounds have left us
with such a clouded view of idolatry that we have raised a man—
Jesus—to a position of equality with God without recognizing this as

an act of pure idolatry. Each Noachide must embark on a long and emotionally painful journey to progress from Christianity to pure monotheism.

A Jewish person might well ask, "How could you possibly place a man on the same level as God and *not* recognize this as idolatry?" To this question, I give the same answer I recently offered to a group of Jewish high-school students. Sadly, tradition has a stronger influence than intellectual reason. If one is told from the cradle that there are three gods or godheads, and this not only from parents but from every pastor or preacher, one believes it must be true.

Second, Christianity is a religion of emotion and community. One is drawn to the feeling of love for God and others that a Christian service offers. When you reach the point where you are questioning basic Christian doctrine, especially the deity of Jesus, you are no longer a part of that community. Instead of a feeling of emotional satisfaction, love, and camaraderie in church, you feel out of place. If you have any illusions about belonging there, they are removed when your new views are expressed. The church is a Jesus-deifying community: love it or leave it. Leaving is painful because there is no alternative community to join.

As Noachides, we are constantly learning to view the Torah from an Orthodox perspective. We are unlearning lessons from the church. Therefore, our most important observance as Noachides is the practice of critical thinking. In church we learned to listen and obey. In contrast, rabbis teach us to question everything, to raise all possible questions, until we are satisfied that we understand what Torah is attempting to teach us. As Christians we were expected to remain spiritual children, not questioning authority or tradition. These rabbis who have taken us under their wings encourage us to become spiritual adults studying Torah and searching in earnest for biblical truth.

With the Noachide movement in its infancy, every aspect of worshiping God is examined anew, including prayer. How do we pray? We open a *siddur* and find beautiful prayers, but many only pertain to Jewish people. Regarding prayer in the *siddur*, we Noachides feel like stowaways on the Jewish boat. Which do we read, and which do we avoid? *Suggested Prayers for B'Nai Noah* was designed as a *siddur* substitute. Its fifteen pages pale in comparison to the beauty of the Orthodox *siddur*, and there is no substitute for the communal prayers in a synagogue. But it is a beginning for us Noachides.

The Seven Laws of Noah have had an impact far beyond the hundreds of new Torah-observant Gentiles. In *The Root And Branch Noahide Guide/5752*, the Congressional Record is quoted as follows:

PUBLIC LAW 102–14—MAR 20, 1991

Public Law 102–14                                    H.J. Res 104
102nd Congress

Joint Resolution

To designate March 20, 1991 as "Education Day USA"

Whereas Congress recognizes the historical tradition of ethical values and principles which are the basis of civilized society and upon which our great Nation was founded;

Whereas these ethical values and principles have been the bedrock of society from the dawn of civilization, when they were known as the Seven Noachide Laws;

Whereas without these ethical values and principles the edifice of civilization stands in serious peril of returning to chaos;

Whereas society is profoundly concerned with the recent weakening of these principles that has resulted in crises that beleaguer and threaten the fabric of civilized society;

Whereas the justified preoccupation with these crises must not let the citizens of this Nation lose sight of their responsibility to transmit these historical ethical values from our distinguished past to the generations of the future;

Whereas the Lubavitch movement has fostered and promoted these ethical values and principles throughout the world;

Whereas Rabbi Menachem Mendel Schneerson, leader of the Lubavitch movement, is universally respected and revered and his eighty-ninth birthday falls on March 26, 1991;

Whereas in tribute to this great spiritual leader, "the rebbe", this, his ninetieth year will be seen as one of "education and giving", the year in which we turn to education and charity to return the world to the moral and ethical values contained in the Seven Noachide Laws; and
Whereas this will be reflected in an international scroll of honor signed by the President of the United States and other heads of state; Now, therefore, be it

Resolved by the Senate and House of Representatives of the United States of America in Congress assembled, That March 26, 1991, the start of the ninetieth year of Rabbi Menachem Schneerson, leader of the worldwide Lubavitch movement, is designated as "Education Day, U.S.A.". The President is requested to issue a proclamation calling upon the people of the United States to observe such day with appropriate ceremonies and activities.

Torah Law has finally begun to merge with modern law. The Seven Laws of Noah are quickly emerging from the depths of ancient talmudic pages.

# 3

# ANCIENT BEGINNINGS

Torah reveals that God has given instructions to man since the days of Adam, a Gentile. When I realized this was a critical aspect of a relationship with God, I began to study the chapters in Genesis before the appearance of Abram. I wanted to know what were the beliefs and practices of God-loving people who were not Jewish.

I began with Noah rather than Adam because little information is given regarding Adam's observances or God's opinion of him. Noah was described as "righteous and wholehearted; Noah walked with God." Genesis does not reveal how Noah earned that praise, however.

Not until Genesis, chapter 9, does God begin instructing Noah and his family how to live. A dietary law is introduced in Genesis 9:4 prohibiting Noah (Gentiles) from eating meat from an animal who had not died. From this verse I also see a prohibition against consuming blood. This command was given to Noah and his descendants, not only to Jewish people. Rabbinic authorities, however, exclude the blood prohibition.

As an ex-Christian, I recognized this blood prohibition from the New Testament, Acts, chapter 15, in a letter to Gentile believers. They were instructed not to convert to Judaism, but rather to observe the following: "You are to abstain from food sacrificed to idols, from blood, from the meat of strangled animals, and from sexual immorality."

There was a direct correlation between the instructions given to Noah, a Gentile, and those expected of God-loving Gentiles in the first century. The church, with its belief that the Jewish dietary laws have been canceled, has never acknowledged these dietary laws given to Gentiles in Acts. I realized that the Seven Laws of Noah, at least a portion of them, had been taught to first-century Gentiles. The connection was clear.

When Abram came out of Ur, it seems that all those who went with him converted to his religion with its additional commandments. This conversion is confirmed later when everyone in his household was circumcised.

From this point in Torah on, references to those different from Abram often come in the form of condemnation for their acts. The men of Sodom were condemned as immoral because of their practice of sodomy. Evidently, this sexual practice was prohibited to Gentiles. Later, Gentiles acknowledge fearing God by avoiding adultery. Gentiles are punished for acts of rape, murder, cruelty to animals, and so on. Between the lines I found the Seven Laws of Noah. Gentiles were often punished for transgressing these laws.

My firm belief that God is just leads me to believe that God would not have punished Gentiles for transgressing laws of which they were ignorant. The pharaoh's avoidance of adultery with Sarah was evidence that he did consider adultery to be a prohibition the transgression of which would bring punishment from God.

As I continued to search Torah for references to Noachide life, I began to see how much of Torah pertained only to Abraham and his descendants. Yet, Moses was mindful of how God was perceived by Gentiles. When Moses asked God not to destroy his disobedient people, his reason was that their destruction might be a poor reflection of God in the eyes of Gentiles. Apparently, God performed miracles not only to build the faith of the children of Israel but also so that Gentiles would know that there is but One True God (Exodus, chapter 10). Monotheism was taught to Gentiles in this way from the beginning.

In Torah, righteous acts of Gentiles are noted by saying they "feared God"; when they behaved contrary to the Seven Laws of conduct, it is said that they did not fear God. However, the observance of these laws did not seem to constitute a separate religion. As I read the Bible, the Noachide Laws did not influence God-fearing Gentiles in ancient times to take on specific rituals or practices. Rather, Noachide Law was a simple system of ethics that God-fearers understood to be authored by God and adhered to by those who feared or loved Him.

The only ritual I noticed that Noah performed was a sacrifice after leaving the ark, and God was pleased by this act. Yet, Noah was not commanded to do it. Sacrifices were common rituals in many world religions. Later in Torah, Israel was commanded to offer them, but extensive instructions were given presumably to avoid cruelty to animals (cruelty was common in heathen religious sacrifices). The glaring difference I found was that Israel was commanded to offer sacrifices and Noachides were not.

I found this lack of religious ritual and practice for ancient Noachides to be unsettling. The Seven Laws prohibit idolatry and blasphemy, which are acts against God. However, the remaining laws pertain only to relationships with others. These laws deal in the realm of ethics. A Noachide leaves behind religious beliefs and practices that are contrary to Torah in an effort to embrace monotheism. Yet, other than belief in God and His Torah, which causes us to abhor idolatry and blasphemy, what religious practices are Noachides allotted that would satisfy our religious emotions? Torah seems void of ritual for Gentiles.

Human history teaches us that religious emotion is natural for all peoples. Therefore, Torah study is required to act as a fence around us, guiding the emotions through intellect and teaching us how to love God without falling prey to idolatry and blasphemy in our zest for Him. Noachides study the philosophy of Torah, the reasoning behind the *mitzvot*, although most of the precepts do not apply to us. Torah does not reveal how God-fearing Gentiles in biblical times remained faithful to God without religious practices or if there were religious practices observed by Noachides.

In Leviticus I found that God-fearing Gentiles were living among the Israelites. Leviticus 24:15–16 makes reference to the prohibition of blasphemy. Though these Gentiles were not required to convert to Judaism, if they blasphemed the Name their punishment was identical to that of an Israelite.

At this point I remind the reader that I am not a Torah scholar. My studies are still at the surface level. As a Noachide I have learned to ask a rabbi about these issues and how they apply to Gentiles. Consuming blood, for instance, is this allowed or prohibited to Noachides? What does Talmud say and why?

Throughout Torah it is clear that many Gentiles were observing the Seven Laws. In the New Testament, references were made to Gentile believers and Noachide Laws in contrast to Jewish believers and the Law of Moses. But what happened to Noachides after the first century?

Throughout the ages, Gentiles have recognized the God of Israel as the One True God and attempted to attach themselves to Israel.

Because of intense persecution, rabbis have always been suspicious and fearful of any Gentiles approaching them. If a Gentile was adamant about his or her religious convictions, the rabbi would concede and allow the Gentile to convert to Judaism. Once converted, the Gentile was clearly no threat to the Jewish community. However, any Gentile who approached the Jewish people without converting to Judaism was considered a threat, both physically and spiritually. Evidently, teaching the Noachide Laws was considered too risky.

It was not until 1895 that any written record can be found of a Gentile embracing Torah without converting to Judaism—but rather through the Seven Laws of Noah. This fascinating account was written by Aime Palliere and is entitled *The Unknown Sanctuary*. It has been translated from French to English and published in the United

States. Mr. Palliere was a Zionist before most Jewish people were, and at one time, he served as vice president of the Jewish National Fund of France. Yet he never converted to Judaism. There is an important difference between the Noachism of Palliere and that of Noachides today. Unlike most modern Noachides, Palliere remained in the Catholic Church and in contact with many Christians. At one point, the pope interceded to stop such meetings. Yet, Palliere remained a Christian until his death. He did not consider Jesus to be a deity, denied the incarnation and virgin birth, believed the Torah to be in effect (not canceled), and did not believe Israel would ever be "replaced" by Christians. Under these conditions Rabbi Benamozegh said Palliere could remain in the church. As a non-Jew who loved Israel, monotheism, and Torah, Palliere could help the Jewish people more than if he converted to Judaism.

Palliere lived in Europe from 1875 to 1949, through both world wars and the Holocaust. Clearly, Rabbi Benamozegh was one of the most courageous men to live in that time, to have reached out with Torah to someone in the Catholic Church. And Palliere, living in anti-Semitic Europe while openly teaching Christians to love Jewish people, also was courageous. Their uniqueness is underscored by the fact that Palliere is the only recorded Noachide living in the Christian era before the 1970s.

Palliere learned Hebrew and prayed in the synagogue on a regular basis. Learning the Hebrew language was the door that opened for Palliere the entire Torah. He also attended church services but did not partake of several rituals that he considered idolatrous. In many ways, he studied and prayed as if he converted to Judaism, but he maintained a connection to the church.

Although there were certainly Gentiles who converted to Judaism throughout the ages, and possibly there may have been Noachides as well, not one case except Palliere's has been documented until now.

# 4

# COMING OUT OF UR

Like Abram, every modern Noachide experiences a coming out from an idolatrous culture. The strength and courage of Abram's act cannot be denied or minimized, but in a way, he had an easier task than do modern Noachides. He left his town and people; his entire culture he left behind. This physical separation allowed Abram to purify his monotheism without the constant pressure of dealing with idolatrous people he knew and loved. He brought many people with him who eventually converted to Abram's beliefs. He did not go to work each day with people whose beliefs now offended him. The lack of physical separation from their past is one of the reasons that make the way of the Noachide so difficult today.

In addition, a Noachide does not live as a convert to Judaism. A convert moves from one well-defined culture (Christian) to another (Jewish). Society today recognizes both as legitimate religions. The convert joins an existing, vibrant group complete with countless synagogues, Jewish Community Centers, and Jewish organizations. He or she leaves the church community, but embraces and is embraced by Jewish people in the area. The convert belongs somewhere, with a religious group recognized as valid in society.

Today's Noachides, with few exceptions, have no congregation to join. Most have stayed in their churches for years, never revealing their newfound monotheism, their realization that Christianity's teachings are more in keeping with idolatry than with monotheism. Most were raised in the church. Announcing their new beliefs or refusing communion on religious grounds would risk the loss of family or friends. If they left the church, where would they go? With whom could they find fellowship each week?

Some Jews would immediately say, "Go to the synagogue. Have fellowship with us." This alternative presents numerous problems. When attending synagogue as a potential convert, I felt that although I did not belong at the time, it would eventually be my home, my community. But as I stepped back to accept the instructions God gave to me as a Gentile, I realized that much of the *siddur* simply did not apply to me. And the Jewish response to a Gentile who is not a potential convert visiting a synagogue is that of suspicion. They are afraid a Gentile is there to convert Jews to Christianity.

Then there is the longer-term problem of Noachides socializing with the Jewish community. We may all be part of the Torah community, but there are Torah-mandated differences between us. Gentiles can eat kosher food; that poses no problem. We can certainly study together. But with the Noachide community being so small in number, where will our children meet future mates who believe as they do? Will Jewish and Noachide children grow together and either the Noachides convert to Judaism or both turn away from Torah and intermarry? Clearly, Noachides and their Jewish teachers must be extremely watchful of such potential problems. The Noachide movement is young, but we have begun to see our children grow up and either turn away from religion altogether or turn back to the church when the time for dating comes. We must search for a way to live out these Torah instructions for more than one generation at a time.

From all the Noachides I have met and in all the stories I have heard, this element of loneliness pervades each conversation. Noachides cannot return to Ur once they have begun to grasp Torah monotheism. They reach for God and study His Torah anew, not as the Old Testament, but as a living reality. And somewhere along the line they find that as one hand grasps Torah, the other lets go of the Christian community. Each day they see friends, relatives, and co-workers, the same people they decorated the office Christmas tree with, the same loved ones they sang idolatrous carols about Jesus with, the same people they studied with in church—and now the camaraderie has been replaced by distance.

It may surprise the Jewish reader that very few Noachides I have met feel any reason to blame or condemn Jesus or the Christian church. Each of these Gentiles came to the Noachide Movement through the church and Jesus. The church exposed them to the Torah, albeit with a contorted view, but it was that portion of the Christian Bible that taught the Noachide to view Jewish people more charitably than did the New Testament.

And with most Noachides, if not all, it was their love for Jesus that planted the seed of a love for Israel, its God, and its Scriptures. Deuteronomy 4:19 taught me that as God allotted the sun, the moon, and the stars to all people, each form of idolatry can and does serve as a stepping-stone to faith in God. One cannot condemn the steps taken toward God.

Each Gentile's path from Christianity to Noachism began with questions, study. Not one Noachide I have met intentionally rebelled from the church. As they read the Bible, they began questioning their priests, pastors, and preachers, asking them to please explain the inconsistencies between the Torah and the New Testament. Their love for Jesus and the strong religious emotion taught by the church backfired on the clergy as they tried to explain away passages such as Matthew, chapter 5, where Jesus said:

> Do not think that I have come to abolish the Law or the Prophets; I have not come to abolish them but to fulfill them. I tell you the truth, until heaven and earth disappear, not the smallest letter, not the least stroke of a pen, will by any means disappear from the Law until every-

thing is accomplished. Anyone who breaks one of the least of these commandments and teaches others to do the same will be called least in the kingdom of heaven, but whoever practices and teaches these commands will be called great in the kingdom of heaven.

Many Christians understandably asked whether Jesus was saying here that the Orthodox Jews are called great and the Christians who teach Jews to abandon the Law of Moses must be least.

Another quote from Jesus seems to contain a similar message: "The teachers of the Law and the Pharisees sit in Moses' seat. So you must obey them and do everything they tell you. . ." (Matthew 23:1–3).

In response to this question, Christian clergy found passages in the New Testament that offered different views of Gentiles and Jews, but they did not help the person in the search for truth. Actually, this response served to create a new problem. Before this, the thinking Christian asked the clergy for help in keeping Jesus on the pedestal when Jesus' teachings contradicted those of the church. Now, contradictions were found between the teachings of different New Testament writers, between these writers and Jesus, and even between different teachings attributed to Jesus himself! The Christian began with a plea for help and ended up with the realization that the New Testament is full of contradictions. The logical conclusion was reached: the New Testament could not be Holy Scripture. And once that was realized, the Christian could see that Jesus only called *Tanakh* (Old Testament) Holy Scripture. This was the first step, give or take a few details, that each Christian took to become a Noachide.

The fundamental belief that severs the tie between Christianity and Torah faith (which includes both Judaism and Noachism) is idolatry. After hearing the stories of many Noachides I have come to a realization. I firmly believe that if the Torah view of idolatry was grasped by all those who profess to be monotheists, believers in the one God, both Christianity and Islam would soon disappear. Noachide communities would abound, Jesus and Mohammed would be placed in perspective, and non-observant Jewish people would be able to grasp their own Torah. Monotheism cannot be truly grasped, by the Jew or non-Jew, without a clear understanding of idolatry. Abram knew this. Noachides know it. It is the basic concept, Torah monotheism versus Torah-defined idolatry, that structures the belief of today's Noachides.

Each Noachide came searching for an Orthodox rabbi when he or she reached this basic level of Torah belief. Why not Reform or Conservative rabbis? These ex-Christians were searching for a purity of Torah faith. They were searching for people who not only knew what Torah said, but who lived it. If Torah/Talmud said to wear *tefillin*, they wanted rabbis who taught and observed biblical commandments such as the wearing of *tefillin*. If Torah said do not kindle a flame on the Sabbath, they looked for Jewish people who did not drive their cars on the Sabbath. These ex-Christians had lived a religion of symbolism and emotion, of abandoning and in effect canceling Torah precepts. They did not want to replace it with another religion that was not based on Torah. Noachides strive to live according to Torah, and therefore they settle for nothing less than rabbis who strive to live according to the same Torah.

The religious practices of today's Noachides are difficult to categorize. There are no rituals for Noachides taught in Torah. The Seven Laws merely include six prohibitions and one positive command to maintain justice, which enforces the other six. There are no commands to keep specific rituals, to say specific prayers at specific times, to celebrate certain holy days. We are allowed, according to the rabbis, to practice nearly all of Judaism's rituals we desire as long as we keep in mind that we are not obligated to do them. And to avoid denying the God-mandated difference between Jew and Gentile, if we keep the Sabbath, for instance, we are told to break at least one precept. Torah is silent regarding Noachide rituals and practices.

This silence leaves a huge void in our lives; it leaves us little room for religious expression, little outlet for the religious emotionalism we dearly loved in the church. An Orthodox synagogue service does fill that void, but there are the potential problems that arise when Gentiles worship with Jewish people. An Orthodox man I recently

interviewed said we must sing songs together to keep Noachides fulfilled, and he suggested some beautiful songs we could sing. He also
suggested that, working with rabbis, we institute rituals for Noachides.
But since these rituals are not commanded, there is a danger of Noachides seeing them as mandatory rather than voluntary. Torah warns
against creating a new religion, so we must be careful.

So how have Noachides been living? It is difficult to structure one's
life only on ideas and prohibitions, without positive practices and
rituals. Therefore, Noachides practice one element of Torah: study.
The rabbis are teaching us to question and study, and every Noachide
I have met tries to read all the rabbinic materials he or she can acquire.
Noachides have formed study groups with a rabbi present either in
person or on the telephone. Noachides are starving spiritual children,
and there are simply not enough rabbis to satisfy this appetite for
Torah. But study is a positive way Noachides find to live Torah.

Other than study, Noachides' lifestyles vary dramatically. Because
it is not a structured religion, some Noachides do little religiously
except study and pray. Most Noachides use the Orthodox *siddur* at
least occasionally. Some Noachides still have one foot in the church,
either because they are not emotionally ready to break the tie from
the people they love or because they stay in the church and try to
teach a Torah perspective. A few Noachides observe many of Judaism's
holy days and rituals.

Most, if not all, Noachides have ceased to celebrate the Christian
holidays such as Easter and Christmas. Some people told me they
actually leave home for a week or two at Christmastime to avoid office
Christmas parties or family gatherings. If they had converted to Judaism, they say, their family could understand more easily their abstain-
ing from Christian holidays; without converting, the Noachide is seen
as rebelling against Christianity or religion altogether or as just being
antisocial. It is simply easier to say, "We'll be out of town."

The social ramifications for each Noachide differ based on how
religious (Christian) their family or friends are. Some marriages have
broken up because the spouse could not tolerate the Noachide's

anti-Christian beliefs and lack of Christian practices. Children are hurt and confused if both parents do not become Noachides. And if the nuclear family stays intact, struggles with grandparents, with the power of their emotional Christian beliefs and the church's support, remain. A mixture of love, concern, and fear combines to ignite tempers, because Christians believe that leaving the church ensures the Noachide's eternal damnation. From my experience, it has not been so much intellectual differences that have caused such anger in Christians as it is their emotional responses. Intellectual differences cannot be possible if Christians refuse to participate in a dialogue.

The most powerful example of difficulties that Noachides have had to face comes from Athens, Tennessee. J. David Davis was a Baptist preacher who convinced approximately half his congregants to reject Christianity and embrace the Torah faith as detailed in the Seven Laws of Noah. Situated in the middle of the Southern Bible Belt area of the United States, Mr. Davis has personally received death threats, there have been threats to burn down their building, and a group threatened to take their building away. Jack Saunders, another ex-Christian pastor and a friend of Mr. Davis, is the head of another Noachide group who also has received such threats. These men and their congregants have shown the incredible courage that comes from their strength of conviction.

The surrounding Christian community considers Noachides to be a threat. Children and teens at school are asked, "Are you involved in a cult? Do you really sacrifice chickens in the basement?" The most severe threats came from people calling Noachides Jew-lovers. The world has hated the Jew throughout the ages, but anti-Semites hate the Jew-lover more than they hate the Jew.

A wonderful couple I am privileged to know, a man and wife both in their seventies, were raised in the church and raised their children and grandchildren in the church. They are grateful that the church had such a moral impact on their family and note the instrumental role it has played in raising two generations. This couple's children and Christian friends do not understand the couple's newfound beliefs, and they are truly concerned for their spiritual well-being. However, these two have a glow about them, a light in their eyes. They become excited when they talk about the Torah or some proverb they have recently learned to decipher. As they have the opportunity, they reach out to family and friends; however, those times when people are open to new beliefs are few. I find this couple admirable because nearly every person they know is connected with Christianity, and yet their Torah faith continues to grow and blossom. Thankfully, they have each other.

I know people who are raising young children with Torah concepts such as justice and encouraging them to question and think through their actions rather than acting only with their emotions. I met a father who began teaching his son not only Torah, but Talmud, when the boy was only four years old. All the Noachides I have met have been pro-Israel and antiracism, whether it takes the form of anti-Semitism or other racism. These people embrace the essence of Torah, to whatever degree they know, wherever they are on their path of Torah learning.

The Noachide movement is dynamic because its members are growing intellectually and spiritually. They are excited because what was once only the Old Testament has now become a living manual on how to live life in the fullest, deepest sense. Some people believe that living a great life means living an easy life or one full of people who like you or with a great deal of money. Millions of people have lived such lives and yet were unhappy. Why? Because the reality is that life is not easy. No one is liked or approved of by everyone. Many of the wealthiest people in the world have committed suicide. It is easier to grow and direct our creativity and productivity when we can clearly see reality. To recognize and live reality is what Torah is all about. This is what the rabbis are teaching us Noachides, and this is what makes our lives fulfilling and dynamic.

The retired couple I spoke with said their greatest concern for the Noachide movement is that, without Noachide communities, the movement may die out in one or two generations. Where are the communities to raise a Gentile family in Torah faith? The pool of potential mates is small. How can Noachides hold on to their faith, let alone strengthen it, if there are only a few congregations in the entire United States? How do we replace the void that remains after one leaves the church community? I echo their concerns.

Another concern I heard expressed more than once among Noachides is the anti-Jesus attitude of most rabbis. Jesus is an emotional issue for both the Gentiles leaving Christianity and the rabbis teaching them. The rabbis are suspect of the motives of Noachides who ask questions about Jesus; they worry that the Gentile may try to convert Jews or that the Gentile really has not left Christianity behind. The ex-Christian simply needs answers. How do you know Jesus was not the Messiah? Why is the virgin birth rejected? Did *Tanakh* say the Messiah must be born of a virgin? Which of Jesus' teachings were in keeping with Torah, and which were not? Were Jesus' teachings okay, but his followers' teachings in error? In what way? If these questions of new Noachides are responded to by their rabbi with emotion instead of factual biblical and historical answers, the Gentile is left with a feeling of insecurity about his or her newfound beliefs and new teacher. This is a real danger to the movement's solidarity and individual growth. These issues must be faced to move past them, as new Noachides will always be coming into the movement with these questions.

Especially for the Jewish reader, it would to helpful to describe some Noachide beliefs here. Gentiles who have recently left the church struggle with questions regarding Jesus and the New Testament. But as they grow in knowledge of Torah and Talmud through the teachings of Noachide leaders and rabbis, they move past these questions to a Torah perspective. Noachides have progressed to the point where they do not believe Jesus was the Messiah, let alone God incarnate; they do not believe that faith in Jesus earns them the World to Come; they reject the virgin birth; they do not believe the Law of Moses was canceled; and they do not accept the New Testament as Holy Scripture. All are earnestly trying to grasp the Orthodox Jewish view of Torah and Talmud. Because of their church backgrounds they must unlearn many church teachings in order to grasp Torah concepts, and each Noachide must progress at his or her own pace. In short, Gentiles in the movement are not Christians, in any sense of the word—they are Noachides who strive to live Torah-based lives.

Those Noachides, who years ago progressed beyond the Jesus questions, grow impatient. They hunger for in-depth teachings, and many resent what they consider to be time wasted on Jesus issues. Realistically, there is and always will be a vast range of Gentiles in the movement, from the disillusioned Christian still in the church to the scholar who daily studies Hebrew, Torah, and Talmud. For the Noachide movement to become stronger and grow, all needs must be met.

The number of adherents to the Seven Noachide Laws is difficult to estimate. The Emmanuel Congregation publishes a newsletter and mails it out to groups and individuals, including a group of 600 people in Africa. In addition, Noachide groups have formed independently in Nigeria, the Netherlands, Belgium, Australia, Israel, and Moscow; each of these groups now receives *The Gap*. Mr. Davis estimated the number reached from 3,000 to 5,000 people in mid-1994. This is approximately twice the number reached in 1992. A listing of Noachide groups, supportive organizations, publications, audio- and videocassettes, press coverage, and books can be found in *The Root and Branch Noahide Guide/5752* by Aryeh Gallin, published by The Root and Branch Association in Jerusalem.

# 5

# ON BEING A LIGHT

Today rabbis around the world are teaching Gentiles; they have answered the Torah's call to be a light unto the nations. They are few in number; many are overtaxed trying to serve both their Jewish congregations and Noachides. But these rabbis see that the time has come, and no one can teach these Gentiles the Seven Laws except those who know and live Torah.

For most rabbis, their involvement began with a call from a stranger: "What can a *Ben Noach* do in regard to the Sabbath?" "What are the Seven Laws of Noah and how do I observe them?" "Can I go to synagogue?" "How do I establish courts of justice?" "How does *halakhah* apply to Noachides?"

Some rabbis have told the Gentiles they have no time to teach them. Some rabbis simply do not have the educational background needed to teach the Seven Laws, some do not know how to apply Torah to Gentiles, and some are simply afraid the Gentile is seeking to proselytize Jews. Some rabbis have mistakenly told Gentiles to practice *halakhah* that pertains only to Jewish people, as though the Gentile was converting to Judaism. Zechariah 8:23 has simply taken most Orthodox Jews by surprise.

Fortunately, there are learned rabbis who have answered the call. Yes, some have had to study the Prophets more or even the New Testament in order to make available the answers Noachides require to turn away from idolatrous backgrounds. These rabbis have made time to call or meet with Noachide groups every week, record tapes of Torah teachings, or write articles for Noachide publications. These contacts have led Noachides to understand the Orthodox view of Torah and to let go of idolatrous beliefs. The rabbis who are involved are dedicated people, dedicated to follow the *halakhah* that compels them, as the priests of the world, to teach Noachides.

Those rabbis who have become involved did not do so blindly. They have asked questions of Noachides to be certain their goal is not to convert the Jew to Christianity. They have studied with them for countless hours, teaching Torah concepts and obliterating false beliefs. Some rabbis have come to respect such Noachide leaders as J. David Davis for his knowledge of Torah, Tanakh, and Talmud. But Mr. Davis is quick to point out that he learns something new from rabbis every week. The rabbis are often challenged by Noachides' questions, but this spurs them to study further and call back with an answer. Both sides benefit immensely from this involvement.

Orthodox involvement is growing steadily. The Noachide Conference in 1992 was the first in which enough Jewish men participated to form a *minyan*. Both Orthodox and chasidic Jews served as teachers. One Orthodox Jewish couple attended just to learn about the movement. They were surprised by the level of knowledge the Noachides had acquired and pleased to witness such a Torah movement among non-converting Gentiles. They felt as though they were eyewitnesses to the fulfillment of biblical prophecy. Indeed, they were.

One young Jewish man told me that he believes we are living in a time before the Messiah, the true Messiah, comes. He said, "When my time is up and I'm standing before God and the Tribunal, and they ask, 'What did you do to bring *Moshiach*?,' I want to say that I did something important. I live Torah and teach Torah to Jews. But to teach Noachides, it's more than an obligation to me. It's like being an instrument of God."

When I inquired about his family's reaction, he told me his father, a rabbi, asked him, "What's more important—teaching Jews or Gentiles"? His reply was, "I can do both." Then he explained the halakhic answer he gave his father. The Talmud asks when you are in the midst of performing a commandment, must you stop to do another? If there is someone else available to do the second *mitzvah*, so that it is done properly, then let them do it and you continue with the first. But if you are the only one who can do it, then you must stop and perform the second *mitzvah*.

"I look at it this way," he continued, "There are very few people who are equipped or willing to teach the *B'nai Noach*. And it is clearly a *mitzvah*. So the obligation becomes more incumbent upon those who feel it's important to them. In Talmud, a person is urged to become a specialist, much like a doctor or lawyer chooses a specialty. You become an expert at something so you can teach others the intricacies of it, so you have something special to offer. The fact that I'm drawn to teach B'nai Noach makes that a special *mitzvah* to me. And in some ways, I'm naive; I want to change the world. We are in the middle of history in the making."

This concept of the special *mitzvah* came to mind as I spoke with a chasidic rabbi from Israel. He told me that twenty years ago, at his *bar mitzvah*, his *parshah*—the Torah portion—was Noach. His concern was that rabbis must educate Noachides regarding Torah, but "they must combine knowledge and heart, leaving neither out. One without the other cannot sustain people."

When I asked how most rabbis view ex-Christians, I was told that they are wary of them. They are wary of Christians' proselytizing efforts, especially combined with their ignorance of the church's anti-Semitic history; lack of knowledge of the Bible, Judaism, and Talmud; concepts of idolatry/monotheism; and lack of historic/realistic views of Jesus. He also noted that Christians carry a Bible they cannot even read in its original language, Hebrew. How can they think they are able to understand it when they cannot even read it? In Hebrew, for instance, the text does not say that the Messiah must be born of a virgin. There is truly a vast chasm between Christianity and Judaism.

Yet with all these apprehensions, the rabbis who are involved in the movement are very supportive of Noachides. One rabbi's wife called her involvement "an exciting adventure" and noted that her family thought the movement was "fascinating." It seems that those rabbis who are secure in their biblical knowledge are not fearful of Noachides trying to convert them.

Both sides look to the strength and knowledge of the leaders involved. The involvement of the Chief Rabbinate of Israel, the guidance of a great scholar like Rabbi Israel Chait, and the knowledge and commitment of J. David Davis reassure all those involved that this movement is in the hands of able Torah-minded people. Of the millions who are afraid to become involved, the consensus of rabbis seems to be that education will remove fear. Zechariah 8:23 will be fulfilled.

# 6

## Our Future

Today is a time to reflect and to plan. I am but one Gentile living in my particular culture in the present age. But I have witnessed the searching faces of Gentiles who have boldly grasped for pure monotheism out of a love for the God of Israel and His Torah. I have scrutinized their faces and words and found sincerity and a great hunger for knowledge. I have listened intently to the inflection in the rabbis' voices, felt their apprehension. There is a longing on both sides to connect and fulfill God's plan for His creation.

This longing, apprehension, love, and enthusiasm are good and an essential part of worshiping God together. At the same time, however, these emotions can work against us. Noachides love the Torah. They see the lifestyle of Orthodox Jews as the Torah come to life, and many Noachides respond by adopting practices of Judaism. Some rabbis know how to convert a Gentile to Judaism but not how to teach the Noachide Laws to Gentiles. But God, in Torah, mandated a difference between His priests (Israel) and laymen (Gentiles). We cannot remove this difference and remain faithful to Torah. The intellect must control the emotions to lead us together along a Torah path.

I am reminded now of an episode in King David's life when his wife criticized him for behaving emotionally in his worship of God. He sang and danced with music in the streets out of his love for God. Emotion, properly directed, is as essential to a relationship with God as is the study of Torah. So we must not deny or suppress these emotions, but rather find appropriate ways to express them. This balance is a challenge for Noachides.

If a Noachide is to worship the God of Israel, the God of Torah, this worship must include many aspects. Primarily, we have a desperate need to study and discuss our findings, our questions, with rabbis and learned Noachide leaders. I see study as the priority for both rabbis and Gentiles involved in the movement today. We must learn a Torah way of looking at life. We need to learn how to apply the Seven Laws to our daily lives. We have to unlearn the lessons taught in the church that kept us in idolatry and away from true monotheism.

There are numerous directions we can take. For Aime Palliere, learning the Hebrew language was the key he needed to unlock the secrets of Torah. We can all benefit from reading the Torah in the original language. Emmanuel Congregation in Athens, Tennessee, has become a clearinghouse for teachings, including rabbinic studies on tape. A school is in the planning stages. As the movement progresses, it is hoped that rabbis will begin writing commentaries for Noachides. Lack of education both among Jewish people and Gentiles has helped keep us fearful of each other and ignorant of God's plan for all of us.

Prayer is also an essential part of worshiping God. But we Gentiles need to learn how to pray, what to pray, and most important, why to pray as we are taught. The beauty of the *siddur* has given Gentiles, who often come from a Christian background of emotionalism in prayer, a longing to pray as a Jew. Some Gentiles have converted to Judaism partly because they feel the need to pray beautiful, biblical prayers, but can find no source of prayers that compares to the *siddur*.

*Suggested Prayers for B'Nai Noah*, a booklet sanctioned by the Chief Rabbinate of Israel, contains a few prayers, but most Noachides find it lacking. It simply does not lead one to a lifestyle filled with the beauty offered by the *siddur*. Though rabbis must be careful not to create a new religion (which is forbidden), the need is clear for a more complete *siddur* for Noachides, or better yet, a guide for Noachides on how to use the existing *siddur*. My hope is that rabbis will create such a guide as soon as possible. We are in great need of one.

The need for the formation of Noachide communities has become increasingly apparent as well. Rabbis will have to train other Orthodox Jews regarding the Seven Laws, the Prophets, and how to answer questions regarding Jesus and the New Testament. Then there will be a growing number of rabbis equipped to serve the growing Noachide population, which will take some of the burden from the rabbis currently working with Noachides. As more rabbis become trained and available, they, like the rabbis already involved, can serve these Noachide communities by engaging in telephone dialogues, writing articles, recording tapes, and so on. Even with an increased number of rabbis, Noachides must begin gathering in groups so that each group has contact with a rabbi.

The second reason for forming larger Noachide communities is that we need communities to sustain us spiritually. Just like Abram's group and like the Israelites who came out of Egypt, we Noachides are in our spiritual infancy in our Torah faith. Daily bombardment from an idolatrous culture wears on the soul. Connection with those of like minds builds us up, encourages us, helps us learn more.

Assimilation is another reason. Our children, with even less Torah knowledge than we have, are more vulnerable and need the companionship of Noachide friends. As they grow older and date and marry, who will they know? Only Christians? Who will they have to choose from when they are ready to marry? The same is true for unmarried adult Noachides. Communities provide friends and a marriage pool; these are necessary if this movement is to last for longer than one or two generations. We have seen what the dangers of assimilation have done among Jewish people. We must recognize that same vulnerability in Noachides.

Jewish people have been scattered around the world, and I am grateful for this dispersion. Who knows but that they were scattered for a time such as this. Through long-distance telephone, any Noachide community can reach a rabbi. But just as they need Jewish communities wherever they are in order to maintain their Torah faith, we Noachides must gather in communities to build and maintain our Noachide Torah faith.

One question arises constantly among those Noachides bold enough to approach the subject: what do we do about Christian friends and relatives? What do we tell them? Will they enter the World to Come? Sadly, the majority of Noachides I have met are not yet equipped to answer these questions. If we do not have the answers for Christians, it means we do not have sufficient answers for ourselves.

It is hoped that Noachide leaders can work with rabbis to develop educational materials to fill this void. Christians whom we know will not ask the rabbis, but they will eventually ask us. Lack of Torah knowledge as it pertains to Christian thought leaves us vulnerable. Learning Hebrew could help in this area as well, enabling us to correctly read passages that Christian people regularly quote as proof of Christian teachings. I feel that until we are fully prepared, until we have the answers for ourselves, it is best to avoid discussing Torah with Christians. If they are genuinely interested in Torah and you are not yet equipped, put them in touch with people who are prepared to help them.

Moses was cautioned by his father-in-law not to take on too much of a burden alone, but rather to train others to assist him. Just as we need more trained rabbis, we need more Noachide leaders. J. David Davis, Jack Saunders, and Dr. James Tabor are learned leaders, but they cannot do it alone. Noachides who are willing and have the time to study must begin to prepare themselves for leadership roles. If the leaders of communities do not have sufficient education, Christian-like developments in the Noachide movement could result within the next decade or two.

The Noachide movement is not one originated by man. Zechariah 8:23 is part of God's plan; He said it would happen, and it is indeed happening today. Individual Gentiles first came to a realization that the God of Israel is the only God, the One True God. These individuals began approaching rabbis. God is not dependent upon us to make this prophecy come true; it already has. Some rabbis were prepared for this to occur in our time, and some were not. Torah and Talmud were ready. There is no need to struggle over creating a new religion filled with rituals and practices that never existed before (which is forbidden). Rabbis and Noachides simply need to study Torah and Talmud so that we can apply existing *halakhah* to this new situation.

I thank God that He somehow gave me and other Gentiles the desire to reach for Him. I am grateful He did it at a time when rabbis were preparing. *Barukh HaShem.*

I thank those rabbis who have prepared, who continue to prepare and work with us, and those who have just begun, perhaps with this book, to educate themselves. Without rabbis and other Jewish people, this nation of priests, we lay people (Gentiles) would not be able to learn, to see the light of Torah. We need you. You are a part of God's plan for us Gentiles.

And I thank Noachide leaders who spend countless hours studying, answering questions, writing articles and books, and leading the rest of us Gentiles out of Ur, our sea of idolatry. Thank you for having the courage to challenge your past beliefs. Thank you for showing us by example that, with education, we too can acquire some of the strength of character you possess.

To every Jewish reader I say, we have taken hold of the corner of your cloak. Hear what the Gentiles are saying to you:

Let us go with you, for we have heard that God is with you.

*Shalom.*

# II

# ONE NOACHIDE'S JOURNEY

# 7

## *BERESHIT*: IN THE BEGINNING

I called on Your name, O LORD,
from the depths of the pit.
You heard my plea:
"Do not close Your ears
to my cry for relief."
You came near when I called You,
and You said, "Do not fear."
O Lord, You took up my case;
You redeemed my life.
—Lamentations 3:55–58

From the day I first read it, this passage has been my favorite one in the entire Bible. It speaks of intimacy with God, of a relationship with him. It is a universal prayer of thanks from every individual who has truly come near to Him.

My spiritual journey began seven years ago, when I made the choice to follow God's will to the best of my ability. But the foundation for that decision was laid, by God, many years before.

By the age of fifteen, I was staunchly atheistic. One of my grandmothers, a pious Christian woman, would patiently explain to me
how there had to be a God. She believed the Bible to be the words of
God, to be completely true. I would continually counter with logical
reasons why that was not possible. We spent many hours discussing,
debating. In my mind, it made no difference; I knew there was no
God.

I remember having a curiosity about religion, however. I read books
about Buddha and other religious figures. They all seemed basically
the same to me: nice men, great men even, who inspired others to be
better people. "That's nice," I thought, "but they don't affect me."

Meanwhile, my heart was filled with the ache of an unhappy childhood. I was four years old when my parents divorced. My father took
my sister and me to Seattle—more than one hundred miles from our
mother. I could count on one hand how many times I saw her over
the next eleven years. She had abandoned us.

When we first arrived in Seattle, my father, sister, and I moved in
with his mother. My grandmother was a harsh woman—quick to
judge and careless with her words to children. She related stories to
my sister and me of how our mother had been neglectful. In these
efforts to be supportive of her son, she robbed me of my only comfort: the fantasy that my mother would have loved us if only she could
have been with us.

After three years with a spiteful grandmother and a series of live-in
housekeepers, my father remarried. Starving for a mother, my sister
and I addressed her as "Mom" before they married. But it seemed as
soon as their relationship was formalized, life changed dramatically.
The cheerful woman who dated our father grew cold and found fault
in nearly everything my sister and I attempted. She often called us
stupid and showed no positive interest in us, so we stayed in our
bedroom escaping her by watching television for hours on end.

My father began leaving for work by 6:00 A.M. and arriving home
near 9:00 P.M., just before my sister and I went to bed. On Saturdays
he worked eight hours, and on Sundays, exhausted, he would fall

asleep in his recliner in front of the television as it reran John Wayne movies. Sometimes I would crawl up into his lap and feel his breathing and the warmth of his body as he slept. It felt as though our father had abandoned us too—to a woman who seemed to view my sister and me as impositions in her life.

The loneliness and sense of abandonment tortured me each night, rendering sleep nearly impossible. I lay there counting ten, eleven, twelve times the cuckoo rang out from three rooms away; the nights seemed endless.

At the age of twelve I began baby-sitting. I loved children, and it felt wonderful to escape my parents' house and go where someone wanted me. Pleased parents referred me to their friends, and soon I was busy nearly every weekend.

My sister and I were not given a weekly allowance, so the fifty cents per hour earned by baby-sitting was an exciting side benefit for me— at first. We quickly learned that we were now expected to use our earnings to purchase our own clothing, shoes, and toiletries.

The meager childhood I had been allotted was over in twelve years. By fifteen, I felt worn out, exhausted from a life that had dealt severe and continual blows to my psyche. The only escape I could imagine was death, so I began contemplating how to commit suicide.

At this time I was working at a senior citizens' apartment building down the block from my home. The ladies there needed visitors more than housekeeping, so I would sit sipping tea, just listening. Nearly everyone complained about relatives.

"They never call anymore," one woman said.

"I haven't seen my son for months. I wonder how his children are."

Some were just plain angry: "At least they could help me with the grocery shopping!"

One woman was different. Mrs. Jenson served up the worst tea and the best attitude in the building. When she spoke of family, she would share a warm moment or some little kindness done for her. She never preached at me, but I did see religious magazines around her apartment. I could not help but notice her kindness.

Shortly after we met, she had a stroke. She was allowed to remain in her home, but she required continuous supervision. Her best friend, who also lived in the building, stayed with her during the day. I slept on her couch at night. In the mornings we would have tea and toast before I left for school.

One night I was awakened by something. There was no voice, no sound, no creaking floor, or unusual traffic out on the street below. I was *internally aware* of a presence. It was powerful, enveloping, and physically warming, and it was communicating with me.

No logic can explain it, but I knew immediately and for certain that it was God. I felt incredible joy; for in that moment, I felt more loved than ever before in my life. Tears streamed down my face as if the love He was filling me with had overflowed, pouring out my eyes. He seemed to be saying (without audible words), "You are here because I love you. Your life *does* have a purpose, so do not end it. *I love you and that will be enough.*"

In later years I would hear very logical reasons why there has to be a God. The world, the elaborate ecosystems, the human body, are all too intricate, too complex for mankind to comprehend. The chemical makeup of a seed can be duplicated by man, but it will not grow. Nature is too orderly and interdependent to have happened by chance.

That night, however, no logic was involved. When someone touches you, you do not question his or her existence. From that moment on, because of that intense love, I had hope for a better future. God gave me hope and the strength that accompanies it.

The next afternoon, I received a call from Mrs. Jenson's friend. She told me that Mrs. Jenson had fallen out of bed during the night. The carpet was so heavily padded that I had not heard her fall. She did not call for my help; instead, she used all her strength to pull herself back onto the bed. In the morning, she did not even tell me about the fall. However, it caused more than a temporary setback; she was admitted to the hospital, and afterward she had to enter a nursing home.

I felt terribly guilty for not hearing her fall, though her best friend assured me it was not my fault. I never heard from Mrs. Jenson again.

Had I still been in that depressed emotional state, the guilt might have sent me right over the edge.

The realization that God existed required that I reconsider religion. Years earlier, my mother had given me a white leather-bound Bible. It was a nice little King James Version with gold-edged pages and a gold zipper that encased those ancient words. It meant nothing to me except as a gift from a mother I seldom saw. I have vague childhood memories of walking to a nearby church for Sunday school, but my sister and I did not like it; they gave us homework. Our parents never went to church, as far as I knew. In our house, religion was unimportant.

After my experience with God, however, I visited the churches of friends. At first I was excited. "These people know the God I just met. They must feel as good as I do," I thought. However, that naive idea was squelched before we reached the church building. In the parking lot, I heard as much gossip as I had at huge family gatherings. I thought, "Don't *these* people have better things to talk about?"

In one youth group, the minister told us not to socialize with members of other denominations. "They don't believe the same way we do," he said.

"How do we believe?" I thought. Surely God would not teach us to avoid other godly people, not the compassionate God I had met. So I stopped looking for God in churches. Other than weddings and funerals, I rarely entered a church building.

Life moved along. I fell in love, married, had a daughter, and got a divorce. Now and then I thanked God for something or asked His help when I felt desperate. I did not exactly forget Him; I simply had little interest in religion in those years. He was still there for me, but I did not turn to Him enough to affect my everyday life. But the divorce brought me to the edge of the "pit" (Lamentations 3:55) again. This time I turned to God for help. He picked me up and helped me start a new life without my husband.

For me, single life was not the unending fun that movies make it out to be. There were noncommittal relationships and conversations of little depth. In some ways, being single stunted my emotional growth too. I did not have to share my room or the decision making. Other than caring for a toddler, I did not have to take into consideration anyone else's needs or desires. And the burden of raising a child alone and paying all the bills myself was a heavy responsibility.

I poured all my energies into raising my daughter and doing my job. I was determined to do my best with what was left of my life. On the job, I worked hard; I was very ambitious. Alecia entered school, so day care expenses decreased, alleviating some of the financial pressure. We were faring pretty well. Then, a series of events turned my attention to God.

One of my grandmothers (my father's mother, not the pious one) became ill. She had always been a "tough old bird" with an incredibly independent spirit. But her bossy, sometimes unkind attitude had pushed most of her family away. Now, as her hearing and eyesight were fading, she seemed powerless and pitiful.

So I was surprised by the telephone call I received one day. She asked my daughter and me to come over to her apartment. During the drive I explained to my soft-spoken little girl that she would have to speak loudly so Grandma could hear. I told her not to be disappointed if her great-grandmother did not understand her or even recognize her.

From the moment she answered the door, I was amazed. Alecia was as quiet as ever, but Grandma could hear every word. She even responded to Alecia's hand gestures; before, she had not been able to see them. I did not know what to think. Grandma was telling me that she was not going to be around much longer, and she wanted to give her possessions to people before she died. "Take what you want," she told me. "You know they'll just fight over it when I'm gone."

Grandma had a new personality. She apologized for whatever wrongs she had done in the past. She tried to make amends with everyone else too, but some refused. It was sad, but she said she understood.

Grandma was enjoying Alecia; watching the two of them converse was a delight. She was insistent with her goal, though: "Take that vase. You want that vase?"

"That's okay, Grandma."

"Kim, you've always admired my antique coffee table. Please take it. It would mean so much to me to know you have it." I felt numb as I carried it out to the car. As I left her standing in the doorway, she seemed the happiest I had ever seen her.

Later, I was told she had "made peace with God" and joined a church. Grandma was in her late eighties and knew she was going to die soon. God had restored her lost sight and hearing. No one understood it; none of us could deny it either. Not only could she see and hear—she was nice too! She passed away shortly after our visit.

Another odd event was that my ex-husband decided he wanted to reconcile. He wanted to remarry right away and have another child. Alecia, then five, felt as confused as I did; neither of us knew how to react. She was only a baby when her father and I divorced. She had no memories of the three of us together. I was apprehensive, but at the same time I wanted to believe it would work. I still loved him.

I did my best to please him, to make him happy. Eventually, though, old problems resurfaced. He still had trouble giving. Verbally, he was proposing marriage; in action, he was trying to keep one foot out the door. It broke my heart to tell him that he would have to give it all or nothing. He left, and I was finally able to close that door for good.

Months later, God began to clean up my life. I had been drinking a lot on weekends when Alecia visited her dad. I smoked over two packs of cigarettes a day. Work was everything to me. I even considered opening my own restaurant. The banker said they would loan half of the $250,000 required; my lawyer began meeting investors with me. I was flying pretty high, not noticing how self-centered and short-tempered I had become. I kept too busy to feel much of anything. How God got through to me with that attitude I will never know, but my life was about to change.

The fact finally dawned on me that establishing the restaurant would require me to work sixteen hours a day for a long time. That was fine except for the amount of time away from Alecia. Sure, I would have the money for day care and maybe even for live-in help. But suddenly I looked at my little girl and realized I wanted to raise her myself. I could not have the best of both worlds; that is a cruel myth. I had to choose. She won. And so did I.

That was the turning point. The restaurant was no longer a consideration. I quit smoking, almost never took a drink again, and shortened my hours at work. Now I could drop Alecia off at school in the morning and pick her up afterward. Some people were irritated with me for dropping the restaurant plans, because they knew I could make it work. However, my priorities had changed. We were poor financially, but we had a good life together.

Christmas that year was the nicest I could remember. Family filled our apartment. I felt close to my father and sensed his approval for the first time in my life. My brother even called from Texas. It was a great day for the whole family.

Four days later I received a call from my grown niece, Lorri, who lived at my parents' house. Dad had lain down for a nap that afternoon and never awoke. He had had a heart attack in his sleep. It was so unexpected that I could not believe it at first. As soon as I put the phone down, I ushered Alecia into her room to play. She had never seen me so upset. I was afraid my crying would frighten her, so I called her dad to come over and pick her up .

Alone in the living room, I said good-bye to my father. He had rarely shown his feelings, though he had suffered a great deal in his life. He was the eldest of six children, and he had to quit high school to help support his family during the Depression when his father had been ill. Of the six children, he had married last; the marriage lasted ten years and ended in a messy divorce. He often wore a tired expression on his face, so it was a treat whenever he smiled or laughed. While I was growing up, it seemed he was either working or sleeping. That is how he wanted it. He once told me that if he could not work, he might as well be dead.

I took comfort from God now. I knew Dad was okay. I was so grateful for that wonderful Christmas. The date of his death is marked on the calendar, and I make a point on that day to remember my dad.

A few months before my father's death, I noticed Lorri reading the Bible. We usually played cards once a week. Now, she had a hard time putting the Bible down when I came. I had not come to watch her read; I came to play cards. "Why can't you put it down when I get here?" I asked.

"You should read it," she said. "It's really interesting."

Right, I thought. She's not shoving religion down my throat! But I said nothing. After a few weeks, she was careful to put it away when I arrived.

Her reading did pique my curiosity, however. Lorri was intelligent and not easily swayed by others. She also read a lot. If *she* found it interesting, well. . . . Eventually I began reading the Bible too. I never let her know, though; no one knew.

Like many people, I began by reading the New Testament. The Bible my mother had given me read like Shakespeare; I had to read it aloud to make any sense of it. Out of desperation, I visited a Christian bookstore to find a modern version. At first I did not trust it; I read the old King James Version side by side with the New International Version (NIV), verse by verse. When I realized they were both saying the same thing, I switched to the NIV. Now I could follow along with ease.

Instead of only taking from God, I wanted to start giving back; I wanted to please Him. That year I mailed out Christmas cards with a religious message. I began donating a few dollars to charity when I could afford to. By the time my father passed away, I had a pretty good (albeit secret) relationship with God.

As I read the New Testament, I met someone new: Jesus. Of course I sang carols at Christmastime and knew he was associated with Christianity, but that was about all I knew of him. Religion was not something I wanted; I was only interested in God. In the New Testament, though, I found that Jesus loved God as I did. He was not like those people in the church parking lot I'd seen in my teens. Jesus had a real relationship with God.

Jesus loved the Holy Scriptures. He knew them so well that he could quote verses from memory when faced with difficulties. Using the Bible in this way was a new concept to me. Jesus apparently knew how to please God, so I began to follow his teachings as best I could.

Jesus told everyone: "Repent, for the kingdom of heaven is near" (Matthew 3:2).

That verse made me take a hard look at my actions. I donated money to charity. My life was cleaned up, and I was a good mother now too. Thanks to God's influence, I had become a person I liked and respected. But I realized Jesus was teaching his followers something more—to go a step further. It was not enough to be nice to those who loved you. Everyone tried to do that. No, he taught that we should be kind even to those who had done us harm. I tried to apply this teaching to my life. With this in mind, I read the following passage:

"For if you forgive men when they sin against you, your Heavenly Father will also forgive you. But if you do not forgive men their sins, your Father will not forgive your sins." (Matthew 6:14–15)

What a scary idea! Now that I had read this passage, I felt accountable to God: if I chose not to forgive someone, God would not forgive my sins. Yes, I took it literally. I did not know any other way to take it. Either you believed the Bible or you did not, and if you did, it had an impact. It was time for reflection. I asked myself, "Whom have I not forgiven?"

Just months before my father's death, I had a long talk with my mother. I began with kind and understanding words, but they were forced and insincere. In all those years I had never shown my resentment about her neglect of my sister and me. This time I opened up the floodgates, and the resentment ran out full force! All the years, all the mistakes—she tried to explain, but I showed her no mercy. The only tie I felt was biological. I informed her that I would have nothing more to do with her. Later, when I related our conversation to my sister at our father's funeral, she nearly applauded. This was the confirmation I needed: I *had* been justified in writing off my mother.

Now God was telling me, "Honor your father and your mother" (Exodus 20:12). Well, Dad was gone. The only way to obey this commandment would be to forgive my mother and love her as best I could.

I argued with God for the first time while writing that letter to my mother. (It was not the last time I would argue with Him though.) I wanted to please God, to receive His blessing and the peace and joy that come from obeying Him. But this time it was too difficult.

"She was wrong, God!" I cried. "She doesn't deserve an apology." Later, when I read about Jacob struggling with the angel for God's blessing, I could relate to his fight. Jacob was not called Israel until he wanted God's blessing badly enough to fight for it.

I knew why God did not speak audibly. It would only give me more opportunity to argue. The Bible contained all He needed to say, and all my objections did not alter the words written there: "Honor your father and your mother." I tried looking for a way out, but the Bible did not say, "When your parents mess up, you're justified in gossiping about them. When they make mistakes, especially big ones, forget them!" I understood. I just did not want to obey.

I did write that letter to my mother, however. I obeyed God just because He is God and because I had faith that His instructions were superior to my fluctuating feelings. The letter was mailed.

Oddly enough, as soon as the letter hit the mailbox and I realized I could not retrieve it, relief poured over me. My mother had not read it nor had she forgiven me yet. There was only a possibility of making amends. And yet I felt an amazing sense of relief!

Though my mind had been convinced that writing her off was justified, the guilt remained in my heart. I had even received my sister's approval, but that was not enough. Just acting on the choice to do things God's way lifted that guilt. "Not my will but Yours be done" (Luke 22:42). Jesus was right; it worked. At that moment, if I had died and stood before God, my conscience was clear. I could say, yes, I acted poorly at first; then I did my best to make amends.

What a discovery! So that is what repentance is all about, I thought. Guilt is such a self-destructive emotion. I realized that God loves us and wants us freed from the heavy burden of guilt. We can rationalize all we want, but it does not seem to change how we feel about ourselves. Now, I found the Bible to be a guide, identifying those actions and attitudes that were self-destructive (causing guilt) and those that bring happiness and peace. Operating my life without this guide had been an exercise in frustration. I was just beginning to realize the value of the Bible.

My mother responded wonderfully to the letter. She was so grateful and kind. Today we have a fairly good relationship, and God gets the credit for it all. Testing God's word through obedience to the Bible caused me to grow in faith and emotional maturity.

Over the course of weeks, similar letters were written to others. I wanted to apply this lesson to everyone I had wronged. In time, I was able to enjoy peace in every relationship in my life. Consequently, I felt cleansed before God.

Now I had fully accepted the Bible as the how-to manual for my life. Jesus laid down the example, and I was following to the best of my ability. But this turned out to be only the beginning of my journey with God.

There remained one item I had not dealt with: the church. From past experience I had not seen much evidence of God's influence there. But it is written in the New Testament that when Jesus was baptized, God was pleased (Matthew 3:17). If I was following Jesus' lead, I would need to find someone who would immerse me in water. Contact with a church became necessary.

"Does your church immerse people for baptism, like they did in the New Testament?" I asked Lorri.

She was stunned. When she regained her composure, she answered, "Yes, they do."

"Well, could you arrange for me to be baptized then?"

We planned to visit her church that Sunday morning. Lorri admitted that she had been praying for me for months but had finally given up. She had no idea I was remotely interested in Christianity. She had been baptized there just six months earlier.

On Sunday, I dropped Alecia off at my aunt's house instead of taking her with me. My desire to be baptized had not lessened my skepticism regarding the Christian community. I rode to the church with Lorri and her boyfriend.

Since that night when I first "met" God, I carried this sense of Him continually being with me. It was as if He was there listening, reassuring, and holding me. Now, as I walked through the double doors of the church building and entered the assembly hall, I could feel an additional dose of God's presence in the room. Skepticism was yielding to curiosity.

People there were quiet but kind. They sang many songs from hymnals: old-fashioned ones I recognized. The sermon was logical and given with a sense of humor that relaxed me. This was a comfortable place with people who loved God and tried to follow Jesus' teachings. I could see that Alecia would be all right here. So would I.

After the service, we began pulling out of the parking lot. I did not want to bother anyone, but there *was* this baptism I needed. As we began to drive away, I timidly brought it up again.

We turned around and drove back to the building. The three of us walked into a young minister's office and sat down. I thought these guys would jump at the chance to get me under that water. Now we were going to discuss it as if he might turn me down.

We must have talked for two hours, or maybe it only felt that long. The minister kept turning to places in the New Testament and asking me what I thought the passages meant. I worried about not passing this test. I kept praying all the time, "God, convince these people to baptize me. It's getting a little iffy here."

The minister was trying to see whether I had counted the cost of following in Jesus' footsteps. I was well aware of the cost: it was arrogance. I had to come to the realization that my Creator knew how to run my life better than I did. Without this acknowledgment and the subsequent desire to obey God, one could never follow in Jesus' footsteps. Finally, the minister was convinced. I was ready.

This ceremony meant more than just being immersed in water before God. In the New Testament, it was a public act—a confession of faith. My faith was not only between me and God anymore. It was time to go public instead of hiding my faith in Him.

That night at the church, Alecia and Lorri went downstairs to the dressing room with me. I changed into the ugly green plastic clothing and waited. When the singing stopped upstairs in the assembly hall, the minister and I walked up a few stairs and then down into the baptismal tank. The entire congregation watched. Down I went, the water enveloping me. As I came up, I heard all five hundred of them begin to sing. Tears were falling. It was overwhelming.

"Well, it's done, God," I prayed.

It was not part of my plan to join a congregation, but they were nice people who accepted me and encouraged my walk with God. Here I found fellowship: praying, singing, studying, and loving God together. No one was perfect; we all just tried our best. In an instant my life had totally changed.

Two major changes occurred because of my new closeness to God. First, I no longer felt utter loneliness. I still wanted other people around but there was no deep void inside me. Second, I lost the fear of death. Pain was not suddenly an appealing concept, but now the afterlife was no longer a scary unknown. I knew I would be with God when my time came to die. Conquering loneliness and the fear of death: this new mind-set was wonderful!

Naturally, when we have found something great, we want to share it. It was not that I thought others' lives were so horrible. My life had not been so terrible either, but how much better it had become!

As a good friend of mine observed years later, when I believe in something, I give it 110 percent. In my excitement, I wrote letters and mailed New Testaments to many people. The letters were not limited to close friends and family; I sent one to each person in my personal phone book, from an ex-boyfriend to my pharmacist. I remember picking up a box of fifty paperback New Testaments at the church office one day for my project. Sincerity and excitement were a powerful combination.

Those early days with the congregation were bliss. I loved every moment. It was as if I had been set free to love others. Suddenly I was a part of this big instant family. Instead of telling me to calm down, they loved my enthusiasm for God, the Bible, and life in general. Alecia loved it too.

Within a few days of the baptism, I attended my first Wednesday night Bible study. It was a nice little gathering in one member's home of about a dozen people. I wanted to go again, but I knew it would be difficult to get a baby-sitter every week and I was not sure I could afford it. No one else in the group had children, so before we left that night, I asked the minister leading the study if the group could meet just a few blocks away, at my home. He was a little surprised, but said they would consider it.

As it turned out, I could not have asked at a better time. The woman hosting the study group had to move, and they needed another place to meet right away.

Within weeks of my baptism, a Bible study group was meeting in our apartment. Every week for the next year, ten to fifteen people would gather in my living room. Each brought his or her own Bible; there were at least six different versions represented. After the potluck meal, we would take turns reading verses from passages in the New Testament. Then we would discuss what they meant to those people in the first century and how we could apply the lessons to our own lives. The open discussions were great. Each week I looked forward to the party and hugged each person as they entered. The only added expense for me was carpet cleaning every three months: potlucks can get messy.

The people in the group soon became like brothers and sisters to me. One night, one of them brought water pistols and had a water fight with Alecia. At one of those first study sessions, I met Cheryl, a woman who eventually became one of my dearest friends. With gentleness and a great sense of humor, she showed me (without preaching) how a godly woman lives.

Aware of my commitment to God, she once rebuked me for gossip. She did so privately, in the kindest way, and I was instantly convinced of my error. I could tell it was love and encouragement she was giving me, not judgment. Since that day, she has continued to play an important role in my life. The people in the Bible study group meant the world to me.

My commitment to God grew and deepened. In the past, work had been too important to me. My ego was so tied up in it that my self-image rose and fell based on how my job was going. I needed to break away and lean on God for a while. So, in faith, I gave three weeks' notice that I would be leaving my job and gave away many New Testaments at work.

I thought that I would not be eligible for unemployment benefits because I was quitting, but I felt certain that God would help me find another job—one that was not going to take over my whole life. As it happened, my assistant assumed my duties as well as hers, and my old position was phased out, so I did receive unemployment benefits after all. I mailed out resumes every week, but I fully enjoyed staying home while it lasted.

Although I was not going to a job every day, I did not waste time. I spent most days reading the Bible, beginning with Genesis and reading an average of twelve chapters a day. In the past I had had trouble reading: my eyes would blur after a page or two, but not anymore. I took Alecia to school, came home, and started reading. Next thing I knew, it was time to pick her up. Some days I would visit my aunt or a friend I had met at church who felt burdened by two young children and a husband who did not care much about God. It felt great to go and encourage her each week. Spring was flying by.

Due to my spiritual experience in my teens, God always came first in my mind. Jesus was important, but God came first. I learned that most others got to know Jesus first; through him, they learned about

God. They prayed to Jesus. In contrast, even though I would add "in Jesus' name, amen" as a matter of form at the end of prayer, it did not feel natural. After all, I was praying to God, not Jesus.

That subtle difference in viewpoint surfaced one night when I met with the two women in my discipleship group. We studied the New Testament along with Bible commentaries, and the content of our joint prayers was on a more personal level than those of the larger weekly group. I felt close to both women. We were talking about our private prayer times, and I shared with them the joy of envisioning myself walking up to God's throne and sitting at His feet. Sometimes, when I needed comforting, I would crawl right up into His lap. They felt uncomfortable with that idea and told me so.

Until then, I assumed they felt as close to God as I did. A little twinge crept into my heart, but I quashed it quickly. I loved these people, and they were the best fellowship available. They were people I could relate to about spiritual matters. I refused to pay any attention to that little uneasy feeling.

By late spring, something else captured my attention. The pastor would be taking a group to the Holy Land (Israel) for a tour in the fall. He had done so two years earlier and now was ready to form another group. I had been reading the Bible and studying Jesus' life in depth. How I longed to go and literally walk in his footsteps!

But I scarcely had enough money to make ends meet. There was no money for a luxury like a tour to Israel, but my desire to go was so strong that I started attending the weekly tour group meetings. It could not hurt just to listen.

After one such meeting, a stranger approached me and said, "If you want to go, I'll pay for your trip."

"That's okay," I replied. "Someday when I can afford it I'll go." As he walked away, I thought, "Right, you'll pay for my trip? And what would you want in return?"

Yes, I was cynical. These Christian people were new to me. I was not accustomed to anyone being that generous to someone he did not know. I desperately wanted to go, but there was no sense in hoping. People who knew the Bible better than I should go; surely they would get more out of such a trip than I could.

Another meeting came and then another. The man kept coming up to me, offering again to pay for the trip. I gave him no reason to think I would take him up on his offer. I still was not sure of his motives. One day he came up to me and said, "You'd better get your passport. Sometimes it takes a while to get one."

I was speechless. Could he be serious? "He probably doesn't even have the money," I thought. "Plane fare, hotels, tour, meals. Well, I *could* get a passport, just in case. Maybe someday I can use it."

Squeezing any money out of our budget was impossible. I sold our new color television to a neighbor. I scraped up every dime I could, but there was not enough. I could not even come up with the deposit for the trip, which was due soon.

Every week, the man kept asking me about trip-related matters. I started asking others about him.

"He's a quiet man," someone told me.

"Yes," someone else said, "He gives money to an orphanage every year for school supplies. He's really a nice guy."

"He works hard and lives quite frugally."

Okay, he's harmless, I told myself. But why me? Why spend that much money on *me*? I had no way to pay him back. Anyway, he was not lending the money, he was giving it to me. No, I could not accept this gift. I would feel too guilty, or I would feel obligated in some way, even if he was not expecting anything in return.

I told Lorri about his offer. She thought it was great! I told her my reservations about accepting the gift, and she rebuked me for being prideful.

"What?"

"You should be gracious about receiving, not just about giving." (I only half-bought that idea.)

Then the day came. He walked up to me during fellowship time at church, patting his shirt pocket. "Our tickets are in here; they're all paid for."

When reality hit that I was actually going to the Holy Land, I sat down and fought back the tears. The lump in my throat was so big I could not sing. It did not matter though. My eyes were blurred; I could not read the words in the hymnal.

Now I began praying for a job. I had not wanted one before; I was enjoying this "honeymoon" with God and the Bible. I had sent out resumes, but nothing happened. Now it was time to return to work.

Also, I wanted to grow spiritually. To do that, I needed to break out of my safe little cocoon and get back into the real world. I prayed, and within a week I started back to work. My new boss agreed to the time off in September for the trip.

Life was busy and good. Sunday mornings, Alecia and I went to Sunday school classes and worship services. Often we would stay in the church building for an hour or more, visiting with people. Sometimes we would go out to lunch with church friends. Occasionally we attended Sunday evening services as well. On Wednesdays, the large Bible study group met at our apartment. Once each week, my discipleship group met. One other weeknight I would have a prayer partner over. Alecia and I also had lots of time together; most church activities began after she went to bed. I was careful not to allow these activities to encroach on our time together.

Preparations continued for the trip. Now we had a little income to save for incidentals on the tour. I wanted to get the most out of this trip, so I read the entire Bible from cover to cover. I arranged to borrow a microcassette recorder to record the tour guide.

Jim, the man who was paying for my trip, was a quiet, shy person and an incredible giver. He not only paid for my trip and his own but he also paid for another person who could not afford it. He used up his entire savings. We found this out during the trip when Jim wanted to buy a watch but did not have enough money.

Jim was also a camera buff and had several nice 35-millimeter cameras. He spent an entire day teaching me how to operate one of his cameras so I could use it on the trip. He taught me so well that I took a shot of a moving train only a few yards away, and the photo

looked as if the train were standing still! He also bought a photo album
and ten rolls of film for me. Photography turned out to be one of the
greatest pleasures of the trip.

Headlines were filled with accounts of hijackings that summer, and
a few people dropped out of the tour at the last minute. Not me. Nothing would keep me from going to the Holy Land if I could help it.

The night before we left, I took Alecia over to my sister's house.
She would spend the first week there and the other with my neighbor. School would begin while I was away.

One of the brothers from the Bible study group called at ten that
night. "When do you leave?" he asked.

"Six A.M."

"Better get some sleep. Done packing?"

"I haven't even begun! I'm so nervous. I don't know what to pack.
It doesn't seem real to be going to Israel tomorrow."

"Well, it is. You'd better get moving."

# 8

# THE HOLY LAND

The night before our tour left, I could not sleep, so I finished reading the New Testament Book of Revelation. All the packing was done. The passport was in my purse. When I heard the knock at the door, it was 6:00 A.M., Wednesday, September 4. Yes, it was really happening.

Nine people from our congregation left for New York that morning. Once there, we connected with other small groups to make a total of thirty, the number required for the tour package. There were some retired people from the Midwest and a few people from Southern California, including an elderly gentleman who spoke only Spanish. By Wednesday afternoon we had all found each other at JFK Airport.

We had plenty of time to get acquainted. Due to mechanical problems, we had an additional nine-hour layover. At 1:00 A.M., a man in our group, Paul, brought out his video camera and I turned on my microcassette recorder. We "captured" some teenagers playing music and dancing to Jewish folk songs. It was great. It was also my second night without sleep.

We finally took off, made it to Brussels for refueling, and then on to Tel Aviv. After the long flight and the time difference (about ten hours from my home), it was past midnight on Thursday when we arrived.

Our Jewish guide, Shep, was waiting at Ben Gurion Airport. He whisked us through customs, gathered up our luggage, and ushered us outside and onto the bus. I was excited, but a bit incoherent (this was my third night without sleep). Down the dark highway we drove from the airport to our Jerusalem hotel.

Our hotel was built on the cease-fire line between Israel and Jordan that remained in effect until the 1967 Six-Day War. This area was now part of the city of Jerusalem. Once up in our hotel room, my two roommates and I began to unpack. Someone placed a voltage converter on her hair dryer and plugged it in. Everything went black. I looked down the hall; all lights on the floor were out. We called down to the front desk; the lights came back on, and a clerk came up to lend us a hotel converter.

Before he left, I said, "And by the way, the toilet runs continuously and the television doesn't work."

"That's right," he replied in a monotone as he walked away. Thus we discovered that not all three-star hotels are created equal.

By this time, all three of us were tired and giddy. We started debating what time it was in Jerusalem. Someone calculated the time difference between Israel and home. Someone else said that 3:00 A.M. was earlier than 2:00 A.M. When we finally laid our heads down, it was 3:00 A.M. on Friday, September 6.

A few hours later, we awoke to a beautiful Jerusalem sunrise. Outside our room at the end of the hall was a large window with a view of the valley that lay between us and the Old City portion of Jerusalem. I watched the sun rise across that valley in awe. "Thank you, LORD, for allowing me to come here. So this is the site You chose for the Holy Land."

When we reached the dining room, we were overwhelmed by the breakfast awaiting us: a huge buffet of eggs and toast, salads, fish, cheese and fruit. They had the largest variety of cream cheese I'd ever seen. Though I love it now, I didn't like cream cheese at the time.

What a waste! After a great meal, we boarded the bus with our recorders and cameras. The first day of touring was about to begin. In preparation for the trip I had purchased a little booklet about the Holy Land. On the tour bus, I leafed through it continually, locating our position on the map and learning the significance of each site before we arrived. That made it easier to follow along when Shep was speaking. I needed all the help I could get. In four days we were going to follow an incredible itinerary:

In Jerusalem, we saw the Western Wall (Wailing Wall), Temple Mount/Dome of the Rock, Old City of Jerusalem, Via Dolorosa/Holy Sepulchre, the model city (of first-century Jerusalem), Gordon's Calvary/Garden Tomb/Place of the Skull, and, the Garden of Gethsemane/Mount of Olives. And throughout Israel, we visited the Dead Sea, Capernaum, Masada, Golan Heights, Qumran, Jericho, Megiddo, Bethlehem, Jordan River, Caesarea, Haifa, Nazareth, Cana, Tiberias, Sea of Galilee, and nearly everything in between.

Our first stop that morning would open the door to first-century Jerusalem. Just a few miles down the road, laid out in front of the Holyland Hotel, was a complete scale model of first-century Jerusalem. The Temple stood here in all its majesty, along with the surrounding hills, valleys, City of David, Temple courtyards, and Antonio's Fortress.

In 70 c.e.[1] Jerusalem covered only eight to ten acres; the model was approximately twenty feet across and thirty feet in length. From the sidewalk surrounding the model, Shep used a long pointed stick to identify each site of religious or historical significance. Except for the lack of inhabitants, this was the Jerusalem that Jesus knew.

From that moment on, Shep was a continual source of information. He knew the Old Testament inside and out; the New Testament he could recite with equal ease. He seemed to know all about the Holy Land: its archaeology, history, traditions, facts, and theories. He could relay not only the beliefs of Judaism but also those of the Islamic faith. As for Christianity, he would diplomatically say that so many "Roman Catholics have this belief" while this number of "Protestants believe that. . . ." Had I not continually recorded this man, I would have missed half the trip.

*History* takes on new meaning in Israel. In the United States we consider something old that existed one or two hundred years ago. In Israel, that is just yesterday. Jerusalem has been destroyed, trampled down, and rebuilt on its ruins again and again. For this reason, archaeologists keep discovering more treasures with each layer they uncover. Built into the stone walls surrounding the Old City of Jerusalem are many huge gates, and a few feet below them lie their earlier counterparts. Stone does not rot; ancient ruins are still there. This week we would see a great deal of Israel's uncovered treasures for ourselves.

At the Model City, our biblical history lessons began. Shep's first topic was the origins of the city of Jerusalem and the Temple. We learned that King David did not establish the city of Jerusalem. "And if you want to prove it," Shep said, "just open the Book of Genesis."

Shep reminded us of the passage in Genesis where we read that approximately 4,000 years ago Abraham met Melchizedek. Melchizedek is identified as the Canaanite king-priest of Salem (*Shalim* in Hebrew). To him, Abraham gave a tenth of the spoils after a successful battle; tithing was a custom at the time. *Shalim*, a form of *shalom*, means peace, and *Yeru* (Jeru) means city. So, in Hebrew, the name is *Yerushalim;* in English, Jerusalem, city of peace. This was the name of Melchizedek's village nearly 4,000 years ago.

One thousand years later, in 1000 B.C.E., David took the village of the Jebusites, Jerusalem, and established it as the capital of Israel. Genesis records that Jerusalem was located in the territory assigned to the tribe of Benjamin. However, Benjamin had not been successful in capturing the Jebusite city, so it remained neutral territory as far as the tribes of Israel were concerned. Later, when David captured Jerusalem and made it the capital of Israel, he was using neutral territory, which pleased all the tribes. For nearly 3,000 years, Jerusalem has been the capital of the Jewish people, regardless of who has occupied its streets.

As we viewed the scale model, I was awed by how large the Temple must have been. I had visions of the masses filling the Temple courts. It was indeed a unique place on earth. God created the whole world, selected this tiny land, and gave it to the Israelites. He then chose a spot at the edge of a village and said that at this site a Temple was to be built, how to build it, the ritual items to use, and how He chose to be worshiped. By Jesus' day, the whole scenario had been playing out for centuries. The Old Testament instructions had come to life, as if God were Shakespeare and the Jewish people had been cast as His players.

The Temple was believed to be built over Moriah, the site where God told Abraham to sacrifice his son Isaac. Connecting a physical place with a passage in Genesis suddenly made the Bible seem more real. Four thousand years ago Abraham had stood here with Isaac; three thousand years ago David walked these streets; two thousand years ago Jesus preached here. And that day we stood within walking distance of the Temple Mount. Moriah means God is my teacher, and we were indeed to learn many things at Moriah.

After David conquered Jerusalem, 2 Samuel relates, God told David to purchase the threshing floor of a Jebusite. God had been punishing David by sending through Israel a fatal plague, and it was at this threshing floor that God stopped the plague because David obeyed God: he bought the site, built an altar, and sacrificed burnt offerings and fellowship offerings. Thus began the Jerusalem Temple.

I had envisioned David buying someone's barn, but actually the threshing floor was a flat, circular area, either of rock or trampled-down earth. Threshing floors were located at elevated open places, often at the edge of towns, which were exposed to the wind. This enabled farmers to toss the grain up in the air and have the wind blow the chaff away.[2] The Temple Mount is located near the outer walls of the Old City, which would place the threshing floor at the edge of Jerusalem as it existed in David's time.

Shep explained the history of the Temple: "Although David's heart was highly esteemed by God, he was a man of war. Jerusalem was the city of peace, and the Temple was to be symbolic of man's spiritual peace with God. Therefore, though David wanted to build a temple for God, He said no. God said it was to be David's son, Solomon, who would build the Temple for Him. God chose where, when, and by whom the Holy Temple would be built. Solomon's Temple was magnificent, and it stood until 586 B.C.E. At this time, Nebuchadnezzar destroyed the Temple and carried most of the Israelites off into captivity.

"Seventy years later, when the people came back from Babylon, they rebuilt the Temple. Zerubabel the High Priest, Ezra, and Jeremiah began to rebuild it. This Temple was known as the Second Temple or Zerubabel's Temple. With few available workers and little money, it was not as glorious as Solomon's Temple; therefore, many cried when they saw it. Nevertheless, it stood just as it was for 481 years.

"In 35 B.C.E. Herod the Great was king of Israel. Herod had a reputation for cruelty and for acting as the Romans' puppet. However, he was also responsible for countless building projects throughout Israel and therefore was called 'Herod the Builder.' It was this Herod who *remodeled* the Second Temple to look as beautiful as it did when Jesus saw it." (A scale model of Herod's remodeled Second Temple is what we saw in the Model City.)

Of course, because of God's instructions, the site of the Holy of Holies remained the same for both Temples, because this was a holy place set aside by God. The Jewish people were careful to keep track of its exact location. The Temple surrounding the Holy of Holies was greatly expanded by Herod, as were the Temple courtyards.

"But Jerusalem is a hilly area," Shep continued. "Herod wanted the entire complex to be on one level, so he dug rock, moved it, and created a huge level area on which to build. It wasn't very stable, so he built four huge retaining walls around the whole Temple area: a northern retaining wall, an eastern one, a southern wall, and the famous Western Wall.

"When the Romans demolished Jerusalem after the Bar Kochba revolt in 135 C.E., they destroyed everything in the city 'to the very last stone' except for the western retaining wall. This wall they left standing to serve as a reminder of the Romans' capacity for destruction." It serves as a vivid reminder to this day.

To bring the topic up to date, someone asked Shep about the Third Temple. "When will it be built?"

As a Christian, the question seemed absurd to me. Jesus was the "final sacrifice"; the Temple would never again be needed. I had been taught in church that after Jesus' ascension, our bodies were the only "Temple" of importance to God.

In Jerusalem I saw a different point of view. I saw bumper stickers that read "Messiah, come soon!" There are many atheists in Israel, but a religious fervor is also stirring. *Yeshivahs* (seminaries for rabbis) are filling up. Although adherents to Judaism do not accept Jesus as the Messiah, they do believe that either a Messiah or at least a Messianic Age will come relatively soon. I have heard that the Messianic Age will be here when "the lion will lie down with the lamb" and there will be "no more wars," and that some people are currently teaching about Temple sacrifice methods. It would follow, then, that these religious Jews would rebuild the Temple soon.

Shep began his answer by citing political objections to rebuilding the Temple. The location God specified for the Temple is now occupied by the Dome of the Rock, which is the third most holy site of the Islamic faith. Moslems would consider its destruction to be an act of war. In addition, the Via Dolorosa and many other Christian shrines are located in the same area. I could imagine that Christians would unite against Israel if these Christian sites were destroyed in order to rebuild the Temple. Shep said that the Israeli government is careful to keep these religious sites in the hands of Christians and Moslems. It is not easy to keep the peace when one city contains vital holy sites for three major religions.

Second, although the Holy of Holies is located on the Temple Mount, no one knows exactly where. It may be at the Dome of the Rock, or it may be at the Ark of the Covenant Dome, a smaller dome with a floor of bedrock located on the Temple Mount several yards

from the Dome of the Rock. The Bible tells us that only the High Priest
was allowed to enter the Holy of Holies; anyone else would desecrate
the holy site. Today, to prevent this possibility, no Jewish people walk
anywhere on the Temple Mount. If they cannot walk on the Temple
Mount, they cannot rebuild the Temple. Shep said, "Now, only God
knows where the Holy of Holies is located. Therefore, when God tells
us to rebuild, He will show us where the Holy of Holies is so we will
not desecrate it."

Someone asked the question again, "When will the Temple be
rebuilt?"

"On the day the Messiah comes," Shep replied, "only on *that* day
will we rebuild the Temple. It may be tomorrow or in two hundred
years. The belief is: not until Messiah comes."

Then Shep pointed out the huge outer courtyard next to the Temple
in the faithful depiction of first-century Jerusalem: the Court of the
Gentiles, designed for all non-Jews who wished to worship the God
of the Jews. Some Gentiles, like Ruth in the biblical book of the same
name, chose to convert to Judaism in order to become biblically
observant of the Law of Moses. However, the Court of the Gentiles
was specifically intended for those God-fearing (God-loving) Gentiles who chose *not* to convert to Judaism. Had I lived in the first century, this is where I would have come to worship God.

Our second stop was Gordon's Calvary, also known as the Garden
Tomb. This site had its own guide, so Shep shared his views about
the site before we arrived. He told us that Gordon's Calvary is one of
two places in Jerusalem thought to be the site of Jesus' crucifixion
and burial. We would visit the second site, the Holy Sepulchre, later.

Before giving his opinion of these sites, he emphasized, "Each one
lives by his belief. And it's not always beneficial to know the exact
site where an event occurred; often when the exact location is known,
the place itself is worshiped and the significance of the event is nearly
forgotten." I thought this might be the reason God is rarely specific
in the Bible regarding exact locations.

First to be considered, Shep explained, was the matter of where a tomb *could* be located in Jerusalem. Because God chose Jerusalem to be a special place, Jerusalem is considered in Judaism to be a holy city. Keeping in mind that in the first century C.E. and earlier, Jerusalem comprised only the Old City area, within the walls of the city (and twenty-five yards beyond) the land was considered holy. Therefore, no burials were allowed inside this area, as is still the Jewish custom today.

The Garden Tomb lies well outside the forbidden area. This means that in the first century, the Garden Tomb might have been a burial site. However, the Holy Sepulchre is located either inside or just outside the first-century walls; one would have to excavate to be certain. In any event, the Holy Sepulchre is definitely *not* twenty-five yards outside the original walls. By this reasoning, then, the Holy Sepulchre could not have been the site of any first-century tomb.

I then learned that crucifixion is a slow, incredibly painful way to die. The Romans placed the crucifixes with their agonized victims at major crossroads, achieving the maximum deterrent effect. In the first century, both Gordon's Calvary and the Holy Sepulchre were located at major crossroads.

Shep explained, "If this rich man, Joseph of Arimathea, (Matthew 27:57) purchased such a lovely garden, would he do so near a popular crucifixion site? Here he would sit in his garden, but he could not enjoy it, because just a few yards away some man is crying out in pain for hours on end. No, I don't believe Jesus' crucifixion took place at the Garden Tomb site. It is a good possibility that this is the place of the tomb and the garden of Joseph of Arimathea, but not the site of the crucifixion."

Although Shep did not believe it was possible for the Holy Sepulchre to be the site of Jesus' tomb, he did think that something important had happened there: "About one hundred years after Jesus' crucifixion, a major revolt took place in Jerusalem. The Temple had been destroyed in 70 C.E., but many Jewish people still lived there. The Roman oppression continued and a leader arose: Bar Kochba. Jewish people from outside Judea came to join Bar Kochba's band of rebels."

Even the great Jewish sage Rabbi Akiva believed Bar Kochba to be the Messiah. Bar Kochba recaptured Jerusalem from the Romans and had coins made in celebration of Jerusalem's liberation.[3] But in just three-and-a-half years, by 135 C.E., the Romans once again defeated the Jewish people, and Bar Kochba died alongside his men in battle.

"Unlike their attack in 70 C.E.," Shep continued, "this time the Romans were determined that Jerusalem's destruction would be complete. The cruel emperor Hadrian Caesar destroyed it 'to the very last stone' and threw salt on the ground to symbolize utter destruction. Next he built two pagan chapels: one over the site of the Holy of Holies and the second over the site known today as the Holy Sepulchre. Hadrian Caesar did this to desecrate the most holy sites of both the Jews and the Christians.

"And remember, just one hundred years after the crucifixion," Shep explained, "everyone would know the exact site of such an event. The Holy Sepulchre site was well-known at the time to be the most holy site for Christians. If it wasn't the tomb, then it must have been the crucifixion site."

I read later that Caesar then proclaimed Jerusalem to be a pagan city and renamed it Aelia Capitolina. Jewish people were forbidden to enter it under threat of death.

When we reached Gordon's Calvary, a British guide took over and told us about this site. He stated his belief in Jesus and how the exact site was not as important as biblical events that had occurred. However, he was very excited about the archaeological evidence found at Gordon's Calvary and how it related to events described in the Gospels.

Throughout the trip, interesting tidbits of knowledge were tossed our way. In this garden, our guide showed us a carob bean tree. In this area of the world, it is known as the locust bean. He felt fairly certain that the carob was what John the Baptist was eating when it is said "his food was locusts and wild honey" (Matthew 3:46).

The first attraction at Gordon's Calvary was a hill, a rock formation really, that looks vaguely like a human skull. Golgotha, "the Place of the Skull," is mentioned in the Gospel of John 19:17–18. The phrase could have meant a place where many deaths occurred, or it could refer to the skull-like rock formation we saw.

Located a few yards from the skull-like hill was a garden, as detailed in the gospel account. Archaeologists know there was a garden at this site in the first century because stones from its wine press were dated to be 2,000 years old. Huge water-holding tanks called cisterns were found here, which were also evidence of a huge garden. One of the cisterns discovered in this area had a capacity of 200,000 gallons.

The third issue in determining the authenticity of the two sites is the tomb itself. The tomb and the lecture made a vivid impression on me. Outside the tomb, I could see a groove running along the front, similar to the channel for a sliding glass door. Though missing now, a huge stone in the shape of a wheel was rolled along in the channel to cover the opening and protect the corpse from animals. This particular tomb was hewn from rock, whereas most tombs were simply modified caves. Only the rich could afford to have a tomb completely hewn from rock, so there are very few like this one in Israel. This was the type of tomb where a rich man like Joseph of Arimathea might have buried Jesus (Matthew 27:60).

In John 20:5 it is said that a disciple (probably John) bent over and looked in the tomb without actually entering it. From this position, he could see where the body would have been lying. According to our guide, this is the only hewn tomb discovered in the Jerusalem area that is believed to be 2,000 years old where one could have viewed the body from outside.

Another interesting aspect of this tomb is that it was obviously used by someone for whom it was not originally intended. The cut carved in the rock where the body was to be placed had been altered; additional rock had been cut away at the foot and the head area. The tomb had been altered for use by someone taller than the owner.

It seems that whenever a viable site is discovered evidence surfaces to refute its authenticity. Recent research has shown that this particular tomb is from the First Temple period.[4] Jesus, however, lived during the Second Temple period, which means that if the first Temple period dating is correct, Jesus could not have been laid in this tomb. But as both guides emphasized, exact locations are not as important as the events themselves.

After visiting the Garden Tomb, we returned to the Old City via Zion Gate, which was riddled with hundreds of bullet holes from the 1967 Six-Day War. We visited Mount Zion, the site of the Upper Room. In addition to being the site of the Last Supper, the second chapter of Acts states that this was also the site of the Holy Spirit baptism at Pentecost. For this reason, Shep felt that it was really the birthplace of the Christian church.

Shep also related the Jewish background to these familiar Christian events. The three biblical holy days on which all Jewish people were required to go to Jerusalem were Passover, Shavuot (Pentecost/ Feast of Weeks), and Sukkot (Feast of Tabernacles).[5] During these pilgrimage festivals, Jerusalem became extremely crowded.

Looking at New Testament events in this light was very interesting. Jesus' crucifixion took place near Passover, the first pilgrimage festival. Seven weeks later came Shavuot (Pentecost), which in Judaism is believed to be the anniversary of the date when God gave the Ten Commandments on Mount Sinai. On this fiftieth day after Passover, the New Testament says, God caused pilgrims to hear of His wonders in their own language (Acts 2:4). In this way, the Sinai experience (giving of the Law) relates to the Christian experience of receiving a message from God.

The building that now stands on the site of the Upper Room also houses the traditional tomb of King David. Shep said that according to the biblical account, David was actually buried in the City of David, which lies approximately a half-mile away in the Valley of Jehoshaphat. Nevertheless, the site was visited by countless people. David's tomb was the first site where men in our group were asked to don *kippahs* (small head coverings usually worn in synagogues).

What fascinated me as I entered the room was the sight of dozens of candles burning at once; it resembled a Catholic shrine. Shep told us that lighting candles in remembrance of the dead is a custom of Jewish origin: "Because the Bible says, 'The soul of a man is like a candle of God.'"[6]

In Judaism, on the anniversary of a loved one's death, the mourner lights a *yahrzeit* candle and recites prayers in honor of the lost loved one. All these candles I saw had been lit in honor of King David. God especially loved David's heart, and the Jewish people loved David. After this experience, I began to take note of the many similarities between Catholicism and Judaism. I began to see Judaism as Christianity's mother church.

This first day of touring was Friday, the Moslem (Islamic) holy day or day of rest. Therefore, even though we were in the Old City, we could not go to the Temple Mount because the Dome of the Rock, an Islamic shrine, is located there. On Fridays, all Moslem businesses in Israel are closed. On Saturdays, religious Jewish shopkeepers close their doors, and on Sunday Christians rest. In Israel, one could usually tell a person's religion by the business days he or she worked.

As we rode the tour bus, traveling only a few blocks gave me a sense of being thrust back into the first century. We passed the Mount of Olives, Garden of Gethsemane, Kidron Valley, and the Valley of Jehoshaphat. Shep casually pointed them out as if the sites were as insignificant as grocery stores or theatres. Thousands of years of biblical events were all accessible within a "Sabbath day's walk."

On the slope of Mount Zion, we saw a church that had been built over the site of the High Priest Caiaphas's house, and just a few feet away was a large cistern where some believe Jesus was held prisoner. The church was named the Church of Saint Peter Gallicantu, which refers to Peter's denial of Jesus three times, after which a cock crowed. Alongside the building was a wide stairway made of stones dated at 2,000 years old. Because of these steps' age and location, the church's guide was certain that Jesus and his disciples must have walked on them. They were now blocked off. I thought it odd that these stairs had lasted 2,000 years, and yet today people felt the need to protect them.

In the afternoon we ventured to the Western Wall (also known as the Wailing Wall). This time we entered the Old City through the Dung Gate. Before entering the Western Wall courtyard, our purses and bags were inspected at a security checkpoint. Again, the men donned *kippahs* and off we went.

Having absorbed so much history that morning at the Model City, the Western Wall seemed all the more awe inspiring. This wall was the only remnant of the temple area that existed in Jesus' day. The Herodian portion of the Wall was made up of massive individual stones, each perhaps four feet high and eight feet long. Below street level lay an additional eight layers of Herodian stones; above street level were layers of newer repairs. The exposed length of the Wall was 200 feet, whereas the entire length was at least 400 feet. Based on the size of this retaining wall, the Temple must have appeared supernatural in size and splendor.

Growing out of cracks between the stones I discovered hyssop (Exodus 12:22). In the Book of Exodus it is written that the Israelites dipped hyssop in sacrificial lamb's blood and spread it around their doorframes in obedience to God's command. The firstborn in each household was thus spared (passed over). In simple ways like this, the Bible constantly came alive for me in Israel.

The voices of the people were another reminder of ancient times. Most spoke Hebrew, the original language of Torah (Pentateuch) and most of the Hebrew Bible (Old Testament). At the Wall, I could hear muffled voices in prayer. Some Jewish men swayed as they prayed, their heads coming within an inch or two of the Wall, their concentration intense. I felt like a little child, observing something I could not quite understand.

I was surprised by the variety of people near the Wall: a young woman in a spaghetti-strapped dress, businessmen in suits, and ultra-religious Jewish people, the *Chasidim*, who wore very modest clothing. The chasidic men and boys had sidelocks, which are uncut sideburns that turn into long curls (Leviticus 19:27). I also saw an elderly Arab man walking slowly down the sidewalk; he wore a long brown robelike garment and the *kippah*-like hat that some religious Moslems wear. The whole scene was so peaceful: a harmony of different people. It felt jarring to exit through yet another security checkpoint.

Late that afternoon we visited the Garden of Gethsemane on the Mount of Olives. Churches abound here; on the Mount of Olives alone can be found two. One is the Church of Mary Magdalene, a beautiful Russian Orthodox church. Its golden onion-shaped domes topped with crosses serve as landmarks identifying the Mount of Olives. Down the hill, closer to the Jericho-Jerusalem road, is the Church of All Nations. Here, a monk from San Diego gave us a short tour of the Garden of Gethsemane, the site of Jesus' last prayers before his arrest. The Mount of Olives is also the traditional site of Jesus' ascension.

The Garden of Gethsemane contains many ancient olive trees; some are 2,000 years old. Because of the garden's location and archaeological evidence, it is certain that there existed a garden on this site in the first century. In any case, as the afternoon sun filtered in through the trees, I was awed by the site. It appeared both mysterious and peaceful.

On our first day, we had seen the Model City, Gordon's Calvary, Mount Zion, the Western Wall, and the Mount of Olives/Garden of Gethsemane site. Throughout the tour we were overwhelmed with history, Bible, archaeology, facts, and traditions. My head was swimming.

Dinner at the hotel was served at seven o'clock. It was nice, as I recall, but a blur. After several days of very little sleep, that bed felt great!

Saturday was an equally beautiful day in Jerusalem. We armed ourselves with film, microcassettes, and videotape. After another great buffet breakfast, we boarded the bus for the second day of touring.

Our Christian tour was scheduled with sensitivity to the holy day schedules of both Islam and Judaism. On Friday, the Islamic holy day, we saw the Western Wall instead of the Dome of the Rock, an Islamic holy site. Today we were allowed to visit the Dome of the Rock, but were asked to avoid the Western Wall, a Jewish holy site. Shep was Jewish and our bus driver was Arab, but neither was totally observant of his religion, so they remained with the tour group on both days.

On our way to the Dome of the Rock, we were asked to respect the Jewish Sabbath in certain ways while inside the Old City. We were asked not to use our cameras or tape recorders and not to smoke or write—acts forbidden to Jewish people on the Sabbath. Years later I learned that most of these prohibitions have to do with honoring God as the Creator, that is, avoiding acts that resemble creating in some manner. Smoking is prohibited because kindling a flame on the Sabbath is forbidden (Exodus 35:3). Out of regard for religious Jewish people present, we observed these restrictions.

Shortly before we reached the Temple Mount, we stopped in a shady area. As a Jew, Shep would not walk on the Temple Mount to be certain not to desecrate the Holy of Holies. When Shep told us that in the Moslem shrine, the Dome of the Rock, we must remove our shoes, I was reminded of God telling Moses to remove his sandals at the site of the burning bush as that ground was holy (Exodus 3:5). We were not allowed to carry anything into the Dome—no purses, cameras, and the like—so Shep would keep watch over our possessions for us.

In the shade, Shep explained Islamic beliefs about the Dome of the Rock. In the Koran, the Islamic Bible, it was Ishmael, not Isaac, whom Abraham was told to sacrifice at this site. Ishmael was Abraham's son by Hagar, Sarah's handmaid (Genesis 16:1–16). The second reason the Moslems consider this huge rock on Moriah to be important is its role in the life of their prophet Mohammed. According to Islam, Mohammed flew on his horse from Mecca, Saudi Arabia, to this rock on Moriah. They believe that from Moriah Mohammed, like Jesus, ascended into heaven.

In remembrance of these events, the Dome of the Rock was built 1,300 years ago. Shep explained that it is a shrine, not a mosque. A mosque is a place to pray and worship, like a church or synagogue, whereas a shrine is built to commemorate an event. Although the structure has been rebuilt many times, the foundation is the original one. The Dome of the Rock is the third most holy site for Moslems; the first two are located in Saudi Arabia, in Mecca and Medina. The Dome of the Rock is a landmark in Jerusalem; its golden dome can be seen from many miles away. Its color is a fairly recent feature, dating from 1966, and is not actually due to gold inlay but rather to gold-colored aluminum. The interior of the Dome is extremely ornate, especially in contrast to the huge gray stone it houses. The outside tile work is also fairly new; it is striking in rich blues, greens, and yellows.

As we left the Temple Mount, we exited the Old City through Saint Stephen's Gate and then boarded the bus for Bethlehem. After an eleven-minute, seven-mile ride, we arrived in Bethlehem, which is located on the West Bank. These two words conjure up images of barbed wire and factions at war, but that is not what I saw. There was no sharp transition from Jerusalem to Bethlehem: one was simply a suburb of the other.

On the short drive from Jerusalem to Bethlehem, we learned that the stone walls surrounding the Old City were built by the Turks during Ottoman rule. We also learned that if we ever wished to visit Israel again more cheaply, we could volunteer to work on a kibbutz and that Hebrew University, one of six universities in Israel, is on Mount Scopus in Jerusalem. Shep told us that Moslems may not be Arab and Arabs may not be Moslem; race and religion are not necessarily synonymous. However, according to Shep, a Jew is Jewish both in nationality and religion. "If he is born to a Jewish woman, he is a Jew. Even if he 'converts' to another religion, he is still a Jew." I found every detail fascinating.

Like the Old City section of Jerusalem, Bethlehem has a population of roughly 35,000. The main road is a large artery with narrow side streets branching off and winding upward through residential areas. Most residents were Arab-Christians. Although most Arab people are of the Islamic faith, there are many Arab-Christians in Israel. Many Christian towns—Bethlehem, Nazareth, and Cana—have mainly Arab-

Christian residents. Along the road from Jerusalem to Bethlehem, modern covered bus stops contrasted sharply with an old Arab man who was riding a donkey.

Bethlehem was the most commercial site I saw in Israel. Our first stop there was at a large souvenir shop where beautiful jewelry, olive-wood carvings, and nativity sets were sold. Everyone was accommodated; signs were printed in Hebrew, Arabic, and English. A few of us took turns having our pictures taken with a handsome Israeli soldier outside the shop in the town square. As I gazed in wonder at this ancient village, a neon star, perched atop a church, pierced my romanticized notions.

Bethlehem is the birthplace of Jesus, so a huge complex called the Church of the Nativity was built over the traditional site of Jesus' manger. Here, we were turned over to yet another guide who led us through the complex and explained its history.

The Church of the Nativity was built in 326 C.E. In 386 C.E. Saint Jerome translated the Bible from the original Hebrew to Greek and then from Greek to Latin. His translation is known as the Latin Vulgate. Saint Jerome died in 417 C.E. His statue stands in the inner courtyard of this complex.

In 614 C.E. the Persians destroyed all the churches they could find in the Holy Land. Over the entrance to the Church of the Nativity the Persians found a mosaic depiction of the three wise men mentioned in the Gospels (Matthew 2:1–2). Since the characters in the mosaic were garbed in Persian-looking clothes, the conquerors mistook the church for a Persian temple so it was the only church to be spared.

One of the most unusual aspects of this church was its entrance. In the sixteenth century, when Turks occupied the Holy Land, they drove their camels and horses right into churches. Christians lowered the entrance to the Church of the Nativity so that neither horses nor camels could get in. This low entranceway also forced visitors to bow out of respect as they entered the church.

The complex is actually a maze of several churches. Inside, at the traditional site of the manger, a brass fourteen-point star lies on the floor. This is a Roman Catholic site, and the star represents the fourteen stations of the cross. (I learned about these stations later when we walked the Via Dolorosa.) Here also are the remains of the mosaic floor that was part of the original building. There were several altars, all incredibly ornate.

Our next stop was the "shepherds' field." In contrast to the ornate churches we had just seen, this was a breath of fresh air.

To lighten things up, our last stop in the area was at the side of the road—for camel rides! One American dollar bought a ride on a huge, noisy, slow camel. One American dollar also bought forty picture postcards! Unlike our later days in Rome, American tourists' money was always appreciated in Israel.

In the afternoon, we drove a few miles back to the Jerusalem area. Here, on top of the Mount of Olives, is the village of Bethany, which means house of the poor. It is assumed that the only rich residents of this village in the first century were Lazarus, Martha, and Mary (John, chapters 10 and 11). There is a tomb here of hewn rock believed to be their family tomb, and a church has been built over the site. Bethany also marks the beginning of the "Palm Sunday Road"; from here, Jesus walked down into Jerusalem just days before his crucifixion.

The story of the raising of Lazarus provides a good example of the way Jewish history sheds light on New Testament passages. In the Gospel of John 11:3, Jesus is sent word that Lazarus is sick. Jesus then understood that Lazarus had actually died (John 11:4). I would have thought that Jesus would have immediately gone to comfort Martha and Mary, or knowing he was going to raise Lazarus from the dead, he would have gone as soon as possible to save the sisters some grief. Instead, he waited several days before traveling to Bethany.

Shep related an interesting belief of first-century Judaism. "People believed that the soul doesn't leave a dead body for the first three days. If Lazarus had been raised from the dead in just seventy-two hours or less, people would have said, 'Ah, he was only sick.' John 11:17 says Jesus arrived after Lazarus had been in the tomb for four days; therefore, there would be no doubt in the witnesses' minds that Lazarus was dead. And this is probably why, though Lazarus was already dead when the news was relayed to Jesus, Martha tells Jesus upon his late arrival, 'If you had been here, my brother would not have died.' Until three days had passed, she still had hope. Jesus' waiting four days made the observers believe that the raising of Lazarus was truly a miracle from God."

Although Shep did not point it out, something about this first-century belief occurred to me later. Jesus died quickly on the cross; Pilate in fact expressed surprise at how quickly Jesus died (Mark 15:44). According to the commentary in the NIV Study Bible[7] it often took two or three days for people to die on a cross. Jesus' body was removed from his cross and laid in a tomb before sundown Friday night, the beginning of the Sabbath. By Sunday morning, one-and-a-half days later, the tomb was discovered empty. If first-century Jewish people believed that death did not occur for at least three days, it is not surprising that many could not believe that Jesus had actually died, let alone been resurrected.

I have often heard Christians talk about belief in the death, burial, and resurrection of Jesus as the ability to accept hard, cold facts. To many, it seems as though the people in the first century who rejected these beliefs purposely blinded themselves to the facts. But I began to see that belief in these things is a matter of faith.

Next, we returned to the Old City of Jerusalem to see the Via Dolorosa, which is Latin for the Way of Sorrow. Since Jerusalem has been built on layers of ruins, we were actually walking several feet above the path Jesus took on the way to his crucifixion. Here, we learned of the fourteen occurrences or sites that are known in Roman Catholic dogma as the fourteen stations of the cross.

1. Jesus was sentenced by Pontius Pilate at the Praetorium, or Antonia's Fortress.

2. Jesus was condemned, given a crown of thorns, beaten, and made to carry his cross.
3. Jesus falls under the weight of the cross for the first time.
4. Jesus sees his mother, Mary.
5. Simon of Cyrene (modern Libya) is told to carry Jesus' cross for him.
6. Christian tradition relates that here a woman broke through the line of Roman soldiers and wiped Jesus' face with a cloth. When she pulled it away, the image of Jesus' face remained on the cloth. *Vero* means "true," and *nika* means "image," so *Veronica* means "true image." The Church of Saint Veronica is located at this station.
7. Jesus falls for the second time.
8. Jesus tells the women of Jerusalem to cry for their children and not for him.
9. Jesus falls for the third time. Stations 10 to 14 are all located inside the Church of the Holy Sepulchre.
10. Jesus' clothing is removed.
11. Jesus is nailed to the cross.
12. Jesus died on the cross.
13. Jesus is taken down from the cross.
14. The last station is the site of the empty tomb.

The last few hours of the day were free time. Six of us chose to stay in the Old City; this was our first chance to fully explore the huge marketplace, a wonderful maze of little shops and a mingling of voices in a myriad of languages. The Old City marketplace was filled with brightly colored fruits and vegetables, unique clothing shops, and many souvenir shops filled with jewelry and olive-wood carvings. No merchant marked a set price. They preferred bartering, and the resulting prices were low. We snacked on fresh fruit as we window-shopped for several hours. When we finished, we caught a public bus to our hotel where dinner was waiting.

The Jewish day begins at sundown,[8] so Saturday night is actually the beginning of Sunday in Israel. That evening, my two roommates went to a folk-dancing event while I stayed at the hotel. Several of us gathered for Sunday service on the roof of the hotel; we held a devotional in the dark. We sang and took communion; the bread and grape juice were given to us by Arab-Christians nearby. We sang often on the bus and elsewhere, but this evening devotional was a solemn occasion.

In my hotel room afterward I reflected on the Holy City of Jerusalem. Few Jewish people believed that Jesus was the Messiah. Our pastor said that the majority of the Jewish people today do not even believe in an afterlife. My heart was breaking over this lack of belief. I could not understand why religious Jewish people did not believe the same way Christians did. I was frustrated that our Jewish guide knew all the history of Jesus, but did not believe he was the Messiah. I thought I had found the truth about God and Jesus, so I could not understand why that truth was not obvious to others. Into my recorder that night I recited the passage from John 20:24–31 regarding doubting Thomas. Persistent Jewish unbelief upset me so much that it eventually led to a quest to find out why they did not believe.

At 7:30 on a bright Sunday morning, we left Jerusalem to see more of the country. How strange that after only two days in the city it had become so dear to me. There is truly no other place on earth like Jerusalem. Our itinerary did not include another visit to it, so as we drove away I felt a loss.

The entire trip from Jerusalem to Qumran by the Dead Sea took only thirty minutes. Not one to waste a moment, Shep was like a television reporter: he had much to say and little time to say it. His talks were always fascinating, but sometimes contained more data than I could absorb. I turned on my recorder, sat back, and relaxed, enjoying the scenery as he spoke.

Shep told us that the State of Israel is very small, long, and narrow. At the farthest points from north to south, Israel is only 300 miles long. Most of the country is less than 50 miles wide, yet climates within the country vary dramatically. Jerusalem, in the Judean hills, has an annual rainfall of twenty-seven to thirty inches; it even gets snow occasionally, and trees and greenery decorate the whole city. Yet, just a half-hour away in the Judean desert, in Qumran it rains only one or two inches per year. When it is cold in Jerusalem, people drive down to a warm beach at the Dead Sea or to the secluded springs and pools of nearby En Gedi, the oasis in the desert where David hid from King Saul.

I learned that the Jewish people of Israel are an extremely diverse group. To escape the Holocaust, millions of Jewish people came from Europe to settle in Israel. Many have also come from the surrounding Arab states, the continent of Africa, Russia, and most everywhere on earth. Wherever there was religious persecution, Jews left for Israel. For this reason, their War of Independence in 1948 was even more difficult to wage: newly arrived soldiers did not speak the same language. Today, everyone learns Hebrew, the language of the Hebrew Bible (Old Testament); the Hebrew language helps unify the Jewish population both inside and outside Israel.

In an area like the Middle East, a large military force is necessary for survival. We learned that Israel has the third largest air force in the world. When they finish school, men and women enter the IDF (Israel Defense Forces). Women are both needed and well utilized in the IDF and the police force.

However, Israel is also very family oriented. If a woman gets married before her time comes to enter the service, she is excused. If after she enters the IDF she marries, she is released immediately. I was impressed with this profamily attitude, especially in a country that needs its women to serve. As we are learning the hard way in the United States, we pay a price when too many priorities are placed ahead of nurturing family life.

Our drive to Qumran continued. On the low hills along the side of the road, we noticed some large, dusty brown tents. Shep told us these were the tents of the Bedouin people. "Although they used to be nomadic, few in Israel are still so today. When they move around, it's difficult to provide free public education for their children, or any other public services. They have begun to form villages, but they still cook outdoors in a hole dug in the ground. They retain tribal ways as much as possible. Even their faith is different from that of other Arabic peoples: they revere Moses' father-in-law, Jethro."

The next set of tents I eyed more carefully. Extending from the top of one of the tents was a television antenna. Nomads with battery-powered televisions? I guess it is difficult to live in the past in a modern country like Israel.

It took less than thirty minutes to reach Qumran from Jerusalem. Qumran was the first kibbutz, a communal-living village. The Essenes, a first-century sect of Judaism, lived here. The name Qumran is actually an Arabic word meaning "two moons." Bedouins saw the moon in the sky and its reflection on the waters of the Dead Sea; hence, two moons.

Unlike the rest of the Jews of that time, the Essenes were strict separatists. They enjoyed a great deal of solitude due to the fact that it took "several good days" (as Shep said) to walk here from Jerusalem. Shep explained, "This is physically and spiritually a *pure* place. No one stands between you and your God. No one stands between you and your way of life."

At Qumran excavations, we viewed the communal meeting and dining area, an elaborate water system, food storage areas, and the *mikveh*.[9] The Essenes lived as self-sufficiently as possible.

Shep believed that the Gospel account of John the Baptist going into the Judean desert probably referred to a trip to Qumran. Shep also pointed out that the first followers of Jesus, who were Jewish people, also formed a kibbutz. This is revealed in Acts 4:32 and Acts 5:1–11.

Like those early Jewish followers of Jesus, the Essenes were intentionally poor. They strove not for monetary riches, but rather for purity of life and worship. However, the Essenes did have some "treasures": a rich library of scrolls. The majority of these scrolls were books of the Bible. To protect them from advancing Romans in the first century, the Essenes hid the scrolls in clay jars and placed them in caves in the nearby hills. After the Roman devastation was completed, however, there would be no retrieval.

In 1947, a Bedouin shepherd boy was watching over his sheep in the hills surrounding Qumran when one wandered into a cave. Fearful of what might be inside, the boy threw a rock into the cave. It shattered something. He got his cousin, and together they entered the cave and found the jars that had been hidden by the Essenes. Today the contents of those jars are known as the Dead Sea Scrolls.

The Shrine of the Book is the Jerusalem museum that houses the Dead Sea Scrolls. Among them was found the Book of Isaiah in its entirety: a 2,000-year-old copy. For those who read Hebrew, this scroll bolsters faith in the authenticity of today's Hebrew Bible, because other than an additional word somewhere in the text, this 2,000-year-old scroll is identical to the Book of Isaiah as found in today's Hebrew Bible. The Holy Scriptures that Jesus loved 2,000 years ago are the very same today.

At this point I realized that in order to emulate Jesus more closely, I would need to read the Holy Scriptures as he did, in Hebrew. When I had questions about the meaning of an Old Testament passage, I wanted to be able to check the original wording. Yet not one of the 500 people in the church I attended knew Hebrew. I became convinced that the Christian community needed more people who could read both Hebrew (Old Testament) and Greek (New Testament). I found it difficult to study in much depth without being able to read these texts in their original languages.

According to Josephus Flavius, the great Jewish historian, it was very difficult to join the Essene community. Shep told us, "First, they rejected you. If you persisted, they offered a reserved maybe. The potential convert was then allowed to join the Essene community during the day to eat, pray, study, and work. But at night, he would have to find shelter in nearby caves. After a few months, if everything was okay, he was allowed to join the kibbutz. Finally, to be fully accepted into the community, he must be baptized."

Shep believed that John the Baptist took the idea of baptism from the Essenes, whose movement began before the first century. We read in Acts that, like the Essenes, those who wanted to join Jesus' movement were baptized: "Those who accepted his message were baptized, and about three thousand were added to their number that day" (Acts 2:41).

Here was yet another example of how knowledge of Jewish concepts sheds light on New Testament passages. The newly converted Essene believers, like the believers in Acts, were not considered part of their number until they were baptized. The first believers in Acts were Jewish people who lived a communal lifestyle, somewhat similar to the first-century Essene community. Now I could better visualize what the life of first-century followers of Jesus was like. But it would take quite a while to assimilate all this new information, let alone have it affect the way I read the New Testament.

From Qumran, we continued down the road that runs along the Dead Sea. On our way south to Masada, we saw groves of date palms and acacia trees; they received water from underground springs. Acacia was the wood used to build the Ark of the Covenant for the Temple. We learned that the eastern shore of the Dead Sea, directly across from Masada, is thought by many to be the site of ancient Sodom and Gomorrah. However, some believe that the ruins of these infamously wicked cities lie beneath the southern tip of the Dead Sea. A guided tour of Israel is really a mobile Bible and history class!

By about ten o'clock we reached Masada. Masada is to Jewish people what the Alamo is to Texans. Masada was one of their last strongholds, where they made their first-century stand against the invading Roman legions.

In 35 B.C.E., two years after he became king, Herod established a palace on top of this huge rock. It would serve as a refuge from his subjects. Though he was legally king of the Jews, he was a slave to the Romans, so his subjects despised him.

Masada is situated 1,200 feet above the Dead Sea along the road to Egypt. It is only a three-and-a-half-hour ride from here by car to the Red Sea, the entrance to Egypt. From this vantage point it is easy to spot travelers while they are still a great distance away. The Romans had no choice but to conquer Masada.

Long after the Romans devastated Jerusalem, they approached Masada. Shep shared this history: "The fate of the Jerusalemites had been known for two years. The settlers of Masada lived in fear of the day the Romans would come. When they arrived, the settlers fought bravely. The Romans laid siege to Masada for six long months: from November 72 c.e. to April 73 c.e. Not wanting to suffer slaughter at the hands of the Romans, as had those in Jerusalem, the settlers on Masada agreed to mass suicide. They finished just before the Romans reached the top: it was a hollow victory for the Romans. The story comes to us because one settler, a woman, hid two children during the mass suicide; she had witnessed these tragic events."

At the foot of Masada, we saw the ruins of first-century Roman army camps. We took a cable car most of the way up the mount. The view was spectacular from this level, but there were eighty-nine additional steps to climb to reach the summit. At the top were excavations of the stone quarry, the bathhouse, Herod's private villa, the synagogue, and a huge cistern. We also saw the ramp the Romans had built to conquer Masada. Shep told us that a maximum of twenty soldiers guarded this palace. What a few soldiers to stand against the Roman legions!

After the tour of the top of Masada, we descended by the eighty-nine steps and cable cars to a restaurant at its foot. Located in the area known as the West Bank, Masada was in Jordanian hands from 1948 to 1967. Yet, no barbed wire or signs of war could be found. Instead, RC Cola signs beckoned a constant stream of tourists.

After lunch, we were on the road again. Our next stop was a beach on the Dead Sea. It was not a long ride, but Shep had time to teach us a little. Someone asked him what the terms *schlemiel* and *schlemazel* meant. (These words come from the opening song of the *Laverne and Shirley* television show.) He said *schlemiel* means clumsy. *Mazel* means luck, like *mazel tov* (good luck). *Schlemazel* means always having bad luck. So, *schlemiel schlemazel* means clumsy and always having bad luck!

These are Yiddish terms. Yiddish is a combination of German and Hebrew, a language spoken by European Jews. Since the Holocaust wiped out two-thirds of Europe's Jewish population, Yiddish is not spoken by many people anymore.

The sand on the Dead Sea beach was unusually clean, white, and extremely hot. The Dead Sea is 26 percent salt, so nothing can live in the water, but even the worst swimmer can float due to the density of salt. However, if that water dries on your skin you itch and hurt, so as swimmers leave the water they take showers in fresh water from pipes that come up out of the sand. As for our desert thirst, every place we stopped sold soda and bottled water.

At 1,300 feet below sea level, the Dead Sea is the lowest point on earth. Masada, at 1,200 feet above the Dead Sea, is still 100 feet below sea level. In contrast, Death Valley, California, the lowest point in the United States, is only 282 feet below sea level. The Dead Sea is 50 miles long and 10 to 12 miles wide, and the present border between Israel and Jordan runs down the middle of it.

In the afternoon we reached Jericho, "the City of Palms," and at 6,000 years it is the oldest *continually* inhabited city on earth. Approximately 3,200 years ago, God told Joshua and the Jewish people to take Canaan as their land, the land He promised to Abraham's descendants (Genesis 13:15). They crossed the Jordan River, left what is today the country of Jordan, and entered Canaan near the city of Jericho.

The Bible tells us that when the Israelites reached Jericho, they marched around the fortified city for six days. On the seventh day, they marched around seven times . . . "and the walls came tumbling down." Shep asked two questions. First, "Why did the Bible say the wall fell 'down'? Wouldn't it have been sufficient to say the walls fell?" Second, "Why did Joshua curse the man who would rebuild the city of Jericho?"

Joshua's curse was that if and when a man began to rebuild the city, that man's eldest son would die. Then, when he finished, his youngest son would die. I realized we were being introduced to challenging Jewish Bible study.

Shep began his answers: "Joshua knew the prevailing custom of victors in a battle: they would conquer a place, destroy it, and rebuild a new city on top of the ruins. Joshua wanted to prevent this from happening because there was something he did not want covered.

"According to Maimonides,"[10] Shep continued, "God gave Israel the victory at Jericho. The Israelites didn't have to fight; they just marched around the walls in obedience. The Israelites didn't push the walls in. The people of Jericho certainly didn't push the walls out, making themselves vulnerable; besides, the Israelites would have been hurt if the walls fell on them.

"Where did the walls go?" Shep asked. "Maimonides believed the word *down* was used because God Himself opened up the earth, and the walls fell straight down into the ground.

"Joshua, a God-fearing man, wanted to be certain God received the glory for His miracle. If someone were to rebuild the city, the holes that provided the proof of God's miracle would no longer be visible. Eventually, Ahab did rebuild Jericho, and he did lose his eldest and youngest sons in the process."

We left the green oasis of Jericho and drove back through the desert, following the Jordan River. On the opposite bank of the river is the Arab country of Jordan. We stopped at a popular tourist spot on the West Bank of the river, which some believe is the site where John the Baptist immersed Jesus. I can still hear Shep's words as he shouted from the front of the bus, "Over to your right are the restrooms. To the left is the snack bar. Everyone who wants to be baptized, raise your hands."

I was appalled at the thought of someone getting baptized with no apparent commitment involved. How unlike first-century baptisms!

Despite this commercialism, though, the Jordan is a beautiful river. It is flanked by trees and thick, lush greenery. I was on the other side of the world, but I could almost visualize Huckleberry Finn and Tom Sawyer rafting down this calm, green river. I stood at the river bank, enjoying this precious moment of peace and solitude. My world stood still . . . but only for a few minutes.

We continued northward through Samaria and up into the northern part of Israel known as the Galilee. In the first century, it was sometimes called Galilee of the Gentiles, though many Jewish people lived here as well. (The southern, dryer portion of the country is called the Negev.) We would spend Sunday night at the Sea of Galilee in a Tiberias hotel.

I missed Jerusalem, but the Tiberias hotel was nice. The television even worked. A few of us were walking past the room of someone in our tour group. We spotted *Bugs Bunny* cartoons on television. It was hilarious to watch Bugs Bunny dubbed in Hebrew!

Reflecting on the day's travels, I realized that the sites we visited—Qumran, Masada, the Dead Sea, Jericho, and the Jordan River—were all located in the West Bank area. Had it been before 1967, we would not have been able to see any of these places. They were part of the country of Jordan until the 1967 Six-Day War when Israel emerged victorious.

I was also surprised to find no war zone here. The only indications of Israel "occupying" an "Arab area" were occasional sightings of Israeli soldiers. We saw Arab villages, but there were also many Jewish villages that had developed over the last two decades. They had not settled their new territory as quickly as we Americans had the Old West, but they were slowly working at it.

If there was any tension between Arabs and Jews, it was not apparent at the time (1985). Visiting the West Bank area myself, I saw that the foreign press must have been exaggerating the conflict. Yes, we saw eighteen-year-old barbed wire from the 1967 war. We also saw abandoned 1948 Russian tanks brightly painted for decoration. But that was all we saw.

That Monday morning, when we awoke in Tiberias, the air was a little hazy over the Sea of Galilee. We were all excited to be here because this was where much of Jesus' healing and preaching ministry took place. On the western shore of the Sea of Galilee that morning we boarded a double-decker tour boat. As we left, I noticed a restaurant sign on the shore; they boasted of serving Saint Peter's fish. People still fish the Galilee much as they did in the first century.

My first surprise was the size of the famous Sea of Galilee. Actually, it is a lake, the only freshwater lake in Israel. It is only seven miles wide, thirteen miles long, and 150 feet at its deepest point. Other names given this lake are Genessaret (Valley of Genessaret), Lake of the Beatitudes, Lake of Tiberias, and in Hebrew it is known as Lake Kinneret, possibly due to its harplike shape (*Kinneret* is the Hebrew word for harp).

The lake is surrounded by mountains: on the west by the mountains of Galilee and on the east by the Golan Heights, which are part of Israel today. One of the mountains of Galilee is Mount Arbel, at the foot of which is found Magdela of Mary Magdalene fame. Magdela is on the old road that Jewish people used in the first century to reach Capernaum.

On a map I saw that Magdela was not along the direct route from the south to Capernaum; the logical path would lead people straight through Tiberias. In 18–22 c.e. Herod Antipas built the town of Tiberias and named it in honor of the Roman Emperor Tiberius. However, he built the town over a cemetery, and Jewish people would not walk there out of respect for the dead. Therefore, Jesus and other Jews traveled to Capernaum via Magdela.

Today, Tiberias is a modern tourist town. Many beautiful hotels have been built along the shores of the lake. The Sea of Galilee has great beaches, and people come from as far away as Jerusalem to swim here. In the first century, after the Romans destroyed much of central Israel (Judea), many Jewish survivors settled in the Galilee. Eventually Galilee became a center for Jewish study and religious life.

According to the New Testament, Jesus healed many people who lived in villages around the lake. At the northern end of the Sea of Galilee were three major cities that thrived in the first century: Capernaum, Bethsaida, and Korazin. We visited ruins of Capernaum including its synagogue. Here I literally fell into the second century— when my foot slipped into a hole at the synagogue ruins.

At Capernaum, Shep told us that with the Ark of the Covenant and the Temple destroyed, the synagogue has taken their place in Jewish life. However, as I later learned, synagogues existed even before the Second Temple was destroyed. Because of the Babylonian exile, only 20 percent of the Jewish nation actually lived in Israel in the first century.[11] Those living too far away from the Temple met together and prayed in the first synagogues.

Archaeologists found evidence that Capernaum was inhabited from the first century B.C.E. and that it flourished in the fourth century C.E. Nearby Korazin also flourished at this time. A group of Judeo-Christians, called the Sectarians, coexisted with the Capernaum Jewish community as late as the second century C.E. A nun who visited Capernaum between 381 and 384 C.E. said these two groups lived in harmony; a church and a synagogue stood here. But by the sixth century, the synagogue was gone.[12]

Today a church stands on a hill above the northern shore of the Sea of Galilee. It was built to commemorate the site where Jesus fed the five thousand and preached the Sermon on the Mount, the Beatitudes. Inside is a mosaic floor that depicts the five loaves and two fishes with which Jesus fed the multitude; but in an effort to form a cross, to mark the place as holy, only four loaves were used by the artist. It was here, overlooking the lake, that one of the pastors in our group read the Beatitudes (Matthew 5:1–12) passage aloud.

I discovered how it was possible for huge crowds to hear Jesus' sermons without a microphone. The hillside below this church was shaped like an ancient amphitheater. Sound naturally carried up the hillside from the shore.

From the Sea of Galilee we traveled north and saw a great deal of the countryside, including Samaria. Samaritans still live in this section of Israel. They accept only the Pentateuch as Holy Scripture, and they believe that Mount Gerezim, not Mount Zion, is the site where Abraham was told by God to sacrifice Isaac. Therefore, the Samaritans pray while facing Mount Gerezim, in contrast to the Jewish people who face Jerusalem and the Temple Mount while praying.

As we drove on, we saw Israel's northern border, the cease-fire line between Israel and Lebanon: we were only a five-minute drive away. Here, Shep told us about the absorption of millions of Jewish people into Israel. He said, "It's not enough to offer them refuge; they also need jobs and shelter." We saw Jewish settlement towns along the road. One was called Kiryat Shmona, which in Hebrew means the city of the eight. This town was named in honor of eight young people who died here in the 1920s. We were now in the Hula Valley, in the Golan Heights area. In contrast to what I thought upon hearing those words, it was lovely and peaceful.

We stopped for a picnic lunch at Banias, also known as Caesarea Philippi. Trees and greenery were everywhere. We ate at wooden picnic tables. I felt as if I were back home at a park in the Pacific Northwest. We found cool fresh water, runoff from the melting snows of Mount Hermon. This stream eventually ran into the river Jordan, the source for the Sea of Galilee. When mentioned in the New Testament, this city is called Caesarea Philippi, named in honor of Herod's son Philip.

Water is such a calming element; we sat down and dipped our feet in. A Jewish couple in their early twenties had also come here to relax at Banias. Paul filmed them with his video camera while one of my roommates played reporter and interviewed the couple. Everyone was laughing and having fun, but we also learned something.

Though both wore swimsuits, the man wore a rifle over his bare shoulder. When we asked why, he told us that Israel had been caught by surprise on Yom Kippur in 1973. Yom Kippur is a day of fasting, praying, and rest, the holiest day on the Jewish calendar. No one was thinking about war on that day.

That year Egypt and Syria took advantage of this lack of prepared-ness, both attacking at once. Unarmed and unprepared, Israel was invaded in the north (Golan Heights) and in the south (Suez). Against these overwhelming odds, Israel emerged the victor. Since that day, all Israeli armed forces wear their rifles even while off duty.

On the drive back down through the Galilee, the bus ride got lively. Shep taught us a few Hebrew words and a song or two. We learned that *shalom* means peace, but people use it for saying hello and good-bye in Israel. *Chaveirim* means friends. *Lehitra'ot* means see you later or we'll see you again. With this limited vocabulary, Shep taught us this little song;

> *Shalom chaveirim, shalom chaveirim, shalom, shalom,*
> *lehitra'ot, lehitra'ot, shalom, shalom.*

Then we sang it in English:

> Good-bye my friends, good-bye my friends, good-bye, good-bye,
> We'll see you again, we'll see you again, good-bye, good-bye.

We also learned, or at least heard, the famous Jewish standard "*Havah Negilah.*" By the time it was done, people were dancing down the aisle of the bus!

We passed the town of Cana, where the New Testament says Jesus turned water into wine for a wedding feast. Just south of Cana we found Nazareth. Nazareth is west of the Sea of Galilee, about midway between the Mediterranean Sea and the Sea of Galilee. Israel is only fifty miles wide at this point. It constantly amazed me that so much biblical history could have happened in such a tiny country.

Nazareth is a little town similar to Bethlehem. Jesus spent the major part of his life here, some say from about the age of eight to the age of thirty. Like Jerusalem, which has the Gihon Spring, Nazareth has only one spring, and a well is built over it. We could be certain that Joseph, Mary, and Jesus came to this well to draw water for their household. With all the scholarly controversy over religious sites, it was comforting to know that this one was certain; this had to be the well people used 2,000 years ago. Of course, now there is a church built over the well: the Greek Orthodox Church of the Annunciation of the Angel Gabriel.

South of Nazareth, on the "Road to the Sea," the Mediterranean, is the ancient city of Megiddo, one of Solomon's chariot cities. Wood was an expensive and scarce commodity, so this city was built of stone. In Hebrew, this place is called the hill of Megiddo (*Har Megiddo*); Armageddon is a mispronunciation of Har Megiddo. Here, at ancient crossroads in the Valley of Jezreel many biblical battles took place. Revelation 16:16 tells of a great battle between good and evil that is to take place here in the future. With twenty-two known layers of occupation, Megiddo is an archaeological delight.

The view from Megiddo was breathtaking. Shep began pointing out mountains and valleys and telling us their biblical significance. In the distance, we could see part of the hills of Samaria. We also saw Mount Gilboah where after several battles with the Philistines, King Saul committed suicide. Across the valley from Mount Gilboah, I saw the hill of Moreh where Gideon fought the Midianites with 300 soldiers who drank water like dogs. A dome-shaped hill to the left is Mount Tabor, the place where Deborah and Cisera fought. From Megiddo we could also see the hills of Galilee. I saw one end of Mount Carmel, which is twenty kilometers long; the other end is at Haifa on the Mediterranean where we would go for lunch.

We took a few photos after lunch, using the city of Haifa as a backdrop. From Haifa we traveled south along the coast of the Mediterranean Sea. On this short trip on our way to Caesarea by the Sea, Shep shared more Jewish insights into the New Testament. I preserved his comments on my recorder, but I have no memory of his saying these things. Had I comprehended what he was saying and understood the ramifications of what it meant, I would have been in shock. As it happened, it went totally over my head. It would be nearly two years before I would hear this teaching again, and that time from a Christian.

Shep relayed the story in Acts, chapter 10, about Cornelius who lived at Caesarea. According to the New Testament, this God-fearing Gentile was told in a vision to send for Peter who was staying just down the coast at Joppa, which is modern-day Tel Aviv/Jaffa. While in Joppa, Peter received his vision of animals on a sheet. Most likely, everyone in our tour group had read Acts, chapter 10, at least once or twice, but I doubt they had heard this exegesis.

Shep told us that this was the vision of unclean animals. "A voice ordered Peter to kill and eat. Peter didn't understand the meaning of this vision, because even today a Jew—and Peter was an Orthodox (observant) Jew—will not eat something which is unclean." He continued, "And then, when they brought him to Caesarea to meet with Cornelius, he understood exactly the meaning of the vision. It meant that Peter was to accept this Gentile, Cornelius, into this new movement. The Holy Spirit 'filled' the Gentiles in Caesarea, and they began to speak in tongues they didn't know.

"This confirmed Peter's interpretation of the vision. In Jerusalem when they spoke in tongues, all the people were Jewish; but here, God was doing the same miracle with Gentiles. Caesarea by the Sea is the place where Gentiles were first accepted into the movement (by Peter anyway). Therefore, *this* must be considered the birthplace of the Christian Church for the Gentile world."

I understood that Peter had been calling *people* unclean, which was not right, but many months would pass before I appreciated the ramifications of that statement. Peter spent three-and-one-half years as one of Jesus' three closest disciples, eating and drinking with him, and long after Jesus was gone Peter still said, "I have never eaten anything impure or unclean" (Acts 10:14). Peter was still following the Old Testament food laws. Jesus had not taught him differently, not even in the forty days before the ascension (Acts 1:3).

I wondered why. I thought Jesus had canceled all these laws. It even said so in one of the letters Paul addressed to first-century congregations (Colossians 2:14). How could Peter have so completely misunderstood Jesus that he would continue keeping kosher[13] if Paul was saying all these laws were canceled? If Peter kept kosher the entire time he was Jesus' disciple, then Jesus must have kept kosher too. Peter was still observing the kosher laws as of Acts, chapter 10; therefore, Jesus had not taught Peter to abandon the Law of Moses at all! Judaism, at least that portion of it, was still valid.

Thankfully, none of this occurred to me until many months after my return home. I was allowed to simply enjoy the trip. Sometimes, ignorance *is* bliss.

Although hotel reservations had been made for us at Tiberias for another night, the entire tour group wanted to stay in Jerusalem Monday night. After all, it would be our last night in Israel. After much discussion (and quick work by Shep) the reservations were changed. Everyone cheered!

Souvenirs were not a big item on my list. I did not have much money, but I did want to bring something to friends back home, so I collected Coca-Cola bottles. In Israel, one side said Coca-Cola in English, the other side in Hebrew. It was not difficult to collect lots of them; our preacher drank at least two with every meal.

In Tiberias, I accidentally left all the bottles I had collected out on the table in our hotel room, and the cleaning staff disposed of them while we were out, so I had to start collecting them all over again. Everyone laughed when we went from place to place with all the bottles in a bag: clink, clink, clink. How embarrassing! But my friends loved them when I finally got them home.

Although Monday was the last official day of our tour in Israel, Tuesday was free time. Some of us went to see the Biblical Zoo. For myself and a friend, there was only one place we wanted to go: the Old City section of Jerusalem. Taxis were cheap, so we took them wherever we wanted to go. Our taxi ride was right out of a 1960s European movie: a high-speed chase for no apparent reason. It was fun though.

My heart longed to be in Old Jerusalem. In many ways this city is the epicenter of the world. Jerusalem saw the biblical events that have affected all civilization. I could almost visualize the powerful figures of history who had walked these roads. More significant to me, I could hear the soft echoes of the ages: the prayers of all the pious of the world rising to the One True God.

Yes, I had touched the ruins of one of Solomon's chariot cities, taken a boat ride across the Sea of Galilee, and felt the warm sand under my bare feet on a beach at the Dead Sea. These were all wonderful experiences. But it was Jerusalem, the city of peace, who left her mark on my soul.

From the arches of the gates in the massive stone walls surrounding the Old City to the apartment buildings springing up all over the new city, she was beautiful. The memory of her majestic Holy Temple had somehow become my personal memory. I loved the maze of walkways and shops in the Old City and the din of voices that seemed to be speaking in a hundred different languages. The faces—all colors, the soft, smooth, glowing faces of the children and the elderly—wrinkles showing the burdens of the years—all captivated me. Instead of reading the Bible as an observer, now I seemed to enter its pages through Jerusalem.

That last morning we explored one of the Old City gates—Gate Golden. This gate had been completely closed off long ago. Soldiers guarded from above. Just below the modern, closed-off Gate Golden, archaeologists had begun excavations. The old gate was there below the surface, and directly in front of it was an Arab graveyard. When we approached the excavation site and my friend tried to lower his camera down into the hole, the soldiers quickly motioned for us to leave.

Recently I read something fascinating about Gate Golden. It is located at the east side of the Old City, and if it had not been blocked off, this gate would have given instant access to the Temple Mount from outside the walls. This gate's predecessor was actually called Gate Beautiful in Jesus' day. Due to its location, directly across from the Mount of Olives, it is believed that Jesus must have entered Jerusalem through this gate on Palm Sunday.

According to the same source, it is a belief of Judaism that the Messiah will enter through this particular gate and the Prophet Elijah will announce the arrival of the Messiah at this site. Elijah is of a priestly family, and priests are not allowed to enter cemeteries because they are forbidden contact with a dead body.[14] I remembered from studies about Jesus' tomb that Jewish law forbade burial this close to Jerusalem's walls.

The Moslems were aware of these Jewish beliefs when they conquered Jerusalem in 1187 C.E. Taking advantage of this opportunity, they blocked Gate Golden and established an Arab cemetery right at its edge.[15] I saw the cemetery that day, and it is quite large. No doubt this is yet another reason for the animosity between Moslems and Jews in Israel.

We walked around Gate Golden to get a look at its back side. As we passed by, I gazed at the Temple Mount. I felt privileged to be at this holy site that God had chosen. However, the soldiers let us know that we were not allowed at the back of the gate either.

Just off the Temple Mount, we heard a school bell ring; children came running from all over the Old City with schoolbags strapped to their backs. A few minutes later, while walking through the Old City marketplace, we heard classroom sounds above the walkway: desks slamming down, children laughing and shouting. I guess the teacher had not entered the room yet. I felt so at home in Jerusalem.

As we began walking out of the Old City, I kept snapping pictures. Money-changing booths were doing a steady business. A colorful old Arab man was riding a donkey down one of the narrow passageways in the marketplace, and I asked him to stop so I could take his picture. He gave a sweet, weathered smile for the camera and then got angry because I did not give him any money. I then gave him a little, but he did not think it was sufficient. That picture is one of the best in my photo album.

We spent our last few shekels on a game in the hotel lobby, waiting for our bus to leave for the airport. Parting with Jerusalem was like leaving behind my heart; my soul would never be quite the same again.

The Holy Land tour included a three-day extension in Rome. If Jerusalem was the source, Rome was the aftermath. The splendor and magnificence of the Coliseum were marred by the form of entertainment people had witnessed from its many tiers of seating: Christians had literally been torn apart by wild animals for the amusement of the pagan masses. Here in Rome, monotheism and paganism clashed with a fury, each eventually influencing the other.

The Vatican is an unbelievable triumph of architecture and art, yet my heart went out to the millions of impoverished Catholics around the world. The Catholic Church talked of tightening its budget while hoarding billions of dollars worth of art. For me, the beauty of the Vatican was made grotesque by shadows of poverty-stricken worshipers. I could almost hear their voices—and that of Jesus.

One sign of paganism has always been idolatry. Making an image and worshiping it or what it represents is idolatry. I stood in St. Peter's, the largest church in the world, and stared at the statue of the apostle. Actually, I was watching the many people who approached it. They either kissed the foot of the statue or simply touched it in reverence. The stone foot had been replaced twice already because of people wearing it away in this manner. Disgusted, I thought, "Is this not pure idolatry?"

I learned from our Italian guide that early Christians in Rome who were hiding in the catacombs used the fish as a symbol for Jesus. The Greek word for fish contains the letters of a monogram that stands for the words "Jesus Christ, Son of God, the Savior." An anchor was also used as a symbol of salvation. It was not until the reign of Constantine in the fourth century C.E. that the cross was used to symbolize Christianity. Before that time, wearing a cross would have been like wearing a little electric chair around your neck.

Early Christians in Rome, like Jews, did not cremate the bodies of their dead; only pagans did that. Instead, early Christians wrapped their dead in cloth and laid them in tombs or in the catacombs. Unlike pagans, Christians believed in the resurrection of the dead and so avoided destroying the body. People believed that Christians mutilated in the Coliseum could still be resurrected; however, a certain respect for the dead was involved. In stark contrast, pagans cremated their dead and placed their ashes in urns. Many would then place these urns along main thoroughfares like the famed Appian Way in Rome.

Rome had beautiful and fascinating sites: the Coliseum, the catacombs, the Vatican, Mamertine prison (where Paul was kept prisoner), and the Forum. In Jerusalem, biblical events seemed to have happened yesterday, but for me, Rome represented the early church, ancient history, and doctrinal discussions far removed from Jesus (who never visited Rome).

Unlike Israel, few natives of Italy spoke English with us, but shopping was still fun: beautiful clothing at low prices. Rome had its own ambience that was wonderful. For me, though, Rome felt distant and impersonal, lacking the spiritual radiance of Jerusalem. It was unfair of me to make comparisons between Rome and Jerusalem. Nothing could compare to the Holy City. I was ready to go home.

It had truly been the trip of a lifetime. I had fully romanticized Jerusalem, but in Rome I became cynical about religion. Great highs and lows characterized my experience. My head was swimming with facts, but they turned out to be just enough to whet my appetite.

The trip would change the way I thought about so many things: the Bible, Jewish people, Judaism, Jesus, Christianity, and God Himself. Though I would have thought it impossible when I left Israel, less than two years were to pass before I was to see Jerusalem again.

It seemed as though I lived an entire lifetime in the first six months after I joined the Christian community. This was enough, I thought; now I could die and feel as though I had not missed a thing on earth. Little did I know that this was just another stone being set in the foundation of what was to come.

# 9

# THE JEWISH CONNECTION

The following twenty-two months were characterized by spiritual growth: I was in a constant state of change. I lived as a modern-day Christian, but found myself drawn to the first-century world of Jesus—an unmistakably Jewish world. I wanted to emulate Jesus and grow closer to God.

Home life was wonderful. My daughter was happy, friends and family were close, and it was a joyful time. I was ready to use the source of strength God had given me to help others, so I kept watch for any possibilities.

An opportunity quickly presented itself. Harry, my employer, seemed to be unhappy and would often come to my office (I was his bookkeeper) to seek advice or simply air his frustrations. His grown son worked for him and they often had loud arguments at work. There was little trust or respect between them. I searched the Book of Proverbs for wisdom regarding his problems and chose two or three verses. He was visibly touched. After discussing how to apply them, Harry thanked me and said he would try.

One day while Harry was in my office, he stood at the window looking sad and far away, and he began to share memories of his childhood in Europe. Looking down on the large parking lot below my window, he recounted how he once watched as Nazis pulled into an area in military trucks. For no apparent reason, they rounded up any Jewish people who happened to be there, including women and children. Only a boy, he saw the soldiers senselessly gun down these people.

I sat in his silence, watching his eyes as he still struggled, fifty years later, to make sense of man's inhumanity to man. Perhaps he was looking to me, this woman who opened his eyes to the Bible, hoping that I might have an answer from God as to why people sin against each other. My only answer would be that we are not robots; we are endowed with free will, the freedom to do good or evil to each other. This truthful answer would remove the blame from God and place it on the people who earned it, but how would that help Harry? No answer would be adequate; silent compassion was the greatest form of comfort I could give him.

Harry proceeded to tell me why he had survived; his family was spared during the first "sweep" because his mother was a Christian. Only his father was Jewish. By the time he reached his teens, he was working in the Underground.

As his thoughts returned to the present, he confessed that he had never been to a church or synagogue. I tried to comfort him and tell him it did not matter. He could read the Bible for himself; God would help him find the answers he needed.

I could not help but wonder what my Christian friends would think if they had overheard our conversation. I did not tell him that Jesus was the answer to all his problems. I did not say, "This world is miserable; just accept Jesus as Savior and you'll be able to look forward to Heaven." Instead, I told Harry to look to God and the Bible, because that is all I believed he needed.

Christmas that winter was my first as a Christian. It felt strange to sing Christmas carols with full comprehension of every verse. By this time, friends and family viewed me as a "fundamentalist Christian." To me, that phrase simply implied that I was trying to live my life according to the Bible, the greatest source of wisdom I had found.

This Christmas held more meaning to me than just family, food, and presents; it was a celebration of God's presence in our lives.

My favorite memory of that season, oddly enough, was a car accident. A lady was driving in the wrong lane and literally turned into my car. I was driving a large, nine-year-old Oldsmobile, and it would take a lot more than a little bump to do much damage to my car.

We both pulled over, and I ran around to her door to see if she was okay. She was frazzled and fretting over her complicated, hurried, stressed-out life. In her nervous state, she began to babble about all the ways this accident was causing her problems. I just looked at her and asked again, "Are you okay?"

She stopped talking and stared at me for a minute. "I just hit your car. I didn't even apologize, and all you can do is ask if I'm okay? Aren't you angry or anything?"

"No," I responded. "It was just an accident. I'm all right. My car's not in bad shape either."

After another pause, she thanked me for caring. Silently I thanked God for teaching me to place people before cars. After exchanging the necessary information, we both drove away into the cold. A few days later, I received a warm note in a Christmas card from her. My return card included a little message, giving God the credit for my attitude. We exchanged cards for several years afterward.

My least favorite memory that first year was the office Christmas party. Most of the employees were in their early twenties, and they looked forward to getting drunk on the boss's liquor. I tried to picture Jesus walking in the door and realized how out of place he would be—and how out of place I would feel. Even the mention of Jesus' name would be pretty unwelcome at this *Christ-mass* party.

As it turned out, I had another commitment that same evening. I told Harry I was sorry, but I would not be able to attend the office party. He was hurt and angry. After that, he seldom came up to my office to visit. In retrospect, I realize I let him down; I should have known what the party meant to him. Wisdom does not come instantly, not even to an eager heart.

Bible studies, prayer, fellowship, listening to Christian talk shows and music on the radio—my life was immersed in Christian input. I loved every minute of it. It was as if I were living in a cocoon; everything in my little Christian world was wonderful.

That is what I thought, anyway. But real life is not perfect and easy. My honeymoon with God was coming to a close, and the marriage was about to begin.

Becoming closer to God and reading the Bible a second time made me aware of the responsibility I had taken on the day of my baptism. I began to realize why religious hypocrisy made Jesus so angry. People were watching me for signs of sincerity and for any hypocrisy. For some, I had become a representative of God and the Bible, so my words and actions might affect the way people viewed God. Following His will suddenly became more important to me. How differently the world would see God if those who claimed to be religious actually obeyed Him!

If pleasing God meant emulating Jesus, I would need to understand Jesus better; my women's discipleship group began an in-depth study of the Gospel of John. When we reached the seventeenth chapter, it was my turn. This passage records one of Jesus' prayers. Throughout the prayer, Jesus kept giving God reasons why He should grant Jesus an affirmative answer: ultimately, whatever Jesus prayed for was intended to bring glory to God.

I realized this was Jesus' motive not only for prayer but also for all his actions, for his whole life. I shared my discovery that Jesus was actually teaching that our purpose, as people who know and love God, is to bring glory to God's name. That being true, anything that causes God's name to be dishonored is to be zealously removed from our lives.

Looking at my life in this context brought about a new sensitivity, an acute awareness: was I dishonoring God in any way? If so, what were people seeing that was turning them away from God? Was I raising my daughter well? Did I work diligently at my job? Was I honest and kind most of the time? This self-examination meant taking a hard look not only at my actions and speech but also at church-related activities in my home.

A weekly Bible study had been held in my apartment for the past year. I loved the people who came every Wednesday and hugged each one as he or she came in the door. Potluck meals were fun and chatty times, like having a party with good friends each week.

The leader of the study was a campus minister; his knowledge of the Bible was excellent. His greatest skill, though, was his way with people; I could ask a stupid question, and he made me feel as though it were an intelligent one. If someone began to gossip or dominate the discussion, he would gently bring the discussion back on track. He made everyone feel good about themselves and each other. Whenever new people came to the study, they received a realistic and loving picture of God. But as much as he and his wife enjoyed being here, they had a commitment elsewhere, and it was now time for them to move away.

Paul, one of the young men with me in Israel, was asked to take over leadership of the Bible study. He did his best, but he was not a trained minister nor was he given adequate instruction on how to lead group discussions tactfully. It soon became apparent that group morale was deteriorating, because Paul would unintentionally say hurtful things and not notice how they made people feel. I spoke with him privately about the problem and he tried to improve, but week after week people left the study feeling upset or angry. I began to get angry too—at the church leaders who had put us in this position. God was being dishonored in my own home, and the only way to stop it would be to hurt a friend.

After much prayer and hesitation, I called Paul to ask if I could come over and talk with him. We both cried as I explained my decision to discontinue the study in my home. We parted with a hug.

Later, the two of us met with a minister on staff at the church. The minister asked me why the study could not continue. I tried to explain that I believed that my friend was not yet ready to lead, and the result was that God's name was being dishonored. I could no longer allow that to happen in my home. The minister looked perplexed. It is not easy to take a stand for God when godly people do not support you.

My first year of Christian life had been one of intense highs and devastating lows. Hosting that study group was extremely important to me; for twelve months those people had served as a constant source of encouragement and friendship. Emerging from such a cocoon of love and acceptance was unsettling and painful, especially because not one of them supported my decision. Although I found another weekly study to attend, the naivete with which I began the year was gone. Once again, I found myself alone with God.

In retrospect, I realize this new independence enabled me to take the next step along the path God had apparently set out for me: independent thinking in Bible study. I still read the Bible and other Christian books, but I no longer depended on church leaders to guide my studies or answer my questions. After only one year I had begun to search for answers on my own.

I was feeding a voracious appetite for biblical knowledge that summer, including an ongoing fascination with Israel. The trip to Jesus' birthplace had only whet my appetite for knowledge of those first-century events. I studied the New Testament and Bible commentaries to discover how Jesus had lived and why, including his practice of Judaism.

One day at work, while listening to a Christian radio station, I heard an advertisement that made me stop and listen. A Jewish-Christian congregation was meeting every week; their pastor spoke of Jesus the Jew and an organization called Jews for Jesus. I was shocked to hear of Jewish people who were pro-Jesus, because I had learned in church that Jewish people hated Jesus so much that they manipulated Pontius Pilate into crucifying him. Yet, Jesus was a Jew, and I knew nothing of this side of him.

Before becoming involved in Christianity, I was apathetic toward Jewish people. To the best of my knowledge, I had never met one. Yet within months of my baptism, just the sight of someone wearing a Star of David necklace would cause anger to well up inside me. My new loyalty to Jesus, combined with the teaching that Jewish people hated him and that Jesus himself called them a "brood of vipers," caused me to view the Jews as my enemy. Christianity had dramatically altered the way I viewed the Jewish people.

Now, just one year later, I was listening to a Jewish man saying he was a Christian pastor; his very identity seemed to be a contradiction in terms. Perhaps this Jewish pastor could teach me about Jesus the Jew. I wrote down the phone number given on the radio, and found out where the congregation met—on Saturdays.

That first Saturday morning I had no idea what to expect. The talks with my troubled boss had given me some compassion for Jewish people; hearing of his experiences with Nazis in Europe made me realize some of the pain Jewish people have lived through. But relating to Jewish people on a religious level made me more than a little apprehensive. Alecia came along for moral support.

We drove to a church building and followed signs up a flight of stairs and into one of the Sunday school classrooms. We were a little early, so there were few people in the room.

The pastor stood up front, smiling through a full dark beard; he was a little pudgy and jolly looking, which served to relax me. As people arrived, he wandered around the room chatting and joking with members of the small congregation. Without making Alecia and me feel like outsiders, he quietly introduced himself and tried to make us feel welcome. As the room filled (about seventy people), single-sheet fliers were distributed. The service was about to begin.

The pastor, Saul, opened the flier and read the week's announcements. Some items regarded upcoming events: potlucks, Jewish holy days, or when a Jewish person was going to give testimony—a personal story of how he or she came to embrace Christianity. Sometimes a member of Jews for Jesus, which is also called Jewish-Christian Ministries, visited to teach classes on how to evangelize Jewish people. I had stepped into a different world; this was like no other church I could imagine. It was so Jewish that, as a Christian, it felt like forbidden territory.

After the announcements, Saul said a blessing in Hebrew. Strangely, just the sound of it was mysterious and wonderful and made me feel closer to God.

After the blessing and between each step of the service, they sang. These songs were different from most of those we sang in my regular church. Instead of being *about* God, these were usually sung *to* Him, like prayers. Some songs were actually direct quotes from the Bible. Many had Christian themes with a little Jewish flavor thrown in. The congregation also sang Hebrew songs like *"Hineh-ma-tov"*; in English the words mean "how good and pleasant it is for all men to dwell together in peace." I loved the emotion of these songs. After the service I felt I had really praised and adored God and came away with this loving awe for Him. These were truly worship services.

After the initial blessing came another one "over the reading of the Torah." A portion of the Pentateuch—Genesis through Deuteronomy—was read aloud after this blessing. The Torah portion was not just a passage chosen at random; in the synagogue, the Torah is divided into weekly portions to be read aloud by the end of the biblical (Jewish) calendar year.

Another blessing was said over the reading of the *haftarah*. The *haftarah* readings are taken from the remaining Old Testament. What Christians refer to as the Old Testament, Jewish people call the Holy Scriptures, the Hebrew Bible, or the *Tanakh*. The word *Tanakh* is really a combination of the first letters of three Hebrew words: *Torah* (Pentateuch), *Neviim* (the prophetic books), and *Ketuvim* (the rest of the writings in the Hebrew Bible). The *haftarah* portions read in synagogue were originally chosen based on their resemblance to the Torah reading for that particular week. The entire *Tanakh* is read and studied by individuals, but only the Torah and *haftarah* portions are read aloud in synagogues.

I heard that long ago Jewish worshipers read only the Torah portions in synagogues. This practice of reading *haftarah* portions began before the destruction of the Second Temple, the temple that stood in Jesus' day. It is said that this practice began about 168 B.C.E. when

"Antiochus Epiphanes, king of Syria and Palestine, forbade the reading of the Torah under penalty of death. The Scribes, thereupon, substituted a chapter of the Prophets cognate to the portion of the Law that ought to have been read that week."[1]

In this Jewish-Christian church we were reading the Torah and *haftarah* portions, just as Jewish worshipers had done for centuries, even before Jesus came. The same passages were being read aloud that day in every synagogue around the world.

Next came the reading of the *Shema,* the central prayer of Judaism. The *Shema* contains the foundational teaching of monotheism that Jesus quoted in Mark 12:29–30. It begins, "Hear O Israel, the LORD our GOD, the LORD is One" (Deuteronomy 6:4–9). The whole Jewish-Christian congregation recited those words in unison. After several weeks, I learned it by heart too.

After the *Shema*, a member of the congregation stood up in front of the group. He chose some Psalms from a thin letter-sized leaflet labeled the "prayer book." The chosen psalms were read aloud in unison.

The children were then called up to the front of the room to recite a Hebrew blessing from memory. (In my later studies of Judaism, I discovered that this was the blessing said over wine during a meal. I never did figure out why this blessing became connected to this part of the church service as no wine or communion was served.) The children then left for Sunday school or, more accurately, Sabbath school classes.

The most unusual practice of this congregation was that they met on Saturdays. They held the traditional Christian belief that Jesus is the Messiah, and like the other church we attended, they also prayed to Jesus or to the Holy Spirit at times. But these Christians told me they accepted only the biblical Sabbath, the seventh day of the week, Saturday. Sunday was not biblical in their view. I struggled with this conflict for many months.

The sermon Saul gave was much like any other Christian sermon: it focused on New Testament passages. However, Saul did not limit himself to the New Testament; often he would bring *Tanakh* passages into the talk and relate them to the New Testament. This brought the *Tanakh* alive for me as never before. Now I could easily see its relevance, rather than thinking of it only in a historical sense. Saul tied the Old and New Testaments together beautifully to help us understand what Jesus was teaching. This was fascinating for me. I found that nearly everything in the New Testament had its origins in the *Tanakh*, and no wonder, the *Tanakh* was the only Holy Scriptures Jesus had.

Although a few Jewish people were members of the congregation, most were Gentiles like me, Christians interested in the Jewish side of Jesus. We wanted to learn about first-century and modern Judaism from someone with experience. It did not occur to us to go to a synagogue; that was still considered off limits. The Jewish members did not talk about the Jewish religion much, and I noticed that Gentiles seemed more interested in conversing about Jesus and Judaism than were the Jewish members.

Alecia and I had entered a new world that Saturday morning. Although I have since discovered that Saul was not unique as a Jewish pastor, he is extremely unusual. He stood at two open doors: one to Christianity and the other to Judaism. He knew both worlds and enjoyed teaching about both. My heart and eyes were opening.

Meanwhile, we still attended our Gentile church, and when I brought up the subject of Israel or Jewish practices there, many were curious. An old woman told me she did not know Jewish people still met in synagogues; she thought synagogues existed only in ancient times. Some Christians told me they were part Jewish or thought they might be. Through reading and personal experience, I was gaining an awareness that Christian interest in Jews and Judaism was growing.

I was told of a man from my Gentile denomination who had moved to Israel. He lived in Lod, a predominantly Arab town on the outskirts of Tel Aviv. I was excited to establish contact with someone in Israel; immediately, I sent him a letter. This missionary had moved to Israel to evangelize Jewish people, but as many who came before and since his arrival, he was not successful. His return letter reflected his frustration with the Jewish people. He remained in Israel, but allied himself with the Arab population. Eventually, he viewed himself as a rescuer for Arabs from their Jewish oppressors.

One day, a guest speaker from Michigan visited our Gentile church. The congregation was told that he would be talking about the Jewish people and the Bible. When he began to speak, he seemed pleasant; part of his teaching was difficult for many of us to grasp, but the crowd was interested and attentive. Our fascination with his subject was evidenced by the standing-room only audience. It was wonderful to hear a pro-Jewish speaker at my Gentile church.

But as the speech progressed, he began to speak harshly. Close friends in the crowd glanced over at me; by this time it was common knowledge that I had become rather pro-Jewish. My stomach tightened as his harshness intensified. Then came the big blow: he announced, "The Jews are a tool of the devil!"

A good friend who had been on the Israel trip turned to me and said, "So *now* what do you think of the Jews?"

My initial response was to swing my arm across his chest and deck him! Instead of lashing out at my friend, however, I silently cried out to God, "How can godly men teach anti-Semitism?"

The worst part of that evening was not the speech; it was the reaction of the audience or rather their lack of reaction. Those people I held so dear said nothing. If the speaker had said, "The black people are a tool of the devil," they would have thrown him out in an instant, but they did not even get angry at *this* racist remark.

When I got home, I wept over the silence in that room. People kept silent in Nazi Germany until it was too late. Egyptian citizens kept quiet while Hebrew slaves were mistreated. My friends, who worshiped the God of the Jews, were silent too. "Why, God? Why the hatred?" I suddenly realized it was the subtle underlying anti-Semitism in that huge crowd of modern Christians that had allowed this man to speak without interruption.

This was *my* church. I was baptized here, and so was my niece; my daughter attended its services. I remember feeling God's Presence when I first came through the front doors. People not only received biblical teaching but they were kind too. They were not racist toward any other groups; there were many interracial marriages and friendships. I could not understand how my friends, my spiritual family, could be silent partners in anti-Semitism, but I resolved to find out why. I began to study the history of the Christian community's involvement in anti-Semitism.

In the speaker's defense, though it does not excuse anti-Semitism, he had very personal reasons for his strong feelings against Jewish people. The explanation for his attitude could be found between the lines of a book written by his father.[2]

In this book his father wrote that he was a religious Jewish man who had been raised in Russia. He was born in 1893, and by the time he was ten years old, pogroms (massacres of Jewish people) had begun. Within months his village suffered a pogrom; fortunately, he was spared. This man wrote in detail of his upbringing in an Orthodox Jewish home, and except for a few questioning remarks, he sounded positive about Judaism.

As a teenager he had the opportunity to come to America. (His homeland was invaded shortly thereafter, and the entire village was wiped out.) Upon his arrival in America he met the relatives with whom he was to live. They did not live as Jewish people of his village had; in fact, they did not practice Judaism at all. They lived like Gentiles and tried their best to fit into the melting pot of American culture. They worked on the Sabbath, ate biblically forbidden foods, and embraced none of the richness of the Jewish culture he had known and loved. He loved God, so this lack of a religious community devastated him.

Eventually he met a Gentile woman, a Christian, who loved God as he did. He fell in love with her, accepted Christianity, and they married. Years later, with two small children, they moved into the Jewish neighborhood of a large city. He began to evangelize his fellow Jews by opening a "Hebrew mission" in the area. The Jewish community deeply resented this intrusion.

The children attended the local school and played in that same neighborhood. Because of their father's activities and their parents' intermarriage, which is forbidden in Judaism, the children were treated unkindly in school and elsewhere. It was a frightening experience for two small children. This was the childhood of a man who would one day say, "The Jews are a tool of the devil!"

After reading his father's book, I understood the painful experiences that had evoked such anger. I could forgive him and have compassion for his pain. But my congregation's silence was deafening.

I turned to my Jewish-Christian congregation to learn more about Christian anti-Semitism. It was one matter for the Egyptians, who were pagans, to deny fair treatment to a people who were their slaves. But for godly people to act racist was incomprehensible to me.

I wanted to know when Christian anti-Semitism began and why. Of course I knew about World War II and the six million Jewish people who were systematically murdered simply because of their race. Hitler's writings revealed that he did it "for the Lord."[3] Many German Christians showed little or no concern when Jewish people were attacked in public. I discovered that the United States and other governments were made aware of Hitler's intentions and activities before World War II; yet, the Christian community and the world in general did not express its outrage until the Holocaust was nearly over. How deeply embedded was the silence of my congregation.

Reading of the time before the Holocaust, I learned of the Russian pogroms of the early 1900s, and that in the latter half of the nineteenth century, Pope Pius IX reinstated restrictions against Jewish people. In 1593, Pope Clement VIII banished Jews from the Vatican state. Martin Luther, after numerous unsuccessful attempts to convert Jewish people to Christianity, said in his tract *On the Jews and Their Lies* (1543) that if a Jew came to him for baptism, he would "tie a millstone around his neck and throw him into the sea." The same monarchs who sent Columbus to America in 1492 banished those

Jews from Spain who refused to convert to Christianity; many forced baptisms occurred as a result. At roughly the same time, Portugal also forced baptisms and made slaves of many Jewish people.

The list of injustices at the hands of Christians seemed endless. The Spanish Inquisition in 1478 was a huge pogrom. Twenty-five years earlier, a Franciscan monk persuaded the king of Poland to withdraw all rights from the Jewish populace. In 1370 a group of Jewish people was accused of defiling the bread used by a church for communion; they were burned alive. Twenty-two years earlier, thousands of Jewish people were murdered, accused of being responsible for the Black Plague that was ravaging Europe. (Due to kosher eating practices, Jewish people did not die from the plague at such high rates as did Gentiles, which made Jews suspect.)

The Middle Ages abounded with anti-Jewish activities. The Crusades, of course, were the stimulus for some of the bloodiest acts against individuals and against entire Jewish communities. As early as the year 613, Spain's history of anti-Semitism had begun. In that year, Jewish people who refused to be baptized were expelled from the country or given to pious Christians as slaves, and all Jewish children over the age of seven were taken from their parents so they could be given a proper Christian education.

As early as 315 c.e., Constantine the Great legalized the Christian movement when his mother converted to Christianity. Suddenly, this previously illegal religion was now the only legal religion in the Roman Empire. A former sun worshiper, Constantine issued a law that everyone should rest from regular work on the "venerable day of the sun" (Sunday). Thus, Sunday took the place of Saturday in the movement Jesus started. But Constantine went a step further in his religious fervor: he issued laws against the Jewish religion and against Jewish people. The break between Judaism and Christianity was complete. Christianity had been cut off from its source by 315 c.e.

These findings convinced me that there was a historical pattern of Christian anti-Semitism, but not *why*. I kept praying; there had to be a reason. Once I understood, perhaps I could begin to fight anti-

Semitism within the Christian community. Modern Christian racists—
this contradiction in terms would give me ulcers in the coming years.

Not willing to give up the people I loved, Alecia and I still attended
the Gentile church regularly. We also faithfully attended Jewish-Christian
services, and I split tithe money between the two. We went to Gentile
Bible studies on Tuesdays and Jewish-Christian ones on Wednesdays.
We also participated in weekend retreats of both congregations.

Life was not all seriousness, however; anyone with a nine-year-old
has to know how to make life fun! As the busy weeks flew by, winter
came, and with it came Chanukah. Having been members of the
Jewish-Christian group for only a few months, this was our first
Chanukah celebration. The party was held in the home of one of the
church members. Nearly everyone came; the house was filled with
people, conversation, and laughter.

"What's Chanukah about?" we asked Saul. First, we learned that
Chanukah was not a Jewish substitute for Christmas. It began in
165 B.C.E., long before Jesus walked this earth. In the Gospel of John,
Chanukah is referred to as the Feast of Dedication; it is also known
as the Festival of Lights (John 10:22).

At that time, Antiochus Epiphanes (the same king who outlawed
the reading of the Torah) had taken over Israel and defiled the Holy
Temple, claiming it for pagan worship. This was a direct attack on
the Jewish religion and on the God of Israel, so a pious Jewish family
led a revolt against the king. They were so tough that they became
known as the Maccabees (the hammers). These Jewish zealots were
ill armed and incredibly outnumbered by Antiochus's army, but they
succeeded in recapturing the Temple. This is the first miracle of
Chanukah.

Jewish worshipers cleaned up the Temple and prepared to restore
Temple services, including lighting the great *Menorah*—the seven-
branched candelabrum. However, there was only enough ritual oil
to burn for one day, and it would take eight days to prepare the new
oil. Yet, God had commanded that the light be kept burning continually. (In synagogues, a light symbolizing the eternal light is called the

*ner tamid.* The lamp continued to burn for eight days. This is the second miracle of Chanukah.

I learned that Chanukah is celebrated for many reasons. First, it honors God and His miracles: yesterday, today, and in the future. Second, Chanukah celebrates the victories God gives the Jewish people, against all sensible odds. Because the great *Menorah* burned miraculously for eight days, Chanukah *menorahs* have eight candleholders, plus a holder for the *shamash*, the candle used to light the others. On each of the eight evenings, candles are lit, and special blessings (prayers) are recited. How wonderful it was to have a holiday to celebrate God's influence in our lives.

Another Chanukah custom we discovered that night was a game called *dreidel*. *Dreidels* are four-sided spinning tops, with each side labeled with a Hebrew letter. In Hebrew, these are the first letters of each word in the phrase "a great miracle happened there." The four Hebrew letters are *shin, hey*, *gimel*, and *nun*. (In Israel, the *dreidels* are different because their letters stand for the phrase "a great miracle happened *here*.")

In the *dreidel* game, one may gamble with candy. As the *dreidel* stops spinning and falls, the letter facing up is read. If *shin* is on top, you put a piece of candy in the "pot." A *gimel* means you get to take the whole pile. A *hey* means you can take half the pot. A *nun* means nothing changes. Alecia won all the candy in our little group. She loved Chanukah!

Later, I heard a *dreidel* story from Russia. In Russia, not so long ago, it was illegal to teach the Hebrew language, so men would gather together in secret. When a Russian soldier came near, they would pull out *dreidels* and gamble with small coins. It was legal to gamble in Russia, but not to teach Hebrew!

That winter Alecia and I began learning the Hebrew language. I wanted to read the Torah in its original language. Every great goal has a modest beginning: Alecia and I would take the little we had learned in class each week and converse with each other. "*Shalom*" or "*lehitra'ot*" were nice for starters. Saul taught lessons in his living room to a dozen people.

Those Hebrew lessons were the reason I made my first trip to a synagogue—an Orthodox one. Saul told me that the synagogue had a small gift shop where I could purchase a Hebrew-English dictionary. Entering this religious Jewish center was like taking another step along the path the LORD had placed me on.

In those days, I was not sensitive to what the cross represented to many Jewish people. Images of burning crosses planted in front yards by the Ku Klux Klan were not things I considered. Many Jews had heard cross-wearing Christians say, "You killed Jesus!" My huge silver cross was worn on a heavy chain around my neck. It hung just beneath my winter coat that day as I walked up the steps and into the building.

The synagogue was in a large, old wooden building. It was late in the afternoon, and no services were being held in the little assembly room. From the stairwell, I could hear voices above. I wondered if they were the voices of rabbis or maybe their students.

The woman in charge of the shop came to unlock the door. The gift shop could not have been much larger than ten feet by ten feet, but oh what riches it held! Yes, they had the dictionary I needed. They also carried flash cards with Hebrew letters on one side and simple Hebrew words on the other. This was all I could afford. But my hunger for Israel and Judaica blossomed in that room. There were tapes of Jewish music: modern, rock and roll, and traditional. I saw Bible commentaries and books on Judaism—on Jesus' Judaism. There were *menorahs*, ritual Passover platters, and *mezuzahs*. I saw beautiful posters, Jewish cookbooks, games, greeting cards, and silver goblets. Every Jewish item I could think of was in that little room.

In the coming months I would return to that gift shop many times. Soon, a Jewish (biblical) calendar hung in my kitchen. I began to buy Jewish books, one by one. The love and curiosity I had for Jerusalem were being nurtured by these Jewish items, and our life was being enriched by these biblical reminders. Jewish commentaries opened a vast wealth of knowledge for me to explore.

Occasionally Saul would teach us about Judaism. He talked of similarities between modern Judaism and the Judaism practiced in Jesus' day. Though Saul had forsaken the Judaism of his parents, he did not mind being a fountain of knowledge for us; he had a captive audience.

Saul told us that the Law of Moses was still being obeyed today. Those who practiced biblical Judaism were in the minority among Jewish people, but many still followed it zealously. To discover that people today were living as Jesus did in the first century was a revelation to me. The fog was lifting as I began to visualize Jesus the Jew.

I had seen Jesus' Israel and his beloved Jerusalem; now I began to identify passages in the New Testament where Jesus and his followers were faithfully practicing Judaism. Saul told us of a practice in Judaism observed in Jesus' day that is still followed today: wearing *tefillin*. In the New Testament, *tefillin* are called phylacteries, and Rabbi Jesus said that wearing showy *tefillin* was wrong (Matthew 23:5). Other rabbis taught the same thing: the standard, rather plain *tefillin* are called kosher, which means biblically fit. Orthodox Jews wear only kosher *tefillin* because they are not worn to impress people, but rather to be a sign between man and God.

One day Saul brought a young man up to the front of the room to show us what *tefillin* look like. The *tefillin* are a pair of long leather straps with small boxes attached; these boxes contain scriptural verses. One set is worn on the head, the Scripture box lying on the forehead; the other set is worn on the left hand and arm, its Scripture box on the muscle of the upper arm directly across from the heart. I found it fascinating to watch the young man put on *tefillin* and count the number of times the straps encircled his arm, tie knots at designated places, and utter blessings (prayers) at each stage of the process.

We learned that the biblical basis for wearing *tefillin* is found in Deuteronomy 6:8. Elsewhere in the Torah, Israel is told to "remember" and "observe" God's instructions; but in Deuteronomy 6:8 they are told to tie them or bind them. Religious Jewish people wear *tefillin*, scrolls of Scripture passages placed in small boxes, placed between their eyes and near their heart in loving obedience to God's commandment.

Through this literal obedience to God's Torah, Orthodox Jewish people were keeping alive the Bible I held dear. Had they changed since the first century, ignoring the literal meaning of Deuteronomy 6:8, I might never have known that *tefillin* were a part of Jesus' everyday life. Now I could see that he wore *tefillin* because of his beloved Torah and his love for God. Now I could see Jesus realistically: as a Jew.

The first few months of 1987 were a blur. My job was going well; Alecia was enjoying school and her many friends. We were busy with both congregations on Saturdays and Sundays, as well as Tuesday and Wednesday nights. One night each week Alecia and I took Hebrew language lessons at Saul's home. In the car, the radio was tuned to Christian music or talk shows. At home, I studied the Bible or books on Christianity or Judaism. We were totally immersed in godly input and opportunities to love and to express our faith.

At my job I worked thirty hours per week. As a single parent, those afternoons off were precious to Alecia and to me. She would tell me all about her school day. We would play games and run errands, or I would help her with homework. It meant paying doctors and dentists only a few dollars per month, but having time with Alecia was worth being in debt. To this day Alecia thanks me for choosing her over money: we grew very close during those afternoons.

I love the Bible. For me, it is the final authority, the truth everyone is searching for in life. When I went evangelizing with members of the Gentile congregation, I simply relayed what I had read in the Bible. There were no doctrines I consciously adhered to, other than my beliefs that God is real and the Bible is from Him—His communication to the human race.

People we met while evangelizing asked me what I believed. Some asked specifically about modern miracles, healings, and "speaking in tongues." The Gentile church we attended was more than skeptical; they were doctrinally opposed to the possibility of anyone speaking in tongues today. As a result, my evangelism partner raised his eyebrows at my reply to this question, "With God, all things are possible. He does not change; so of course, if He did something in the first century, He can do it again."

It was not rebellion against church leadership that prompted me to speak those words. And it was not the influence of the members of the Jewish-Christian congregation who were adamant in their belief in "tongues," some to the point of questioning a person's salvation if he could not speak in tongues. No, my answer was based on my belief that the all-powerful and limitless God I had met was capable of anything.

For me, evangelizing simply meant talking to people about God and His Bible. I love Him, so it was easy to do. The people we spoke with saw my enthusiasm and became curious. I was honest with them. If I did not know the answer to a question, I said so. Sometimes I would relay thoughts from the Bible and say, "Maybe it's like this . . . or, on the other hand, because of this passage here, maybe the answer is. . . ." God gave us the Bible to read, and we could find the answers there on our own. That sums up what I taught as we evangelized.

I found that some people were intimidated by the Bible. The language in some versions seemed archaic and confusing, but today there are versions in modern English that are easy to comprehend and are equal in accuracy to the traditional versions. I believe the Bible is God's gift to us, so I taught people that this gift should be opened and enjoyed. "Then, when you've read it," I would tell them, "go find a congregation to worship with."

I loved going door-to-door, visiting with people this way. It surprised me how many asked us into their homes. We all enjoyed the conversations. Most people we met were interested in spiritual matters and wanted to discuss them. Since the topic is taboo in most work places and in other social situations, many people are hungry for spiritual conversation. We simply fed them.

I once heard a preacher say, "We each have a God-shaped hole in our heart. We attempt to stuff it full of all kinds of things, but nothing satisfies. We never become fully satisfied until we find God and place Him in that hole." There is no substitute for God; using substitutes is like trying to fit a square peg in a round hole.

Amidst all my enthusiasm, two ideas were still threatening to burst my bubble. The first conflict I felt was between the Word of God and the beliefs of Christian people I knew. I found that sometimes people were teaching doctrines that did not agree with what I read in the Bible. I feared losing friends over theological differences that were developing between us.

The second problem was the nagging feeling that God wanted me to make a second trip to Israel. I had no idea why, but I felt there was an urgency in His desire for me to go. For months now, these two ideas kept intruding into my perfect little world. I prayed to God for answers and hungered for His truth, but as He began to reveal it, I became fearful of where that discovery might lead.

I felt confused about the teachings that differed between the "Old" and "New" Testaments. For instance, God said the seventh day was the Sabbath; it was to be an eternal sign. Now most Christians ignored Saturday and worshiped on Sunday. The Christian community was convinced that all these *eternal* commandments in the *Tanakh* were canceled. I could not find where God had changed His mind about them or even where Jesus had taught this. If God changed His mind about things He said were eternal, then I could not count on what He said, and that did not make sense to me.

When I asked ministers about these things, they could not give me a clear answer about how to choose what to obey and what to ignore in the *Tanakh*. I simply wanted to read it and obey, but I was often told, "We don't need to do *that* anymore." As a purist, I had to know why we did not obey the Bible as written.

Both congregations taught that Jesus canceled the Saturday Sabbath and kosher laws, and that the New Testament rendered the *old* obsolete (Hebrews 8:13). But as I read the Gospels, I read of Jesus' actions and words (Matthew 5:17–19) and found no evidence of his cancellation teaching.

I noticed something else strange about this line of thinking: Jesus

practiced these *Tanakh* commandments. Both congregations, in de-
claring the *eternal* instructions of God invalid, were in effect condemn-
ing Jesus' behavior. If the Judaism Jesus practiced was replaced by
Christianity, I had to wonder why. After all, God created Judaism; if
people thought something was wrong with it, then they were insinu-
ating that God made a mistake. He authored all the commandments
in the *Tanakh*. I could not believe that God made a mistake that anyone, even Jesus, would have to *correct*.

I began to see Jesus as loving biblical Judaism and practicing it out
of a love for God and His perfect commandments. As I studied the
New Testament, it became apparent to me that it was only the flaws
in the way some people practiced Judaism, not the commandments
themselves, that Jesus disapproved of. Over the course of a year I
gradually felt myself drawn to Judaism. It was as if Jesus were pulling me in one direction while the Christian community pulled me in
another. Popular Christian belief about Jesus did not seem to fit the
Jesus I found in the Gospels.

All the while, my heart and spirit were being prepared for a truth
my mind could not yet comprehend. Yes, I was still asking God for
answers, begging Him actually, because of a confusion that would
not allow me any peace. Yet at the same time, I was afraid His answers
might cause worse problems, that His "truth" might come between
me and the friends I had found in both congregations.

I had innumerable questions about Jesus, the Jewish people, Judaism, and modern Christian beliefs. Saul, the Jewish-Christian pastor,
taught that Jews and Gentiles are to come together as if there were no
biblical differences between them, but I began to see that the New
Testament did not view Jews and Gentiles in this way. My Gentile
church went further in its teaching, insisting that the Christian community was now the "New Israel," replacing the "Old Israel" (the Jews),
and that Jewish people must now join Israel by converting to Christianity. Out of loyalty and a desire to be accepted, I wanted to believe
the people I cared for in both congregations. But my mind could not
ignore the discoveries I was making. I did not know what to believe.

Meanwhile, work and Alecia were my anchors. The patterns of everyday life are so reassuring. Each day I worked as a bookkeeper, a wonderfully unchanging world of black and white. Either numbers are in balance or not; if not, they are easily corrected. And listening to my daughter relate her simple world of playground social events was a breath of calm sweet air.

During this time of searching and confusion, I purchased a tape through Jewish-Christian contacts. The title intrigued me: *Israel the Nation*.[4] Though the speech was recorded almost ten years earlier, its message was new to me and radical in the eyes of most Christians. Concepts raised in that sixty-minute tape would challenge me for years.

A Christian man, David Pawson, began his speech to a Christian businessmen's conference with a prayer that God might help him, "a mere Gentile," speak on behalf of "Your people" (the Jews). His purpose was to reveal how God feels about the Jewish people. According to Pawson, there was no New Israel, because the Old Israel was still alive in God's eyes. He spoke as if there was a God-intended difference between Jews and Gentiles. Rather than helping me decide which of my congregations' doctrines to believe, he was giving me a third, entirely different point of view.

He began by reading aloud Jeremiah, chapter 31, a passage I would come to know intimately. It speaks of God's everlasting love for Israel, of Ephraim, His firstborn son. The passage said God will gather them whom He scattered, returning the Jewish people to the land of Israel. Pawson felt God had indeed begun this work of gathering them back to their land: the re-formation of the State of Israel.

As he read Jeremiah 31:31, about a new covenant, I immediately thought of Jesus and the New Testament. But as he continued to read, I realized God had been talking about something else, something that had not yet occurred.

> "The time is coming," declares the LORD, "when I will make a new covenant with the house of Israel and with the house of Judah. It will not

be like the covenant I made with their forefathers when I took them by the hand to lead them out of Egypt, because they broke My covenant, though I was a husband to them," declares the LORD.

"This is the covenant I will make with the house of Israel after that time," declares the LORD.

"I will put My law in their minds and write it on their hearts. I will be their God, and they will be my people. No longer will a man teach his neighbor, or a man his brother, saying 'Know the LORD,' because they will all know Me, from the least of them to the greatest," declares the LORD.

"For I will forgive their wickedness and will remember their sins no more."

This is what the LORD says, He Who appoints the sun to shine by day, Who decrees the moon and stars to shine by night, Who stirs up the sea so that its waves roar—the LORD Almighty is His name:

"Only if these decrees vanish from My sight," declares the LORD, "will the descendants of Israel ever cease to be a nation before Me."

This is what the LORD says:

"Only if the heavens above can be measured and the foundations of the earth below be searched out will I reject all the descendants of Israel because of all they have done," declares the LORD (Jeremiah 31:31–37).

Jeremiah 31:34 says we will know when Israel's new covenant has begun because they will *all* know God; no rabbis or pastors will be necessary, not for Jewish people anyway. And the same verse says Israel will not be replaced because they had sinned in some way; God said they will be forgiven. As far as replacement theology goes, Jeremiah 31:36 removed all doubt for me: the descendants of Israel will never cease to be a nation in God's eyes, as long as one copy of the Bible exists.

Some Christians theorized that the Holocaust was God's way of punishing the Jewish people for rejecting Jesus of Nazareth as the Messiah. However, according to Jeremiah 31:37, regardless of what they have done, God will not reject the descendants of Israel. Perhaps this punishment theory served as an excuse for the inaction of Christians while Jews were suffering and dying.

Because of this passage in Jeremiah, instead of feeling sad about my congregation's silent partnership with anti-Semites, I grew fearful for them as I thought of what God told Abram:

> I will make you into a great nation, and I will bless you; I will make your name great, and you will be a blessing. I will bless those who bless you, and whoever curses you I will curse; and all peoples on earth will be blessed through you. (Genesis 12:2–3)

The Christian community has a long history of *not* blessing the seed, the physical descendants of Abram. Instead, using Jewish rejection of Jesus as an excuse, the Church has been "cursing" Israel for centuries.

While I was still pondering this situation, Pawson began to tell us how Genesis 12:3 has proved to be true—that all peoples (Gentiles) on earth will be blessed through the Jewish people. The fulfillment of this prophecy was not dependent on the faithfulness of Jewish people; many blessings have come from non-religious Jews. He named inventions that had originated in Jewish minds: digitalis for heart problems, vitamins, insulin for diabetes, aspirin for pain, polio vaccine, and a cure for syphilis. He named a few of the many gifted Jewish entertainers: Irving Berlin, the Marx Brothers, Neil Diamond, Barbra Streisand, Goldwyn and Mayer, Mel Blanc, Milton Berle, and Al Jolson. And three of the most influential thinkers of our time were Jewish: Albert Einstein, Karl Marx, and Sigmund Freud.

Pawson proceeded to explain how the Jewish upbringing of these great thinkers had contributed to their discoveries. Albert Einstein believed in the monotheism of Judaism, that since there is but One God, there must be a unified equation: $e=mc^2$. Karl Marx, although an atheist, gained his social consciousness while being raised in a Jewish home. And Sigmund Freud said that he began his studies of human behavior in the pages of the *Tanakh*.

As a Christian listening to a Christian, this sounded like a mixed message. This man said that Jesus was the Messiah and Christianity was God's plan. Yet, he also said that the world was blessed by these

Jewish people because they were raised as Jews, not as Christians. If Einstein had accepted the teaching of the Trinity, for example, he might never have discovered the unified equation. Pawson said that we Christians should encourage "Jews to be Jews," holy days and all. In my thinking, that means they should be practicing biblical Judaism. And if that were true, then we should stop evangelizing them and start sending them to synagogues, because we do not teach or practice Judaism in the Christian community. Yet, Pawson also said he disagreed with those who said, "Don't evangelize the Jews." The longer he spoke, the more my confusion grew.

Now Pawson began to speak in terms of coincidences. The Jewish people flourished in many societies in the Diaspora, but each time they "blessed" their host country, that country "cursed" them in some manner. After this curse, the host country suffered either economically, politically, or both. Germany in the early 1900s served as an example in this endless chain of similar events. Though just one percent of Germany's population, the Jewish people had provided an extremely high percentage of its professionals, including three-fourths of its professors. When Germany chose to curse its Jews, it was left the loser in World War II and was destroyed financially. Pawson sounded a warning to America that American Jews were settling in, and a new tide of anti-Semitism was sure to follow (ten years later this has proved true). If this pattern continues, I wonder if America will be cursed by God for its tolerance of anti-Semitism.

Just as I was feeling a bit self-righteous as an American whose country was basically good to its Jewish population, I received a lesson in history I would not soon forget. President Franklin D. Roosevelt had called an international conference in Evian, France, on July 6–15, 1938. By this time, world leaders were well aware of Hitler's anti-Semitic attitude, intentions, and actions.[5] The conference was called to discuss who would take in Germany's Jewish refugees before the "Final Solution" could be set into motion. Of the thirty-one countries represented, only the Dominican Republic took in a substantial number of refugees. The United States said they could take in no more than they had already accepted.

Four months later Hitler had clearly understood this Evian lesson: the "nations" (Gentiles) did not care what happened to the Jewish people. Therefore, in November came *Kristallnacht*, the Night of the Broken Glass, when Jewish businesses, synagogues, and homes were destroyed.

I should not have been surprised to find that the Evian conference[6] was practically ignored by history books. We could not accept the guilt. It took the Japanese bombing of Pearl Harbor to bring America into the war; so much for this self-righteous attitude I had about America's involvement in World War II. Perhaps it was partially this guilt that resulted in our financial support of the re-formed State of Israel in 1948; it was the least we could do after standing by for three-and-one-half years while six million Jewish men, women, and children died.

Pawson's British audience, aware of the growing tide of anti-Semitism in their country, was reminded that Europe had now been nearly emptied of Jews. Even today, the few remaining European Jews are being persecuted. The speaker believed that it was a response from God, not a coincidence, that Europe had suffered through two world wars. Pawson's message to those Christian businessmen was to stop dealing with Arab businesses whose contracts stipulated a boycott of Jewish products: bless the Jews, do not curse them, or Genesis 12:3 will continue to work against Europe.

As I thought over his speech, I realized the conference in Evian was perhaps the pinnacle of the world's turning against the Jewish people. And yet, just one decade after the conference, against insurmountable odds, the nation of Israel had been reborn. The countries of the world could no longer say they would have nothing to do with the Jewish people: Israel had become a force in the Middle East at the exact time the world became gluttons for Middle East oil. Now, how would we deal with God's decree "I will bless those who bless you, and whoever curses you I will curse" (Genesis 12:3)?

Pawson emphasized that "the Christian community has all but forgotten that the God we worship is the God of Abraham, Isaac, and Jacob" (present tense). His words reminded me of Romans 11:28–29: "As far as the gospel is concerned, they are enemies on your account; but as far as election is concerned, they are loved on account of the patriarchs, for God's gifts and His call are irrevocable."

As I studied this passage in Romans, I saw that Paul was speaking of those Jewish people who did *not* follow Jesus: "they *are* loved"; *their* gift and *their* call from God will never be revoked. God is the same yesterday, today, and forever; so too His Bible does not change. Whatever He instructed the Jewish people or the nations—the Gentiles—to obey was still in effect today. Therefore, Jesus' coming could never change how God viewed Jewish people or Gentiles or the Holy Scriptures. According to Jesus, God's Scriptural call and love for the Jews would stand firm:

> Do not think that I have come to abolish the Law or the Prophets; I have not come to abolish them but to fulfill them. I tell you the truth, until heaven and earth disappear, not the smallest letter, not the least stroke of a pen, will by any means disappear from the Law until everything is accomplished. Anyone who breaks one of the least of these commandments and teaches others to do the same will be called least in the kingdom of heaven. (Matthew 5:17–19)

These passages in Romans and Matthew I found on my own; however, Pawson did seem to be saying that Jewish people could accept Jesus as Messiah and still observe biblical Judaism just as they had in the first century. He also seemed to feel that Christians would come closer to first-century worship if they repaired the severed ties to their Jewish roots. Because of this cutting off of our roots, we have lost the meaning of a great deal of Scripture and the significance of the biblical holy days. Instead, the Christian community turned away from Jesus' Holy Scriptures, the *Tanakh*, and turned to pagan holidays and practices.

I wanted to find out how Gentile Christianity differed from Judaism, to see if we had indeed allowed paganism to enter the Christian movement. I began my study with the Christmas holiday. We celebrate Jesus' birth on December 25 of the Gregorian calendar. I found that Christmas had its origins in a week-long winter festival called Saturnalia and that the 25th day of December was a celebration of the birthday of Mithra, the Iranian god of light.[7] Mithraism was a religion that began earlier than and existed in competition with Christianity.[8] Placing Jesus' birthday on December 25 had nothing to do with the actual date of his birth; it was related more to observing pagan mythology.

I found that Easter was another pagan-based holiday. The pagan goddess Astarte (Beltis), the "queen of heaven" (and Baal's wife), was known as Ishtar in ancient Babylonia.[9] Even modern-day Lent had its origins not in the first-century Christian movement, but rather in the Babylonian forty-day spring festival. At this time of year, the death and resurrection of Tammuz were celebrated.[10] The use of Easter eggs during this spring festival has a great deal of pagan symbolism; one story is about a large egg that fell to earth, and when it hatched, out came Venus, who is synonymous in this story with Astarte, Ishtar, or Easter.[11] Obviously, early Christians had traded the biblical Passover celebration for pagan Ishtar observances.

All this talk of pagan practices in church reminded me of an incident that occurred one Halloween. Alecia and her friend searched our Bible concordance one afternoon, looking for words associated with Halloween, such as witch (sorceress), witchcraft, magic, sorcerer, and spiritist. They read the referenced biblical passages to see what God had to say about these words and discovered that God forbids His people to indulge in these pagan practices. God's people are to represent God and His views, not paganism. Philippians 4:8 instructs followers of Jesus to meditate on all that is good, not on evil, death (skeletons), and frightening others. At the library Alecia discovered that Halloween is actually a high holy day in the satanic church. This study was enough to cause Alecia and her friend to decide that Halloween was not to be celebrated by those who love God.

On October 31 that year, Alecia and I happened to visit the home of one of the church deacons for a Bible study. Upon entering, we saw Halloween decorations all over his house. Every room displayed reminders of this satanic holy day. My nine-year-old was confused by what she saw in this "godly" person's home. I was disgusted.

As I read *The Two Babylons* by Reverend Alexander Hislop, I discovered that a multitude of pagan legends, symbols, and practices had been absorbed into the Christian community. I was striving to obtain a fuller understanding of the One True God, studying the Bible to learn how to please Him. The Bible taught that we should eliminate all forms of idolatry and symbols of paganism from our lives, but these things had become a large part of everyday Christian and American cultural life.

The Bible-based worship and practices of first-century Christians made it clear that they were a sect of Judaism, but modern-day Christianity no longer resembled Judaism. To religious Jewish people, Christianity looks like the paganism God warned them to avoid.

Finally, Pawson summarized how he believed Christians should respond to Jewish people today. In Genesis 12:3, the Bible says to support the Jewish people; Pawson included practical ways such as business dealings and conversation. The Bible teaches supplication: to God, "pray for the peace of Jerusalem" (Psalm 122:6), and to people, as Esther did. Finally, Pawson said to bring the message of salvation through Jesus to the people of Israel, but not with arrogance. Instead, he said to approach them with humility (acknowledging *their* God, *their* Messiah), in penitence (accepting our share of guilt for society's anti-Semitic attitude and actions), and in love. But he reminded his audience that if one takes a biblical stand for the Jewish people, he or she may one day be considered by many to be a traitor. In the coming years I would experience this truth personally.

My life before choosing to follow God had basically been an unexamined one. I had simply done my best at life, paying little attention to any available sources of wisdom. When I read the Bible, wisdom suddenly became valuable. This was my spiritual infancy.

Entering the Christian community had been a natural step, implementing a desire to be with people of like mind. My relationship with God was primary, but fellowship with Christians created a loyalty to them that sometimes conflicted with the Bible's teachings. I had begun to lean on the teachings of people, accepting their viewpoint as God's without thoroughly testing their teachings with the Bible. I loved the God I met; I wanted to live as His Holy Scriptures taught, and not by pagan practices and anti-Semitism (or any racism). When I finally accepted that what the Christian community taught and practiced was not necessarily in keeping with a biblical viewpoint, the spiritual child inside me died.

It was time for me to go beyond doctrines, to return to God for fellowship and guidance and to the Bible for His truth. I was confused about where I fit into God's plan and about the Jewish people—how any today could remain "Jewish" and still accept Jesus as Messiah. I did not know whose view to believe or where I might find the answers I was seeking. Ultimately I knew I must be faithful to the truth of the God I loved, regardless of the consequences. It was time to set aside a childlike faith based too heavily on emotion; now I must thoroughly engage my mind in study and decide for myself what I would accept and reject. Spiritually speaking, I had entered my young adulthood.

When I was a child, I talked like a child, I thought like a child, I reasoned like a child. When I became a man, I put childish ways behind me. Now we see but a poor reflection as in a mirror; then we shall see face to face. Now I know in part; then I shall know fully, even as I am fully known. (1 Corinthians 13:11–12)

# 10

# TRUST AND OBEY

Not quite two years had passed since my baptism. The trip to Israel had been nearly eighteen months ago, yet I felt God tugging at my heart to go again. I kept passing it off as a personal whim: I loved Israel, and maybe I was merely missing it. But the *tugging* grew stronger.

One Sunday afternoon in early March I found myself in fervent prayer for four long hours. I tried to be still and "hear" God's will, but He seemed to be saying something I did not want to hear. I kept telling Him, "I have no money, no contacts, not even a reason to go! Is the reason evangelism? Then send someone else, someone with more experience. Send people from Jews for Jesus." I did not think His reason was evangelism, but I could not figure out what it was.

Why, God? I kept asking. No answer. Is this You, God? Is it just my idea? How can I be certain? Anyway, how can I find a job there? It would take so much money for Alecia and me to get to Israel, and for what? For how long? I gave Him all the reasons I could not go. It just was not humanly possible!

At that point in the prayer, I felt almost physically pressed down by God. I cried, begged, pleaded, and reasoned, but He would not allow me any peace. After battling for hours I finally understood. There was no audible voice, but the message was as clear as it had been when He first revealed Himself to me in my teens. I felt that He was saying, "You know I want you to go. Will you follow My will or not?"

The argument was over. I had no choice: to say no to God at that point would have meant leaving Him altogether. For me, to love God means to follow His will as best as you can discern it. Sometimes we are wrong about what His will is, but I had to do what my soul told me He wanted. Now, peace swept over me like a blanket.

Somehow I would get to Israel again. But I would have to take care of the financial arrangements and explain this spiritual demand on me to others in a manner they could accept. Most important, I had to communicate to my daughter the need for such a drastic disruption in our life.

Just as I knew He wanted me to go to Israel again, I also knew the time: the last week in July. On Monday I visited a travel agent picked at random from the phone book. When I arrived, I asked to book a trip to Israel, and the woman asked if I was Jewish.

"No."

"Do you speak Hebrew?"

"A little."

"Oh, who taught you?" she asked in a positive tone, thinking we might have a mutual acquaintance.

I gave her the name of my Jewish-Christian pastor.

Obviously she recognized Saul's name. She looked a little shocked and tried to conceal her anger. Most Jewish people are very offended by a Jew converting to Christianity. Saul had been raised religiously, which added to his offense. The agent quickly asked, "Oh, could you wait a minute while I make a call?"

She dialed and spoke excitedly in Hebrew. I do not know exactly what she said, but she was obviously upset. She probably thought I was some *goy* (Gentile) whom a converted Jew had taught to convert other Jewish people, and in Israel, no less! As I sat there in silence, all her frustrations came spilling out. When she got off the phone, she asked when I wanted to leave for the trip. Two seats were reserved for a July 26 polar flight to Copenhagen and then a connecting flight to Israel.

"Do you know anyone in Israel?" she asked.

"Not really."

Here I was, a Christian, going to Israel without any contacts, not even knowing the language. Surely she thought I was planning on evangelizing Jewish people, and in her view, I knew nothing and had no business going to Israel. But there was nothing more she could say. She made the reservations.

As I left, I prayed, "Well, God, You must know what You're doing. I sure wish You'd let me in on it."

A few weeks later, I went to another travel agent to compare prices; it would be a very expensive trip. The second agent gave me a quote that was $200 higher than the first price. Aware I was comparing, the agent asked where I got such a low price. I told her the name of the travel agency where I had made the reservations. She said that particular agency gets the best deals because they book more Israel trips than any other agency in the city. I could not help but wonder if it was a coincidence that I had gone there first or if God had His hand in all this.

Preparations began. I asked people from both congregations to pray for Alecia and me. Most people did not think the trip was going to take place (as a friend informed me later). Others thought God was sending me to Israel to evangelize. Some even thought that perhaps God was telling me I was Jewish. I had no idea why I was going; I began to wonder if they were right.

This brought to mind an odd thing about Jewish-Christian congregations; most members were Gentiles like me, and the idea of a Christian being pro-Jewish was not well accepted in most Christian circles. I heard some in the Jewish-Christian congregation say they found out, after confronting family members, that one of their grandfathers was Jewish. One man even said he had vague memories of his family acting in "Jewish ways" when he was little. This provided pro-

Jewish Christians with an acceptable explanation as to why they turned out to be pro-Jewish. I was not sure if these Christians were jealous of Jewish people (God's chosen people) and so wanted to be Jewish, or if they felt the need to provide an excuse to their Christian friends who were not accepting of their pro-Jewish attitude.

One woman told her children that people can not convert to Judaism: "You must be born a Jew." I happened to be teaching the Sabbath school class the day her children told me this. I asked, "But what about Ruth the Moabite who converted to Judaism?"

"Oh, yeah," they replied with perplexed looks on their faces.

There is a wide range of ideas in Jewish circles about who is a Jew; the same is true in Jewish-Christian groups. When I was on tour in Israel, our Jewish guide told us that according to Orthodox Judaism, one is a Jew only if his or her mother was born Jewish. The only exception to this, biblically, is if someone converts to Judaism as Ruth did.

If I were to immigrate to Israel (even temporarily), it would be easier if I were Jewish; if so, I wanted to know whether I was indeed Jewish. By biblical definition, then, my mother and grandmother had to be Jewish. I wrote to my grandmother; she told me in no uncertain terms that I was definitely not Jewish, nor was anyone in my family! My aunt later sent documentation of our family lineage, and added that they were all Christians. (Well, I had to ask.)

In the meantime life moved along smoothly. I had not given notice at work yet because I was waiting for God to provide additional proof that He wanted me to make the trip. I was waiting to find contacts or a job or money before I was willing to tell my employer I was leaving.

Both congregations held their spring retreats. The Jewish-Christian group celebrated Purim, the Feast of Lots. Purim occurs about four weeks before Passover, and it is based on the biblical Book of Esther. As Chanukah refers to an attack on the Jewish religion, Purim is about an attack on the Jewish people—an act of pure racism. On Purim God's acts of deliverance are celebrated. Those who oppressed and threatened the Israelites in the Book of Esther were themselves killed. This reminded me of Genesis 12:3: "I will bless those who bless you, and whoever curses you, I will curse." God is just: He does exactly as He says.

The July 26 deadline was still four months away. We found a four-piece luggage set for only $50. We held a yard sale. There was not much money, but we did not owe anything either; that was the best I could hope for at this point.

I purchased a three-month bus pass for April, May, and June to save gas money. However, we still needed a car for many things. This was our first financial problem: the car required major repairs (over $300), and we had to keep it running. That financial obstacle was minute, however, compared with what happened next.

One evening near the end of March I began to feel sick; as the evening progressed, I felt worse. Alecia went to bed, and my room-mate came home and went to bed, but the pain grew stronger. By morning I was scared; the pain had become intense. My roommate was only nineteen years old and did not know what to do, so I asked her to get my neighbor Lori.

Lori and I were close friends, and she kindly took over. She asked her husband, Paul, to take me to the hospital; by then, I was no longer able to drive. Alecia stayed with Lori and her two children. Without Lori, I do not know what we would have done. I thanked God for her love, help, and presence of mind.

By the time we reached the hospital, I was in no mood for emergency room questions. "What kind of insurance do you have?"

"None."

"None whatsoever?"

"No." Part-time employment usually means no medical or dental insurance, no paid holidays, no paid sick leave, no benefits. This was the price I paid to be there for my child before and after school.

Within two hours I was in surgery with an appendix that was ready to burst. Now it was no longer a matter of how to save money for the trip to Israel; I had to figure out how to feed us. There would be no income until I returned to work, and hospital bills were piling up quickly. If God wanted me to go to Israel, He would have to provide the way. It was clear these things were beyond my power; maybe God just wanted to be certain I knew that.

Friends told me how fortunate it was that the appendicitis hit when it did; at least I was in the United States when the illness struck. Still, "fortunate" seemed an odd choice of words.

After I returned home, a friend dropped off several bags of groceries, knocked on the door, and left before I could answer. Later he gave us $600 to help make up for the loss of income and to help pay some doctor bills. Our friends came through for us. I cried prayers of thanksgiving for their generosity and emotional support.

I returned to work as soon as possible. My health was not the best (I walked bent over), but I was alive. Godly friends had helped us through the storm. I could relate all this, in a small way, to Passover. That spring, death and poverty had indeed "passed over" us.

We continued to make plans for the trip as best we could. The church we attended on Sundays had a congregation in Jerusalem, in addition to the one in Lod. I wrote to the Jerusalem congregation about possible assistance in finding housing or a job in Israel. This proved to be a dead end; not one of the resources or contacts was helpful. We just did whatever we could to prepare, trusting God for the rest. I still did not give notice at work.

As always, my learning continued. A friend at our Jewish-Christian congregation told me about a newsletter issued by another Jewish-Christian congregation in the area, Beth Ha Shofar; she put my name on their mailing list. Their newsletter was intriguing. They offered pamphlets entitled *Messianic Judaism* and *Becoming a Proselyte*. I knew about Ruth the Moabite, but this message was different; this group taught that Gentiles could convert to messianic Judaism (Jewish-Christian beliefs) and thereby "become Jews." This was a form of converting to Christianity, not Judaism, as far as I could tell from the Bible. But I loved reading about anything Jewish, so I continued to read their letters.

Meanwhile we had been selling everything we could, but we still did not have enough money for the trip. Realizing that time was running out, I informed my roommate that we would have to give up our apartment at the end of May to save money. She was getting married soon, so she made plans for temporary housing. Alecia and I made arrangements to stay with my stepmother.

That apartment had been our home for four-and-one-half years. Our home, landlord, and neighbors had been wonderful; giving up our home was like relinquishing my security. The first brand-new sofa I ever owned was sold; the big bookcase and most of my books were gone; dressers, tables, and nearly everything except Alecia's toys were sold or given away. One very large box of kitchen items and a few other things were placed in the basement of my sister's house. The song "Trust and Obey" often ran through my mind.

Passover was now one month behind us. We had entered the days on the Jewish calendar known as the counting of the *omer*. An offering from the harvest was made on the first day of counting; the commanded offering was a sheaf (*omer*) of barley. The fiftieth day after Passover is holy: it is Shavuot (Leviticus 23:15–21). That year, those fifty days between Passover and Shavuot proved to be some of the most eventful days of my life.

As I studied, I realized these special days played a crucial role in Israel's history, as well as in the life of Jesus. Passover was the time the Children of Israel were taken out of Egypt, whereas Shavuot was the purpose for the rescue: it is believed that Shavuot is the date God gave Israel the Ten Commandments. In the New Testament, Jesus' death occurred near Passover. Acts 1:3 states that after the resurrection, Jesus accompanied his followers for forty days. Approximately one week after the Ascension, Acts, chapter 2, records the Holy Spirit baptism on Pentecost (Shavuot). All these events occurred during the counting of the *omer*.

I too felt as though I were counting down days to an important event, trusting that God would provide whatever we needed. An Ingathering (Jewish-Christian retreat) was scheduled for Memorial Day weekend. The Ingathering sounded wonderfully restful—a break from the mounting tension. But that was not how it turned out.

Several Jewish-Christian congregations came together for the Ingathering. I had no idea there were so many people involved in the Northwest's Jewish-Christian movement. People came from a similar congregation in Oregon, and some from the local Jews for Jesus chapter as well. One speaker traveled all the way from Colorado.

The worship assemblies were large, and the singing was joyful and inspiring. The variety of classes proved to be an eye opener, representing the wide range of beliefs within Jewish-Christian circles. Some speakers encouraged interest in a more Jewish way of life: celebrating the Saturday Sabbath and lighting candles on Friday evenings. This group played musical instruments during worship assemblies and sang songs about Israel. They were from Beth Ha Shofar, the congregation that published the newsletter I had been receiving.

The speaker from Jews for Jesus talked about evangelizing Jewish people; her class was mostly about what not to say. Although Jewish people give more to charities per capita than any other ethnic group,[1] the stereotype of the "cheap Jew" still exists. She relayed a recent experience she had had in a souvenir shop while wearing her Jews for Jesus T-shirt. The shop clerk had leaned over to her and commented, "That Indian over there tried to 'Jew' me down." Disgusted, she responded, "He did not try to 'Jew' you down! I'm Jewish," she said, pointing to her shirt. "If anything, he tried to 'Indian' you down!"

There were many other Jewish sensitivities she mentioned, as well as very specific ways to inform Jewish people about Jesus. She listed many *Tanakh* references that might convince Jewish people that Jesus is their promised Messiah. In general, though, she taught that loving actions, sensitive speech, and patience could win many Jews over to Christianity.

Bert Yellin, the speaker from Colorado, was the most radical of the group. He wore a *kippah* such as those worn in synagogues. His wife, a Gentile, wore a scarf covering her hair as some Orthodox Jewish women do; she considered herself a convert to Judaism (a proselyte). They observed many more practices of Judaism than did other Jewish-Christians.

Like the pastor of my congregation, Mr. Yellin had been raised in a religious Jewish home: he shared his early memories of observing the Sabbath, eating kosher food, and celebrating the holy days of the Jewish calendar. Like many Jewish people who convert to Christianity, he mocked many practices in Judaism he now considered legalistic. Yet at the same time, he was gradually absorbing more and more of these practices into his life. His speech reflected a bittersweet feeling toward his past.

I was impressed by his knowledge of the Bible; he seemed to know the *Tanakh* and the New Testament extremely well. Also, he had begun to study the Talmud (Oral Law), where he searched for verification that Jesus was the Messiah. In the Talmud Bert had found quotes from great rabbis that sounded remarkably similar to the words of Jesus in the New Testament. He told us he discovered that in the Talmud some sages held views similar to Jesus on certain issues while maintaining differing views on others.

Hearing this Jewish viewpoint on the New Testament was like graduating from silent movies to talkies. Acts, chapter 20, was a great example of this "enlightened" view Mr. Yellin gave us. In Acts Paul is speaking until midnight. Eutychus fell from the third floor window, and Paul revived him and continued speaking until daybreak. I have heard Christians quote Acts 20:7 as proof that the Sabbath was changed from Saturday to Sunday in the New Testament, but in the Jewish context we learned something different.

I began to realize that the whole setting of the New Testament was Jewish. Jesus' entire ministry took place in Israel, the land God gave the Jews. Peter, James, and John were all Jewish; so was Paul. The twelve disciples were all Jews, and the majority of the multitudes who gathered to hear Jesus speak were Jewish people.

In a Jewish country, the Jewish calendar was in use, and the day was reckoned from sundown to sundown. The Sabbath began on

Friday evening, and ended at Saturday nightfall. Saturday night was the start of the first day of the week, Sunday. The handling of money is forbidden on *Shabbat* as are most daily affairs. Because money could not be handled on *Shabbat*, the custom arose to collect money for the poor and handle other synagogue business on Sunday, the first day of the week. The Sabbath day was devoted to God and to spiritual business.

Today, as in the past, at the close of *Shabbat* on Saturday evening there is a service called *Havdalah* (separation). Prayers and blessings are said, and a special braided candle is lit. *Shabbat* is bid farewell, and the new week is ushered in. Often someone preaches at the *Havdalah* service.

Now I saw the Jewish setting for the events related in Acts 20:7–11. Paul was the chosen speaker for the *Havdalah* services that Saturday night. Verse 6 sets the time of year as just after the Feast of Unleavened Bread—in late spring when the days were getting longer. The *Havdalah* service could not begin until sundown, so Paul must have begun speaking about nine or ten o'clock. (The breaking of bread here simply meant to eat together.) Paul spoke until midnight, rescued the young man, then continued speaking until dawn. This means that Paul probably spoke for seven to ten hours; quite a feat for anyone!

When I ignored the Jewish context and returned to the modern Christian one, a strange picture emerged. Verse 7 says they came together to break bread: here they are on Sunday morning partaking of communion. Paul speaks that morning and all day long, continues speaking until midnight, then rescues Eutychus, and speaks until Monday morning. This would mean that Paul spoke for nearly twenty to twenty-four hours with only a few meal breaks. That does not make sense, even for a speaker like Paul.

I wanted to understand Jesus' teachings, but I realized that without a knowledge of Judaism and the Jewish cultural background of the New Testament, it was nearly impossible. I could now see how easily Christians could misunderstand passages like this one in Acts.

After Mr. Yellin's talk, I told him how sad I thought it was that we

Christians were cut off from our Jewish roots; we lost a great deal of insight and understanding. In addition to losing the nurturing spiritual root, Jesus' movement was turned into a tool of racism; century upon century of heinous acts against Jewish people had been committed by the church. I said to the pastor, "Maybe Gentiles, upon entering the movement, should have converted to Judaism."

"No," he quickly responded. "What did the leadership say to the Gentiles?" He quoted James:

> It seemed good to the Holy Spirit and to us not to burden you with anything beyond the following requirements: You are to abstain from food sacrificed to idols, from blood, from the meat of strangled animals and from sexual immorality. You will do well to avoid these things. Farewell. (Acts 15:28–29)

In this passage, there is a difference between what the apostles were teaching the Gentiles to do and what they told Jewish followers to practice. Jewish believers were taught to be "zealous for the Law" (Acts 21:20–24), whereas Gentiles were told they need not observe Judaism to join this Jewish religious movement. Instead, they need only observe the few instructions mentioned in Acts 15:28–29. Later, when I learned of the Noahdic Covenant, it sounded similar to Jesus' instructions for God-loving Gentiles.

Mr. Yellin said that although Gentiles were not required to convert to Judaism, they could do so if they wished; he seemed to be encouraging it. But he did not keep kosher; like Christians, he too was picking and choosing which parts of the *Tanakh* to practice and which to reject. I wondered what kind of Judaism he was encouraging.

I sought out Bert's wife, Sylvia, told her about my planned trip to Israel, and asked for her viewpoint. She believed God was sending me to Israel to evangelize Jewish people, but that I was not prepared for the task. She thought it might be best if Alecia and I moved to Colorado to study and train with their congregation before going on to Israel. They could prepare me for a life of evangelizing Jewish people; surely there was no other reason for God to send a Christian to Israel. I did not know why God wanted me to go, but I did not believe it was to evangelize Jewish people.

I left the retreat a day early to pray. Through that prayer, even though I was now emotionally exhausted, God was teaching me to trust and obey. If the second trip to Israel was truly His will, He would open the way; I had to be patient and look for the door that He would open. We were moving in just a few days.

As Cheryl, my dear friend from the Bible study group, said, God does things for me in the "eleventh hour." Moving out of our apartment and getting rid of most of our possessions were scary steps of faith. If I were going to take these steps of faith, there could be no foot left in the door. By the time we turned over the keys to our home and moved our few remaining possessions into one small bedroom of my parents' house, it was definitely 11:59 P.M. The door to my old life slammed shut behind me.

On Monday, June 1, my nine-year-old daughter and I found ourselves in the bedroom where I had grown up. My father had passed away several years earlier, but the house looked the same. Here I was at the age of thirty, back in my little bedroom with virtually nothing: no home, furniture, or money; no connections to Israel; and a car on its last legs. I just kept praying, "If You want me to do this, God, You'd better do something soon."

Two days later, the counting of the *omer* was finished; it was Shavuot, and I was about to be given the Torah in a way I had not imagined. God was ready now to answer my prayer, or rather, I was ready to receive His answer. In any case, a new period in my life was about to begin.

While reading Beth Ha Shofar's newsletter, something caught my eye: two visitors from Israel were scheduled to speak at Friday evening services—only two days away. I wanted to hear what I could about Israel—and perhaps they might know someone who could help us get there.

Unfamiliar with that part of the city (and wanting some moral support), I asked Cheryl to go with me. We found the little church and walked up its wooden steps. Everything outside looked serene and traditional, but appearances can be deceiving. Once inside, I noticed some marked differences from a traditional congregation. Most of the men wore *kippahs*; only a few had worn *kippahs* in the Jewish-Christian church we usually attended. The women here wore scarves covering their hair; this I had not seen Gentiles do, except for Sylvia Yellin. This church had also adopted more synagoguelike practices into their services than had any other messianic churches I had visited.

The assembly room was crowded, and many non-members were present, including a local bishop. Cheryl and I took our seats in the second row. Having read about Judaism, I recognized some terms the pastor was using. He welcomed everyone to the *Erev Shabbat* (eve of *Shabbat*) service, the Friday evening services that introduce the Sabbath day. Other messianic congregations were led by pastors who had been born Jewish, but this man was a Gentile. While other pastors related childhood experiences of being raised in Jewish homes, this man spoke of a Judaism he had only read about. We were in for a unique experience.

A young woman lit *Shabbat* candles, an act usually done in Jewish homes before going to *shul* (synagogue) on Friday night. After lighting them, she sang a little song; her words came from the *siddur*[2] blessing recited when *Shabbat* candles are lit. However, this woman added something about "Yeshua," the Hebrew name for Jesus. Everyone said amen, and the congregation broke out in a song about Yeshua being the light of the world, "even in the darkness," just like *Shabbat* candles.

This congregation, instead of ignoring their Jewish roots, practiced as much Judaism as they knew. But they did not stop there. They spoke as though every Jewish practice symbolized Jesus, ignoring whatever meaning these practices held prior to Jesus' coming—whatever meaning they had to Jesus himself. Because of this viewpoint, their service was a greater insult to Orthodox Judaism than was a standard Christian service.

After singing a few songs in Hebrew, the first of two speakers began. He was a third-generation native Israeli Jew and a believer in Jesus as the Messiah. He had the olive-tone skin and black hair of a *sabra*, a native Israeli, but actually his ancestors were from the Bukhara area of then Southern Russia. Though smiling and joking, this middle-aged man's face looked as though it carried much pain.

His name was Shlomo (translation: Solomon). He pleased his audience by saying "Praise the Lord!" many times. Then Shlomo introduced the main speaker, Goran (pronounced Yoran), and said that this Swedish minister was a blessing to both Jews and Christians in Israel. "His great mission is to help Christians understand Israel."

As part of his introduction, Shlomo told us of a booklet Goran had written.[3] After the talk, copies would be given out "free of charge, because I want to be a good Jew from Israel; I don't want to sell you everything." His comment made me think of those misconceptions about the "cheap Jew." Then Shlomo quickly hid his pain by saying, "Listen: we don't understand everything. Paul said we are looking through a dark glass, but one day we will see face-to-face." Without explaining his reason for the reference (1 Corinthians 13:12), he introduced Goran.

Goran was already a very learned theologian when he first visited Israel in 1972, and in the following fifteen years he learned a great deal more. For the last seven years, he had lived in Mea Shearim, an ultra-Orthodox Jewish neighborhood in Jerusalem. Exactly what he had learned there was the topic of his speech.

Goran began by saying "*Shabbat shalom*" (Sabbath peace to you); then he continued in Hebrew. "Oh, I thought I was speaking English; excuse me. Well, it all sounds the same anyway: Swedish."

He began describing what he felt he had in common with the audience: a love of Israel, of Jerusalem, of the Holy Scriptures, of the One True God. He spoke of his arrival in Israel in 1972. He had never before entered a synagogue, nor had he met one Jewish person. This highly esteemed theologian said, "I didn't know very much." Almost immediately, though, his words and expression told me that he now understood Jerusalem, Judaism, and the Jewish people as completely as any Gentile was able.

As I sat there, I felt my heart and soul absorbing his message, but my mind was barely following his words. This Swedish minister spoke of Judaism with love, the way I pictured Jesus loving it. Goran spoke of the Sabbath as a sign between "God and His people forever" (Exodus 31:17). There it was, that word: forever. Forever and everlasting in the Old Testament seemed like a paradox to me; how could God really mean forever if He sent Jesus to cancel His instructions (Colossians 2:14)? But here was a Christian saying it was true: the Sabbath is to last forever, just as it says in Exodus.

Like David Pawson, Goran believed the very existence of the Jewish people constituted a miracle. I was beginning to agree. The Jewish people are a small persecuted group of people, and in every generation it seems another power arises to annihilate them. From Haman in the book of Esther to Pharaoh in Egypt, from Hitler to today's Neo-Nazi party, Church of Aryan Nations, and Arab-bloc countries, many have been the devout enemies of Israel. With such continual and organized efforts to exterminate the Jewish race, their survival does seem miraculous.

Goran spoke of his Swedish relatives who came to North America during Sweden's potato famine. They assimilated into the melting pot of American culture. "They don't speak Swedish; they don't know from where in Sweden their families came. Only one hundred years and their Swedish identity is nearly gone. That's okay, though," he said. "It was not God's purpose that the Swedish people should be the holy people of Michigan."

However, Goran believed the people of Israel received a different task from God: to be an eternal people, to be a holy people forever. And as they are a permanent part of God's plan, He ensures their survival. I was reminded of Jeremiah, chapter 31.

Next, he introduced a concept to which I had given little thought. Goran emphasized that we should take note of how God preserved this people, that He did so with very special signs that serve to keep Jewish people separate from other nations. The tools He uses include the Sabbath, an eternal sign in time; dietary laws specifying which foods Jewish people are and are not allowed to eat; a sign in the flesh, circumcision; and a tiny country in the Middle East given to be an "eternal possession." All these signs were given in the Torah, and they serve as a fence around the Jewish people, maintaining their unique identity as Israel. In this way, Jewish people were keeping God's Torah alive.

Goran went on to clarify the terms *holy* and *sanctified*, giving an explanation that was new to me. He said we must understand the meaning of these words in Hebrew if we wish to comprehend God's purpose for Israel. He told us that in Swedish as in English, *holy* means a sort of quality, a superior spiritual quality, but this is not so in Hebrew, the language of Torah. *Holy* and *sanctified* simply mean to set something apart for a specific purpose. God gave Israel a special task, one that would require their continued separation from all other nations (Genesis 12:1).

There are many misunderstandings of this idea of God's choosing. In Exodus 19:5, one version of the Bible says that Israel will be a special treasure *above* all people. Goran said this is an erroneous translation, and is not at all what is written in the Hebrew text. No, Israel is to be a "peculiar" [different] treasure "because all the earth is Mine," God says. Israel is a different treasure, but not God's *only* treasure among His creation. I realized that God created and loves us all equally; He had the whole earth to choose from. He had to choose one nation to accomplish His plan, so He did.

By comparison, most Christians know that they too are to be a "kingdom of priests, a holy people." For some, their recognition of God makes them feel superior to pagans, but beliefs do not make Christians superior. I realized that being holy to God simply means to choose a different way of life from that of non-believers. Living by God's instructions makes all God's people different. This was the biblical concept of *holy,* and it changed the way I read the Bible from that day forward.

As I studied the Bible with these newfound insights, I began to understand Goran's teachings regarding *how* God kept Israel holy (separate). All the laws in the Torah guarded against pagan influences. Though they were scattered, their strict monotheism and unique practices maintained Jewish nationhood so that one day God could unite them and bring them back into their land.

It was painful to think that, although their observance of the Torah has kept alive the meaning of God's revelation (the Bible), these same commandments also cost the Jews much suffering. Being different and being scattered have made the Jewish people an easy target for violent people. In recent generations, many Jews have chosen to assimilate: to abandon the Law of Moses and live as Gentiles. Perhaps those who choose assimilation believe that they will avoid or at least delay the suffering of persecution. We learned from the Holocaust, however, that although religious Jews were persecuted first, assimilated Jews were also murdered.

I could see that Christian anti-Semitism was more than simple xenophobia, however. Some Christians talk as though the Jewish people have somehow earned the horrible treatment they have experienced throughout history, as if God has been punishing them for rejecting Jesus as the Messiah. However, this was not Jesus' reaction to their unbelief; rather, Jesus said, "Father, forgive them, for they do not know what they are doing" (Luke 23:24). The very few Jews in the first century who brought Jesus to Pilate did so because they believed Jesus had blasphemed God; in the Holy Scriptures blasphemy is punishable by death. The Romans would not allow Jews to carry out the death penalty on their own, so Jesus was turned over to Pilate. Those few Jewish men involved in this act were simply applying the Law given by God. No one can justify racism on this basis.

Goran's next words hit harshly on many ears in that room. Here, as in many messianic congregations, following some Jewish practices is a common trend; it has become popular to perform Jewish folk dances and sing Hebrew songs during Christian services. Goran related how in the first century some Gentiles were trying to live as Jews, considering themselves more like Jesus the Jew. But Jesus *was* a Jew, commanded to observe those laws; Gentiles were never commanded to observe them. Goran's teaching was not well received in a room full of *kippah*-wearing Gentiles.

This pro-Jewish minister said he did not keep the Sabbath or wear "fringes" (Numbers 15:37–41 and Mathew 23:5). He did not wear these signs because he was not a Jew. Goran's message was not to *be* Israel, but rather to recognize the biblical differences between Israel and the Gentiles and then, because of the Bible, to speak and act in support of Israel. After all, God said He would bless those who bless Israel and curse those who curse Israel.

Yad Vashem, the Holocaust memorial museum in Israel, was his next topic. Yad Vashem stands in memory of those who died in the concentration camps of World War II and also serves as a reminder of the continued threat of anti-Semitism. Goran told us of a beautiful picture that hangs in the entrance to Yad Vashem. It was taken in the early 1930s somewhere in southern Germany, where they put up crosses to mark crossroads. The sun was shining; trees and flowers filled the scene. The words on the cross were written in German: *Juden verboten*—"no Jews allowed here." To Goran, this was one of the most horrifying pictures in all of Yad Vashem.

Goran asked, "How could such a sign be placed on the cross of Yeshua (Jesus)? Why was it that the first Christian with a living faith didn't tear it down? No, the hour of destiny for the Jewish people was not when the gas chambers of Auschwitz began to operate, for by then it was too late. It was in the beginning of the 1930s, when it would still have been possible to do something. But they did nothing." (His words reminded me of the silence of my Gentile congregation.)

Goran took us back to 140 C.E., to the main source of Christian anti-Judaism and subsequent anti-Semitism—Marcion of Pontus.[4] In a work entitled *Anti-Thesis* (contrasts), Marcion taught that Christianity and biblical Judaism were direct opposites: Christians were good/ Jews were bad; Old Testament Law was bad/the New Testament was good; Israel's God was bad/the Christians' God was good. His two-gods theory finally convinced the Church fathers to call Marcion a heretic, and Polycarp called him "the firstborn of Satan."[5]

Until 70 C.E., Jesus' movement was headquartered in Jerusalem and led by James; it was clearly a movement within Judaism. When the Romans attacked Jerusalem, most people left the city. Then the movement's Jewish influences were forced into direct competition with pagan influences. Marcion's theology apparently developed in that battle zone.

If the Church fathers had simply labeled Marcion a heretic, he might have caused little harm, but according to Goran, the Church Fathers went a step too far. Marcion wanted to throw out the Old Testament because it was too Jewish, but the Church Fathers knew the *Tanakh* was Jesus' only Holy Scriptures. Combining Marcion's teachings with Jesus's Holy Scriptures, the Church Fathers now said that the *Tanakh* was not Jewish, but Christian, and all literal meanings were now to be ignored as being merely symbolic of the newly revealed Christian interpretations. Gentiles were now called the New Israel, and whatever Jews did the Church declared a heresy. Jewish people who kept the Sabbath or were zealous for the Law were now called heretics: enemies of the Christian community (Acts 21:20).

Goran said, "The Church began to preach like Haman in the book of Esther. They said, 'You Jews are different, so you are bad (a threat). You must now become as we are. We will accept you if you abandon Moses (Acts 15:21) and become good Gentile Christians.'"

The early Church developed a train of thought that would prove deadly to the Jewish people even into this century:

Step 1.  You cannot live among us as Jews (no Judaism).
Step 2.  You cannot live among us (no Jews allowed).
Step 3.  You cannot live.

This was the progression followed by Hitler's Nazis in World War II. Is Step One how Jews are viewed in most Christian churches today?

Goran spoke of his mission of opening Christian eyes to Holy Scripture and mending relations between Jewish people and Christians. He was preaching Judaism for Jews and Christianity for Gentiles. Unlike David Pawson, Goran did not believe in evangelizing Jewish people, possibly because the Christian community will not allow them to be faithful to the eternal commandments God gave them. Goran said that God Himself will take care of their salvation. "His gifts and His call are irrevocable" (Romans 11:26–29). They *are* loved by God. Goran emphasized his point by saying, "What God has said here (in the Old Testament) is the same as He has said here (in the New Testament), because there is One God who does not change."

> Oh, the depth of the riches of the wisdom
> and the knowledge of God!
> How unsearchable His judgments,
> and His paths beyond tracing out!
>                                    (Romans 11:33)

Goran felt that we must bring Christians to Jerusalem and teach them how religious Jews live today in order to remove the bias Marcion implanted in the Church. He stressed that we must go to the root, to the Jewish people, the very source of Christianity. From them and from ancient Jewish commentaries, we can begin to understand Jesus. Goran said that God has put a hardening on the hearts of most Jewish people (Romans 11:25) so they will not accept Jesus as Messiah. Since God has chosen to do this (His will, not that of the Jewish people), then God will not take away their eternal salvation for not believing Jesus is Messiah. Salvation lies in God's hands alone.

That night all this information was like a paradox to me. Yet, as I listened, I felt I was drawing closer to the truth. My heart was being swept away, but the canvas Goran was painting was much too large for me to see. God had given me my own task, and somehow I had to find a way to obey Him. I could see that Goran's teachings were important, and later I would read the booklets. But for now I had to continue along the path that God had laid out for me.

When both speakers were finished, the congregation's pastor announced their next service, to be held the next morning, and then invited everyone downstairs for tea, coffee, cookies, and conversation. I thought, here's my chance.

I walked up to Goran, introduced myself, and thanked him for the fascinating lecture. Then I took a deep breath and told him that I needed to go to Israel.

"Why?"

"I'm not sure."

"Uh-oh, better talk to Shlomo!"

Shlomo did not seem bothered that I had no idea why I needed to go to Israel, other than God wanting me to do so. He told me about his Christian center in Jerusalem where many people lived, worked, and studied on a short- or long-term basis. He asked, "What work can you do?"

"I'm a bookkeeper and I can do all kinds of office work."

He thought perhaps I could work in the Jerusalem office. This was my first ray of hope. He would need to see my resume and call his branch manager in Jerusalem to find out if there was an opening for me.

That evening I stayed at Cheryl's apartment a few miles from the little church. In the morning, after service, I planned to drive home, get my resume, and come back to the church building to meet with Shlomo. That evening he called, asking many questions and telling me of the work they were doing in Jerusalem. It sounded fascinating. I was excited and hopeful, especially after such a long time without leads.

Then he told me there were no children at the center.

"Not yet" was my response. I could not imagine leaving Alecia behind.

The next morning, I went alone to hear Goran and Shlomo speak. The congregation's pastor said they normally read the weekly Torah portion (as in synagogues), but this time they would postpone it until Sunday. Instead, they moved directly into the worship service.

Their Saturday morning service included the short prayer we had recited the night before and the *Shema*.[6] They only said the first few words of the *Shema*, however. Instead of completing it, they began to sing a Jewish-Christian song about Jesus and the *Shema*. It sounded like an evangelistic song directed toward Jewish people. Tiny pieces of synagogue prayers were scattered throughout the songs.

The worship service lasted for only a half-hour. The congregation passionately believed they had one piece of knowledge religious Jews were missing. With this Jewishness in their evangelistic message, the Jewish people would surely be able to see that Jesus is the Messiah; then they could become "completed" Jews. The singing was beautifully sincere, but sincerity does not necessarily indicate truth. We were about to meet one of these "completed Jews."

Shlomo rose to introduce his friend Goran again, but first he had something to say. He began by telling us about his childhood: he was born into an Orthodox Jewish family in Jerusalem. The pain and anger he had been hiding during the previous evening's speech began to seep through his forced smile. He was responding to those who believed in evangelizing Jewish people: the majority of the audience. Some were perhaps casting a critical eye on Shlomo for not evangelizing his fellow Jews, and he was well aware of their feelings.

"One mention of Jesus' name," Shlomo blurted out, would cause a rush of anger and resentment from his relatives in Israel. Shlomo's offense against his people was that he had joined the enemy: he accepted Jesus as the Messiah. However, he was still a Jew, so he was tolerated in the synagogue and among family, but only if he kept quiet about Jesus. Shlomo spoke of the "rivers of Jewish blood" shed in the name of Jesus. "How can I go to them, my fellow Jews, my people? What do I tell them about a religion that has caused them such grief?

"I can go to *shul* every day, but what can I say to them?" Jesus' message of love, of comfort, of hope—that is not what Jewish people have *experienced* at the hands of Christians. "People want to go to Israel to evangelize the Jews. What will you tell the Jews when you get there?" Shlomo asked. "All of a sudden, this pro-Jewish movement in Christianity has appeared. What are Jewish people supposed to think about it? For two thousand years you didn't look at us or think of us. You looked at us as cursed for eternity. What happened?"

Shlomo's pain was now revealed: he was a Jew, in Jerusalem, with his family there for three generations and thousands of relatives there, but Shlomo did not fit in because he believed that Jesus was the Messiah. Among Christian friends he could not act like a Jew, and among his fellow Jews he could not talk of Jesus. Perhaps this was why God had hardened the hearts of most Jewish people, that they might not see Jesus as the Messiah (Romans 11:25).

"I'm cut off," he said, fighting back tears. "People say I am the enemy of Israel, of the Jew. We will come, bring Jews to church, assimilate them, and there will be no more Jews."

Hitler destroyed them physically; evangelizing is seen by many Jewish people as destroying Jews spiritually because modern Christianity calls Jewish people to abandon the Law of Moses, to stop obeying the Torah.

"Sometimes—I'm sorry, you may not like this—but sometimes I wish God had allowed me to be an ordinary Jew." Shlomo wished that God had "hardened his heart" too. All his pain came pouring out at once.

None of us, except perhaps Goran, could understand Shlomo's pain. We could not appreciate the background from which he spoke. We had been taught in churches to view Judaism as obsolete and incomplete, replaced by a fuller knowledge—Christianity. After studying Judaism, I was afraid the opposite might be true: perhaps there was actually a richness in Judaism, our source, that had been whitewashed out of the Christianity we knew today.

All I knew for certain on that Saturday morning was that this man was suffering. He was stuck between two worlds and belonged to neither. The part of him that defended Jesus as the Messiah might have been uppermost in his mind around his Jewish people, but now, among Christians, the other part surfaced, the part that defended his people. As a Jew, he took offense to the same things any religious

Jewish person finds offensive: terms such as "messianic congregations" or "messianic Judaism." Jewish people believe in a Messiah, so they are all "messianic." They just do not think Jesus was the promised one. As Shlomo spoke, I realized how little I knew about the Jewish people.

"During World War II many of my people did everything they could to deny the fact that they were Jews, in an effort to save their lives. After Israel's Six-Day War in 1967, now everybody's a Jew!" (The modern Jews for Jesus movement began then.) Shlomo continued, "Israel is in the headlines every other day; it is a dynamic, exciting country. So now everybody wants to be a Jew for the first time in two thousand years. How long will these new Jews be Jews? Perhaps when again there's a price to be paid to be a Jew, then they will no longer be Jews."

Thinking this over, I realized that Christians strive to be people of action. That is the reason for evangelism. The very idea of waiting for God to move the hearts of Jewish people seemed foreign. Christians are told to become involved in the lives of others; show them you are a good person, and they will appreciate it and ask how you came upon this attitude. Tell them the reason is Jesus, and they will become Christians too. But this teaching is not compatible with Romans, chapter eleven, where we are told that God has control over what Jewish people believe about Jesus. Accepting that as truth, then, those beliefs are part of God's plan and God's timing. Consequently, evangelizing Jewish people would not only be pointless, but evidently against God's plan.

However, the standard Christian message regarding Jewish evangelism is different. Judaism, and even the Jewish people have been regarded as an enemy of the Christian community since the days of Marcion. This is so deeply embedded into the Christian mindset that it has surfaced in even the most ardent pro-Jewish Christians I have met. For them, Christianity is right, so Judaism must be wrong. To attempt to comprehend that God may have a reason for keeping biblical Judaism alive until the "end of days" is considered a treasonous concept in the Christian camp. Yet, I read Revelation, chapter seven, where the "saved" people are described as two groups: first, the tribes of Israel and identified separately, the multitudes in white robes— the Gentiles. That morning I was convinced that I needed to rethink everything I had learned so far.

Shlomo sat down and Goran took the podium. Goran stood there, empathizing with the pain and confusion of both sides: the Torah-observing Jews and the Christian audience. Both wanted to love, both sides wanted to be biblically correct, and neither side wanted to yield to the other and so be marked as a traitor in their own camp. Shlomo and Goran stood in the middle—Shlomo standing with his Jewish people and Goran with his Gentiles—and both men were wounded deeply by friendly fire.

Goran told us that it took him many years to understand Shlomo. He spoke of first coming to Jerusalem in 1972. He had so much to tell the "poor lost Jews of Israel." Instead, it was Goran who learned. Goran, who was far away from the God of Israel, had now come close to God because of Jesus. He did not think the prophets or rabbis would have gotten their message regarding the God of Israel all the way to Sweden, because that was not their perspective. Fortunately, the Gentile followers of Jesus brought the God of Israel to Sweden.

Only once in the Old Testament did a prophet go to the Gentiles. Jonah went to Ninevah, but he was a reluctant missionary to the Gentiles. The mission God gave Jonah was to become a sign for the future: Jonah did not tell the Ninevites to convert to Judaism and so become Jews; they were simply told to repent. They repented of heinous acts against each other and developed a fear and respect for the God of Israel. And though God created us all, He was still to be called the God of Israel.

Goran did not believe in evangelizing the Jewish people. "And I know very well it is said in the New Testament, 'first to the Jews.' Yes, I know it." But he spoke of the many stumbling blocks the Church had placed in the way of the Jew. He told of Christian anti-Semitism today and in the past and of Christians calling eternal commandments canceled, thus showing disrespect for the Holy Scriptures. He spoke of Jesus, the Jewish Messiah, "Gentilized" beyond Jewish recognition. Rather than evangelizing then, Goran said that Christians must first repair the way.

The question of evangelizing Jewish people has been a difficult one in the Christian community. I realized that if people think God made a mistake in His creation of biblical Judaism that Jesus needed to fix, then Jesus' own words in Luke, chapter ten, were inexplicable.

> On one occasion an expert in the law stood up to test Jesus. "Teacher," he asked, "what must I do to inherit eternal life?"
>
> "What is written in the Law?" he replied. "How do you read it?"
>
> He answered: "'Love the Lord your God with all your heart and with all your soul and with all your strength and with all your mind'; and 'Love your neighbor as yourself.'"
>
> "You have answered correctly," Jesus replied. "Do this and you will live." (Luke 10:25–28)

Then, a few verses later, at the end of the parable of the Good Samaritan, Jesus asked the Jewish man:

> "Which of these three do you think was a neighbor to the man who fell into the hands of robbers?"
>
> The expert in the law replied, "The one who had mercy on him."
>
> Jesus told him, "Go and do likewise." (Luke 10:36–37)

Jesus did not condemn the Law of Moses or say it was canceled (Matthew 5:17–19). Rather, Jesus told the man to love and obey God (the Law), and then he would receive eternal life. Evidently Jesus did not feel the need to convert the man in any way. Instead, he said, "Go and do likewise." The man was practicing Judaism as God had commanded him, so Jesus did not correct him. I had to reconsider what Jesus' message *really* was. This was not what I had been taught in church.

There was more, much more than any of us in the audience could handle. The message was too deep; it was too much to learn in one day, and it cut against every Christian grain. How many ears were closed at that point, I wondered. Many minds slammed shut because they could not grasp the message. We needed milk, not meat. This biblical meat gagged and frightened most of the people in that room. For the audience that day, like some Jesus had spoken to, the preaching attacked some basic beliefs. We were fascinated, but upset.

Goran spoke of Gentiles evangelizing Jews and teaching the commandment of love, for instance, as if the Jews did not know it. Christianity comes from Judaism; the teachings originated there. These concepts were not new to religious Jewish people. Heaven, hell, paradise, a one-on-one relationship with God, humility, resurrection, the Messiah, mercy, sin, forgiveness, and baptism—all these ideas originated in Judaism. Goran told us that it insults religious Jewish people when Christians share these concepts as though they originated in Christianity. It is a sad thing to realize that non-religious Jews might believe these misconceptions when they hear them from Christians.

Goran proceeded to teach us the Jewish concepts of God's grace and righteousness. These are both complex concepts in Christianity, but quite simple in Judaism. Goran showed us the basic meaning of righteousness: a cup filled right to the top, to the brim, where not one more drop will fit. "A righteous merchant sells you something right up to the top, because that is what you paid for." And grace Goran explained by raising his hand above the filled water glass: "You can't pay for this" (this immeasurable gift from God). "God is righteous; He gives His promises to the full. However, He also gives more: He gives grace.

"Since You, God, have promised to give grace to sinners," Goran continued, "we call on that promise; we are dependent on grace. This is good Judaism. There are legalistic Jews and there are legalistic Christians, but that is not the correct teaching of either faith." We learned that legalism is not synonymous with obedience and that religious Jews obey out of their belief in and love and respect for God.

I have heard preaching about the Pharisee and tax collector in the New Testament; that the Pharisee is legalistic (Jewish) and the tax collector is pious (Christian). However, Goran taught that this passage is not a comparison of Judaism and Christianity. Instead, it is a warning to *all* religious leaders of the dangers of piety, of feeling superior to others and above the temptation to sin. According to stories I read in newspapers, many Christian leaders should heed this lesson.

Then Goran brought up a problem, a response some Christians have when they hear these positive teachings about Judaism. They see the value of the rabbis' teachings and that they were the same as Jesus' teachings. Then they ask, "Then why did we need Jesus?"

It is as if they believed that if Jesus did not oppose everything in Judaism, it was not necessary that he come at all. Goran taught that Jesus was not the antithesis of Judaism, but rather, he was the confirmation of Judaism and of Holy Scripture, the declaration of the God of Israel. Jesus was the method God used to carry the message of His grace beyond the Jewish people and out to us Gentiles.

Goran told us of a survey taken among Christians. It listed many characters in the *Tanakh* and many from the New Testament. The Christians were asked to identify which ones were Jews. Most labeled people in the *Tanakh* as Jews, but only one figure in the New Testament was identified as a Jew: Judas. Though almost every person mentioned was Jewish, Christians only thought of the traitor as a Jew. This is the epitome of Christian anti-Semitism.

That Saturday morning I learned of New Testament passages that accounted for the answers in that survey. In the New Testament, Jewish people were often identified as Jewish only when they were doing something "wrong." In the Gospel of John, for example, whenever something negative was attributed to Jewish people, they were called "the Jews." It was not written, "those particular Jews" or "a few Jews." No , it was written, "the Jews," as though all Jewish people were terrible. When Jewish people were doing something "good" in the Gospel of John, praising Jesus or saying "*hoshannah*," they were called "the people." The vast multitude of people mentioned in the New Testament were Jewish. Only a few considered Jesus to be a threat, but they were hesitant to act against Jesus for fear of the multitudes of Jewish people.

The revelation of these subtle anti-Jewish messages in the New Testament cut me like a knife. Eventually, as I understood the viewpoint of the New Testament writers and the world in which they lived, the reasons for what they wrote became comprehensible. But that morning all I could see was the damage done by writing with such a slant.

I was beginning to see where many Christians were getting their anti-Jewish point of view, and I was stunned. I began to understand that this is the reason why rivers of Jewish blood had flowed at the hands of Christians. I cried for the Christian community. Then I began to pray, "Father, forgive them, for they do not know what they are doing" (Luke 23:34).

Sometimes it seems that God makes it tough to obey Him in order to test you. Immediately after the morning service, I spoke with Shlomo. I had to drive home to get my resume, I said, but I would return in an hour. He said he would be waiting.

I drove all the way home, found the resume, and returned as quickly as possible. After looking for Shlomo all over the church building, I was told he had left. Apparently he could not wait one hour!

I drove home in mourning. I sat in the little bedroom my daughter and I now shared. "What are we going to do now, God?"

Just then, the phone rang. "Why aren't you here?" Shlomo demanded. I explained, and he specified a place in the building to meet. I was on my way again.

We sat together in the large basement where we had shared coffee and cookies the night before. All I could think of was that I *had* to get to Israel; I was desperate now. Shlomo asked again, "Why go to Israel?"

Though I tried hard not to show it, all the stress, the fear of going, the fear of not going welled up inside me. Tears ran down my face. "I have no idea why I'm going. All I know is God is pressing me to go. I have to."

Shlomo looked over my resume. Letters of recommendation would be required from pastors of both congregations and from my employer. After we talked for an hour, Shlomo said he would find a way; if there was no opening in his center in Jerusalem, he would still find a way to help me. He seemed to understand why God wanted me to go.

Later, taking another step of faith, I flew down to Southern California while Alecia spent the weekend with her father. Once again I met with the two speakers from Israel—my only hope of getting to the Holy Land on schedule. Though intrigued by their Bible knowledge, I still found some of their ideas difficult to accept. Perhaps my heart was resisting whatever contradicted the teachings of my two churches. I struggled with the possibility that these men might be correct and both churches wrong.

Returning home, I reflected on all that had happened in the previous two weeks. There was so much to take in, so much to comprehend. When time allowed, I listened to the tapes of Goran's and Shlomo's speeches. Biblically, much of what they said made sense, but how could nearly 2,000 years of Christian thinking be wrong? Still, they had faith in what I was doing, so I felt there must be a connection between their faith in me and my going to Israel. But nothing was certain, and time was running out.

At this time I began writing a ministry letter for Christian friends; I was bursting with new insights to share. The first letter was a single sheet filled with information about Jesus and Judaism. Reactions were positive. The more I learned, the more I enjoyed sharing with others.

The weekly Bible study group that Cheryl attended helped us by praying for Alecia and me. They also took on the ministry of reading over the newsletters to let me know if something I had written was unclear or biblically questionable. I was grateful for the supervision. In the months to come, these people became a great source of emotional support and encouragement.

I sent copies of the first letter to the elders of the Gentile church and to pastors of both congregations. I requested their guidance and critique. There was no response.

Preparations continued. Both Alecia and I had medical checkups. My family, worried about conditions in the Middle East, insisted I buy life insurance. Study continued as time allowed. Prayer was nonstop.

In the meantime, things were not working out well at my step-mother's house. There were misunderstandings and hurt feelings. Near the end of June, I realized we would need to find another place to stay. The night of that discovery, I sat with my little girl in our shaky car at a nearby park. Silent tears ran down my face. Only three weeks remained before the time to leave for Israel, and still no word from Shlomo. We found another temporary place to stay.

On Monday, July 6, I received a call at work from the travel agent. The plane reservations for Alecia and me must either be paid for or lost. With no confirmation of a job in Israel, I forfeited our seats. There we were, twenty days before the date I felt God had wanted me to go. I had no job in Israel, no way to get there, and no home in the United States. "Well, God," I prayed, "if You're going to do something . . ."

Three days later the call finally came—a job was open at the center in Jerusalem; I could live there too. However, Alecia would have to stay in the United States; there was no place, yet, for us *both* to live. No children were allowed where I was to stay, and I would not be receiving enough income to pay for housing outside the Center. I had waited so long for an answer, for a way to get there, and now I had to leave my child behind. We were both devastated.

If you have ever been separated from your child for a long time, you understand how I was feeling. It was like having your right arm cut off and then being told to function normally. "How can I give her up, even temporarily? Who will care for her, God?" I cried. "How can You ask this of me?"

But He did ask, and I obeyed.

As Cheryl said, God was acting in the eleventh hour again. I went back to the travel agent. She did not bother to look it up; she told me the reservations were lost. I knew it was God's timing, so I asked that she check anyway. Her mouth dropped open as she read her computer screen: one seat (not the original two) was available on the flight we had chosen.

"Thank you, I'll take it," I said, as she sat there, stunned.

Cheryl charged the ticket on her credit card, along with a ticket for a second trip to Southern California for my orientation to the Jerusalem Center. God had provided the way, at 11:59 P.M., but not according to my plan.

Without consulting me first, Saul, the pastor for the Jewish-Christian congregation, held a family meeting. His family wanted to take in Alecia while I was away. There were four children in the family already; one more would be welcome. Alecia would have "siblings" for the first time in her life, including a big sister. In addition to being a home where Alecia wanted to stay, this family was supportive of what I was doing. No one else in whose home she could have stayed was supportive of my trip. I could not blame people for not understanding why I was going—I didn't either—but that attitude would have made my absence much more difficult for Alecia. In any case, the arrangement with the pastor's family was for three months. At the end of that time, either Alecia would join me in Israel, or I would return home.

Every remaining detail had to be arranged in less than two weeks. This time, no romanticism was attached to my trip to Israel; maybe that was a necessary element in God's plan, I do not know. I finally gave notice at work. Though I could only give two weeks' notice, my boss wrote a good recommendation letter. Quickly now, papers were prepared and signed for the pastor's family to authorize medical care for Alecia in my absence. I paid premiums for three months on Alecia's medical insurance. Cheryl became a cosigner on my checking account so she could handle my finances while I was away.

After so many months of planning and making preparations together, the coming separation was breaking my heart and Alecia's. From the day she was born, I often sang to Alecia, especially at bedtime. Before I left, I recorded a tape for her; I thought she might take comfort in hearing my voice. (Long after I returned home, Alecia told me that she could not listen to that tape while I was gone; it was too painful for her.) Though I tried to console her and explain, she began putting up a self-protective distance even before I left. She was only nine years old.

Alecia and a few friends from each congregation saw me off at the airport. It would be years before my child would understand why her mother had to go. To board the plane, I had to walk down a long hallway that was separated from the waiting area by a glass wall that stretched all the way up to the ceiling. My little girl stood at the other side of the glass; I pressed my hand to hers. Neither of us let the tears fall in front of the others, but the tears were there inside, drowning us both.

As I took my seat, I could not help thinking back to the conversation I had had with the minister before my baptism, less than three years earlier. We had discussed the New Testament passage where Jesus said, "Carry your cross and follow me."

"What do you think that means?" he had asked.

With tears of understanding in my eyes, I replied, "It means that one day I may have to give up everything, even my daughter, to follow Jesus."

He said my answer was correct. Now I hated that answer, as I sat on a plane, moving farther away from Alecia.

# 11

## ISRAEL

First came the short trip to California for my orientation to the Jerusalem Center. Emotional and physical exhaustion rendered the first
afternoon useless for work. Instead, I visited Shlomo's second home
and met some of his family: his sister, niece, and his daughter, Naomi.
Shlomo's home away from Jerusalem was small but nice.

In the morning, Shlomo picked me up at my hotel and took me to
the San Diego branch of the Center. The manager instructed me in
the use of their word processor, which was identical to the one I would
be using in the Jerusalem office. I read all I could about the Center,
and the manager explained its goal: to build a bridge of understanding between Jews and Christians. I felt privileged to be working toward
that goal.

Already, I felt alone; I missed Alecia. The San Diego manager
warned me that the Jerusalem staff was rather close-knit. Visitors like
me came and went, staying only a few months or weeks. He told me
the longer-term employees might not attempt to get close to me. "But
don't take it personally," he added kindly. The only person I knew,
Shlomo, would be traveling most of the time I was to be in Jerusalem. God would be my companion.

That evening Shlomo took me to visit a temple (the Reform denomination's counterpart to a synagogue). The equivalent in Christian denominations to a Reform temple is the Unitarian or Unity churches, which emphasize a sense of belonging over biblical doctrine. In contrast to Orthodox and Conservative branches of Judaism, the rabbi here was a woman, and she wore a *tallit* (prayer shawl) and a *kippah*; in my experience, only men wore these items in the other branches of Judaism. The Reform service resembled a Jewish-Christian church service, but more Hebrew was spoken in temple.

A *bar mitzvah* was celebrated during the service. In Judaism, at the age of thirteen a boy is considered ready to assume responsibility for his spiritual life. The *bar mitzvah* ceremony marks this milestone in his life. Before assuming this responsibility, he studies the Bible and biblical commentaries by great Jewish sages.

This boy's parents had spent a great deal of money on the grand party after the service. Shlomo wanted to stay for the festivities and soon wandered off into the crowd. Although I was feeling out of place and nervous, I tried to mingle as best I could. A kind-looking man asked if I came to temple often.

"No, I'm not Jewish," I responded.

Understandably taken aback, he fell silent.

I continued, "No, I just think that Christians should know more about Judaism. So many awful things have happened due to misunderstandings."

He smiled. Then he went on to introduce me as "one with a Jewish soul" (or perhaps heart). I can not remember his exact words—I only remember how wonderful they made me feel. A work had begun in me. I felt as though I were in the middle of some great plan of God, and I thanked Him for this privilege.

The following morning, we accompanied a young woman to the local Orthodox synagogue. The congregation had no building of its own; it met on the second floor of a small office building. The young woman with us was Jewish, but she knew as little about Judaism as I did.

We sat on the women's side of the partition, Shlomo on the men's side. When the rabbi spoke, I listened intently. Thinking of my first trip to Israel, I reflected on our Jewish guide. He'd had much Bible knowledge, and yet he did not believe Jesus was the Messiah. This rabbi knew the Bible well too, and he did not believe Jesus was the promised Messiah either. In church I had been taught that Jews just did not understand the Bible and that if they did, they would realize who Jesus really was.

The congregants knew Shlomo well; he was welcome in synagogue, as is every Jewish person, but the people were aware of Shlomo's Christian beliefs. Now, here he was, bringing this Gentile to synagogue. I wondered if the rabbi considered my visit as building a bridge of understanding between Christians and Jews. All the unsaid words and the conflict between Shlomo and the rabbi were hiding behind smiles and loud words of welcome, and yet they were somehow holding onto each other for dear life. All this hung in the air that Saturday morning.

As the rabbi spoke, he studied me as much as I did him. I was absorbing his words, the atmosphere, everything around me. He made eye contact so often that I became self-conscious; what was it he saw in my eyes? Again, I felt that God must have a purpose for me in all this. We ate a little after the service, or as some Jewish people say, "We noshed a little." The young Jewish visitor said little and seemed to feel as out of place as I did. As we were leaving, the rabbi invited us to visit again, with cordial goodbyes and intent eye contact.

Lunch after *shul* (synagogue) was a quiet one in Shlomo's home. It began with a blessing said over the wine:

Blessed art Thou, Lord our God, King of the Universe
Who created the fruit of the vine.

*Barukh Attah, Adonai*
*Eloheinu, Melekh Ha'olam. Borei pri hagafen.*

Next came the blessing over the bread. Pieces were dipped in salt (a sign of the Covenant) before being passed to each person at the table.

Blessed art Thou, King of the Universe
Who brings forth bread from the earth.


The experience was fascinating, but there was tension in the air.
Shlomo's sister and niece were visiting from Tel Aviv, and a family
squabble was going on: there was lots of arguing in Hebrew. Thankfully, I did not understand a word.

Some Christian visitors were staying in Shlomo's home. Unfortunately, the visitors had not only worn out their welcome but they were
also causing a battle between family members. Some wanted the
visitors to stay; others wanted them to leave. Naomi seemed overwhelmed, growing up in a home where visitors came and went constantly, never able to count on privacy. For the sake of the ministry,
Shlomo's home was often turned into a free hotel. I could hear echoes
of Shlomo's "free" speech: "I want to be a good Jew from Israel." Yet,
his family suffered as he tried to combat this "cheap Jew" stereotype
among Christian "friends."

The whole family was torn between two worlds: one Jewish and
one Christian. Naomi seemed to be having an identity crisis. My heart
went out to her, but I was not in any position to take sides. I simply
said, "Blood is thicker than water."

This experience served as another part of my orientation to the
Jewish-Christian world. Everything I had experienced up to this point
had been from a different perspective. The Jewish people I knew who
had converted to Christianity were completely assimilated: they lived
like Gentiles. They saw value in some Jewish culture, but drew the
line well before practicing biblical Judaism. Jewish-Christians I knew
did not consider God's commandments in the *Tanakh* to be eternal
any more than Gentile Christians did. Messianic Judaism, as they
called it, was actually Christianity with a little Jewish flavor. But this
experience with Shlomo was different; his was the perspective of a
Jewish person who loved Judaism.

Shlomo accepted the *Tanakh* as written: he believed that the commandments still applied to him, even though he had accepted Jesus

as the Messiah. In the first century, Jews like Shlomo received much encouragement from the leadership to remain Jewish (Acts 21:20, 24); but in today's world, everything had changed. A Jewish believer in Jesus now had two choices: the synagogue or the church. Shlomo belonged to both and neither. Because of his personal turmoil and his attempts to further Jewish/Christian relations, Shlomo's family was placed in the battle zone. I could not get that picture of their struggle out of my mind.

Soon I was back in Seattle, boarding the polar flight to Copenhagen; it was going to be a long flight—nine hours. I was lonely, apprehensive, and scared. The situation was too somber to feel excited. No tour guide would escort me through customs or lead the way. I brought no camera, no microcassette recorder; paper, pen, and books were the tools for this trip. I kept envisioning Alecia's face at the airport. "God, help us through this. Show me what I need to do."

"Excuse me."

It was the passenger sitting beside me. Having my thoughts interrupted was a relief. Here I was, a Christian on my way to Israel, the land of the Jews, and sitting beside me was a young man from Saudi Arabia who had been studying in the United States.

His faith was Islam, as I was about to learn. At great length he told me about the Muslim religion. It was his belief, he said, that it was Ishmael, not Isaac, whom Abraham was to have sacrificed. He spoke of Mohammed and the Koran, the Islamic Bible.

He was on his way to visit family in Saudi Arabia; on this trip he would also be making a pilgrimage to Mecca, the holiest city in the world to Muslims. He told me that each believer must make this pilgrimage at least once in his lifetime. This man loved his family and his country. He enjoyed learning and visiting in the United States, but when he finished college, he would move back home to Saudi Arabia.

In addition to the nine-hour flight, I had a seven-hour layover in Copenhagen. My new friend had a four-hour layover before his connecting flight to Saudi Arabia was scheduled to depart. Having someone to converse with made time pass quickly, and the Copenhagen airport was a great place to spend a few hours. The airport had the atmosphere of a small, expensive shopping mall. We browsed through the many shops, joking about unique souvenirs and postcards.

When we sat down to have a soda, a deeper conversation began. We spoke about Judaism, Christianity, and Islam. In particular, we discussed the concept of an eye for an eye (Exodus 21:22–27). From Goran's speech I had learned that in Judaism, this passage was known as the law of compensation, not the law of revenge. A minority in the first century had taught the latter concept, and Jesus had corrected them. However, the Pharisees and the bulk of Judaism taught this passage as the law of compensation.

Goran had said that this passage was not directed toward the offended party: the law instructed the offender to replace or compensate for any loss incurred by the victim. Only in the case of murder was the death penalty invoked in biblical Judaism, for there is no possible compensation for a life taken intentionally. And yet, to avoid executing an innocent person, the rabbis only utilized capital punishment if there were two eyewitnesses to a murder. That being nearly impossible, this punishment was rarely used.

In Islam, the same passage is taught differently. This young man explained to me that American leniency toward criminals was the reason we have so much crime. In Saudi, if a man is caught stealing, his hand is literally cut off. Others see that he is a thief and are more careful around him. If he steals again, the other hand is severed. He cannot steal a third time.

The Christian point of view is that although the Old Testament taught revenge, the New Testament teaches mercy. Consequently, I was horrified by this Islamic doctrine. "How cruel!" I told him.

"It is justice," he replied. "It is safer in Saudi Arabia than in America."

People seated nearby were obviously shaken by our candid discussion, but we were enjoying ourselves. We parted by promising to exchange holy books by mail. I would send him an Arabic translation of my Bible, which I did, and he would send me an English version of the Koran. (I never received my Koran.)

When my plane landed in Tel Aviv, it was late Monday evening, July 27. On the biblical calendar it was the first day of the month of *Av*. From notes on my calendar, I learned: "This period in time is called the *nine days* (within the *three weeks*). This is a period of intensified national mourning for the two destroyed Temples and the ensuing persecutions in every generation."[1]

No one greeted me at the airport. Ben-Gurion Airport looked the same as it had two years before—like a huge decorated warehouse. People were pushing around metal shopping carts filled with baggage and small children. I managed to find my luggage and make it through the barrage of questions that a lone visitor receives from airport officials.

I began to feel nervous again. Reality was setting in. I was alone, on the other side of the world. I stood on the sidewalk in front of the airport terminal, my coat and purse heavy on my arm, my suitcase standing beside me. All I could do was hope and wait.

After a few minutes, a new white Volkswagen van pulled up. "Are you Kim? I'm so sorry we're late. Hope you weren't too worried. Here, I'll help you with your bags."

"No, I wasn't worried," I lied, as I breathed a huge sigh of relief.

Two people were in the van with me. We drove from Tel Aviv to Jerusalem as they chatted away about the house "where we all live" and how nice it was to have someone visiting from America.

"How long will you stay?" was the first question.

"I'm not sure."

"Oh, well, you'll love it here; it's wonderful; we're like a big family. And of course, Jerusalem is incredible."

As we drove along the freeway in the darkness, I saw that everything was modern as in Europe or America. Could this really be the same country I had read about in Genesis, I wondered. On the tour, twenty-two months earlier, I had seen a country filled with Christian sites and churches. I was now about to see Jewish Israel.

Freeway lanes united to form a single street that led directly into Jerusalem. It was late; the streets were nearly deserted. We passed through two or three traffic lights. Then I saw them—the majestic walls of the Old City. The walls seemed to be glowing due to the many floodlights along their base. My heart responded as though greeting a lover returned from the war. "Thank You, God, for allowing me to reach this moment." I felt an overwhelming sense of coming home.

We passed Zion Gate and turned up a street that led to a hill in West Jerusalem, a predominantly Jewish area of the city. All the homes, including the one we parked in front of, were built with Jerusalem stone. Due to Jerusalem's violent history, the building code now required all homes to be built in this particular stone to better withstand attacks. This code certainly did make for a beautiful city.

The black wrought-iron gate creaked as I pushed it open. At the top of the stone staircase, I saw other employees of the Center who had stayed up to greet me.

"Welcome, welcome. Would you like some tea? Here, sit here on the couch, the news is on. Did you have a good flight? You must be tired after so much travel."

There I sat, sipping hot tea from a clear glass cup, watching the local weather report on a large color television. The announcer narrated as the screen showed panoramic views of the Galilee, Samaria, and the Negev. It was the most beautiful weather report I had ever seen.

The people at the Center were literally from all corners of the globe: Japan, Austria, India, England, Switzerland, Sweden, Holland, Syria, East Germany, and America. We were all employees of a unique Christian organization that gave away Bibles and biblical literature in a dozen different languages. Our other purpose was to promote good relations between Christians and Jews, mainly by educating Christians. I was reminded of Zechariah 8:23:

> This is what the LORD Almighty says: "In those days ten men from all languages and nations will take firm hold of one Jew by the hem of his robe and say, 'Let us go with you, because we have heard that God is with you.'"

Yes, I had made it to Jerusalem, but not without great personal sacrifice. God brought me here at the specified time, because God is faithful. Within a few months I would understand why He chose this particular time for me to come to Israel.

In the next day or so, the Islamic friend I had met on the trip over came to mind as I watched news footage from Mecca, where he had gone for his pilgrimage. Violence had erupted among the crowded worshipers, and there were many injuries. The violence was blamed on the United States. The Saudi Arabian government proclaimed a "National Day of Hate" against America. Perhaps to stop them from rioting and killing each other, it was safer to unite people against a common (outside) enemy. This served as my introduction to Arab politics.

The warm sun and fresh air roused me from slumber long after most everyone had gone to work that first Tuesday morning. My room was simple, neat, clean, and modern, as was the rest of the house. Furnishings were crafted of light Danish woods: in my room were a twin bed, night table, wardrobe, and a cabinet complete with shelves for books and a flip-down writing surface. In the weeks ahead, I would spend many hours in this room writing ministry letters and studying.

As I lay there, I thought this must be the nicest room in the house. Its windows stretched up to the high ceiling and opened like French doors. From my room I could see the front walkway and lovely trees in the garden. Decorative yet functional wrought-iron bars in the window opening enabled me to feel safe even with the windows open.

My room was located on the main floor along with three other bedrooms, two bathrooms, a small sitting area where the television was kept, and a large open dining area. At those dining tables, anywhere from ten to twenty people would gather for the noon meal each workday. The kitchen on our floor was large, sunny, and complete with a dishwasher.

Off the entryway, two steps led down into a sunken room—the library. Its collection of Jewish Bible commentaries and other Jewish and Christian books would fascinate me for hours on end in the coming months.

Israel was no longer a rough frontier; I was staying in a beautiful modern house. Two more floors were above me, each with bedrooms, baths, and smaller kitchens. The top floor had access to the roof, which looked like a large stone deck. From the roof I could look out over the city of Jerusalem. The view was spectacular, especially at night, when the city glowed with scattered lights.

Back on the main floor where my room was located and out the main entrance, I reached street level. Down a second stone staircase, I found the floor of offices. Traffic along the street reminded me that this was just another day for the residents of Jerusalem.

Down another flight of stairs was a completely finished basement area, where Bibles were stored, packaged, and labeled for mailing. From these two floors, Bibles, letters, and other literature were mailed all over the world. The washer and dryer were also on this level, though most people hung their clothes outside to dry in the heat of summer. This large house served as home to a dozen people and as a workplace for several more.

In the record-breaking heat of that summer, the air-conditioned offices were a welcome relief. Some employees (like me) typed on a word processor. One woman translated pro-Jewish Christian Bible studies into Japanese. An Arab woman from Bethlehem, who was originally from Syria, read and answered Arabic correspondence. A teenager from Austria handled German mail. The branch manager was a woman from Sweden. Shlomo's grown son supervised everything. Though much quieter than his father, Amit still acted as an ambassador for Israel and the Jewish people; we all did, each in his or her own way.

People from all over the world wrote letters to this center. Some asked about Israel or specifically about Jerusalem; some had questions about the Bible. Many gave money to support the work, the purchase of Bibles, staff wages, and the like. A monthly newsletter was mailed to all correspondents. From here, Israeli news from a religious point of view reached Christians in dozens of countries.

Living with such a diverse group of people was a rich experience. The woman whose room was closest to mine was from Japan. Her name was Yoshia. I learned that Japan is known for its negative view of Jewish people; Yoshia translated a Bible course into Japanese to promote better Jewish/Japanese relations. She did not match my conception of a traditional passive Japanese woman. She was kind and patient, but she was also very funny, intelligent, resourceful, quite independent, and she rode a motor bike.

Yoshia shared a cute story about a shopping trip in the Old City. Though dealing with an Arab merchant, she began conversing in Hebrew. (She was fluent in Hebrew and spoke little Arabic.)

He said, "Please, I am Arab. Speak with me in Arabic."

She quickly apologized. "Oh, *slihah!*" which means "I'm sorry" . . . in Hebrew.

Hebrew is not just the language of the Torah (Pentateuch) or the major part of the *Tanakh*. It is also the national language of modern Israel. Because Jerusalem is host to many English-speaking tourists, nearly everyone in the city also spoke English, so I had little difficulty communicating. Jewish people moved to Israel from all over the world, and tourists hail from countless countries, so many languages are heard in the Old City. Jerusalem is truly an international city.

A standing joke among the employees was that when one of us said something that did not sound intelligent, everyone else responded with "*Boker tov!*" In Hebrew, *boker tov* simply means "good morning." However, we meant it in the sense of "Wake up! Smell the coffee! Think! That was a stupid thing to say!"

One evening several of us were walking down the street together, when someone said something silly. The rest of us immediately rang out, "*Boker tov!*"

A passerby said reprovingly, "*Erev tov!*" which means "good evening"; it was rather dark out at the time.

One of the most interesting people I met was a chasidic rabbi who lived in Mea Shearim, the ultra-Orthodox neighborhood of Jerusalem, with his wife and many children. In addition to being a teacher and a religious leader in his own community, he also wrote Bible studies for Christians. This was his work at our office. His vast knowl-

edge of the writings of Jewish sages was applied to a Christian correspondence course. Sometimes I helped enter text into the word processor for this new course. The Bible was a reference book at my desk.
I was constantly learning.

Mea Shearim became my favorite part of Jerusalem. I could walk there
from where I lived. Its bookstores carried a wide assortment of Jewish
and biblical literature. Music tapes were sold by vendors on the sidewalks in front of their stores; we could listen to a tape before deciding
to buy. Judaica, jewelry, clothing, and souvenir shops lined the streets.
Children played safely, as though it were a small town. Mea Shearim's
atmosphere was bustling, but always warm and inviting.

One of the rabbi's children, a twelve-year-old girl, adopted me. I
missed my own daughter, so it was nice to have this child around.
She would play with my long hair or take my hand while we talked.
She asked many questions about Alecia and told me how wonderful
her school was and how Alecia would like it too.

From this young girl, I learned the very spirit of Judaism. A trip to
the airport was an excuse to travel outside Jerusalem, and one night
several of us piled into the van to pick up some visitors. The rabbi's
daughter sat in the back seat beside me. When we got on the highway, she put her head out the window. The window opened hori-
zontally, and she closed it as far as possible against her neck. She began
gazing out at the vast plain in the dark, and although it was greatly
muffled, I could hear her singing.

I tapped her on the shoulder. Her head came in.

"What are you doing?" I asked.

"Singing to Him."

"Why not sing so we can all hear?"

"We don't sing in front of men." (This is a belief of chasidic Judaism,
to be certain a woman does not cause a man to lust after her.) She seemed
so happy, elated, really, bursting with love for God. "Some people just
don't understand," she continued. "They think following God is just a
lot of rules. They don't see the *beauty* of God!" The window closed against
her neck again, as her spontaneous song continued.

Legalism was not part of her lifestyle. Yet, in 100-degree weather, she wore high necklines, sleeves below her elbows, and colored stockings to avoid revealing her legs in public. All chasidic Jewish people dress this modestly. Jesus warned against lusting after someone "in your heart." The way many people dress, especially in hot weather, makes it difficult to follow this teaching, but everyone in Mea Shearim takes it to heart. This twelve-year-old girl not only learned to dress modestly for the good of society but she also learned the love of God in this neighborhood. So did I.

The work week in Israel runs from Sunday morning to Friday afternoon (one o'clock for us). I learned that Israel has the highest number of paid national holidays of any country—fourteen—so the five-and-one-half day work week is not severe. Our day of rest was Saturday, the biblical Sabbath (Genesis 2:2 and Exodus 20:8–11). Though many Jewish people in Israel are not particularly religious, the residents of the area of Jerusalem where I lived were. Therefore, people in our house behaved in a manner sensitive to our neighbors' Sabbath observances.

On my first Friday afternoon, I visited the grocery store like everyone else; the neighborhood store would be closed for *Shabbat*. I took a shower (no major bathing was allowed during *Shabbat*), cleaned my room, and helped clean the house. We were going through some of the same motions as our neighbors. No one in the house was Jewish (Shlomo was gone and Amit did not live there), but we were in Jerusalem to learn and experience all we could.

And on the seventh day God finished His work which He had made. He rested on the seventh day from all His work which He had made. And God blessed the seventh day and hallowed it, because that in it He rested from all His work which God in creating had made. (Genesis 2:2–3)

God "hallowed" the Sabbath. Like *holy* and *sanctify*, *hallowed* means that God set the Sabbath aside to be different, for a different purpose than the other six days of the week. He "blessed it." When the Sabbath is observed by resting, praying, rejoicing, and ceasing to create in honor of the True Creator, one experiences a blessing. I learned about the Sabbath and its biblical purpose while in Israel.

Participating in *Shabbat* in a religious Jewish neighborhood is an awe-inspiring experience. A distant siren sounds each Friday afternoon, and traffic outside ceases. Because of the biblical injunction against kindling a flame on *Shabbat*, cars are not driven. Candles are lit before the Sabbath begins. In a Jewish home, the woman of the house and sometimes the daughters say a blessing while lighting these candles.

Outside my window, I heard families and friends walking home from synagogue each Friday evening. Other than the sound of chatting or laughter, it was quiet until Saturday night. Then, all at once, I heard traffic out on the street and loud music coming from a hotel a couple of blocks away. The public buses began to operate again. The unity of the city, at least that portion of it, was amazing to me.

At first I kept to myself on *Shabbat*. I simply prayed, studied, and rested. However, after a couple of weeks, I began visiting a nearby Orthodox synagogue on Saturday mornings. Many synagogues were within walking distance.

My first step into that old synagogue was like taking a step backward in time. Men worshiped on the first floor, the women above in the balcony. Most basics of an Orthodox (biblical) synagogue service had not changed in 2,000 years, so I heard what Jesus had heard, and I heard it in the same language. Synagogue worship was a part of Jesus' lifestyle I was just beginning to discover.

Some Jewish families observe the custom of inviting a stranger met in *shul* to Friday dinner, the first of three *Shabbat* meals. Once, when I visited a synagogue on a Friday night, I was privileged to enjoy this custom. A young woman who stood beside me during the service invited me and my friend to her parents' home for dinner after the service. Since my friend David and I were both Gentiles, her parents patiently explained each custom of the meal and the prayers. Her mother taught us how to use the *siddur*. They made us feel relaxed and welcome in their home.

The meal was lavish, and the entire evening was a joyful experience. Psalms were read, prayers were said, and special Sabbath songs were sung. God's blessing was asked upon their daughter and the father read Proverbs, chapter 31, to his wife. I witnessed how the Sabbath binds a Jewish family together and strengthens its ties to God.

It soon became my custom to go to synagogue on the Sabbath. In this way, I was following Jesus' footsteps (Luke 4:16). Books about Judaism are informative, but nothing compares to an actual synagogue experience.

Jesus taught what we refer to today as the "Lord's Prayer" to his followers so they could recite it together. It incorporates many beautiful words we long to say to God, but may not be able to compose on our own. Incorporating such words is also the purpose of the *siddur*, the Jewish prayer book. The *siddur* contains the prayers recited in synagogue, at home, and for special occasions in life. I received my first *siddur* from Shlomo, and I still love using it; both Alecia and I find that praying the bedtime prayers at night helps us feel closer to God and at peace: ready for sleep. The "Lord's Prayer" is simply an appetizer for what the *siddur* has to offer.

In an Orthodox synagogue, both prayers and Bible readings are recited in Hebrew. This was a great challenge for me, because I wanted to participate in the service and comprehend as much as possible. Hebrew is the universal language of Orthodox synagogues around the world. The Torah was recorded in Hebrew, so naturally people would want to understand the Torah in its original language and get the fullness of its meaning.

There is another reason why Hebrew is spoken in synagogues: unity of the Jewish people. People who know Hebrew can enter any Orthodox synagogue in the world and worship with that congregation. They can converse with people there, regardless of the language of that land. So, even though Jewish people have been scattered for centuries, the Hebrew language serves to unite them.

The first time I entered my soon-to-be regular synagogue, I knew almost nothing about the service. When I sat down in the ladies section, an elderly woman sat beside me and noticed that I was not turned to the correct page in the *siddur*. She found the page and traded *siddurs* with me, to help me get started. Though I tried my best to sound out the words and turn pages when others did, she soon noticed that I was on the wrong page again.

She tried to converse with me in Hebrew; about all I could say was, "*lo Ivrit*," which means "no Hebrew." Undaunted, she tried Spanish. We were in a Sephardic synagogue, and Sephardic Jews are of Spanish descent; many spoke Spanish as a second language. I replied feebly, "No habla Español" (no Spanish either). Normal communication was abandoned.

As a chasidic rabbi once told me, "You don't look so non-Jewish." The lady thought I was a Jewish woman trying to return to my faith; she became determined to help me. Each week we sat side by side. She placed her left shoulder in front of my right one and laid the *siddur* between us in our laps. She ran her fingers below each line of print and whispered the words in my ear just before the speaker below uttered them. Week after week she patiently taught me. By mid-September, I could almost follow the service on my own.

Shortly before I was to leave Israel, I wanted to thank her. After asking around, I discovered she was known to be one of the most pious women in the congregation. I wanted to get her a special gift, and she reminded me of the epilogue of Proverbs, chapter 31. I found a plaque with that passage written on it in Hebrew. It described her beautifully:

> She speaks with wisdom
> and faithful instruction is on her tongue
> She watches over the affairs of her household
> and does not eat the bread of idleness.
> Her children arise and call her blessed;
> her husband also, and he praises her:

"Many women do noble things,
but you surpass them all."
Charm is deceptive, and beauty is fleeting;
but a woman who fears the LORD is to be praised.
Give her the reward she has earned,
and let her works bring her praise at the city gate.

(Proverbs 31:26–31)

By August 4, I had been in Jerusalem just over a week. The date was the ninth of *Av* on the Jewish calendar. God's timing for the trip was becoming clearer.

Each morning our workday began with a "devotional." All the employees gathered together to sing songs and read a chapter from the Bible, a few verses each, each in our native language. Though we each took turns leading the study portion of the devotional, the format was flexible. On the day before the ninth of *Av*, Shlomo's son, Amit, suggested that someone research the day and share his or her findings with the group. No one else volunteered, so I decided to try.

I went down to the library that night and learned the following about the ninth of *Av*. Like Chanukah, the ninth of *Av* was not a biblically commanded holy day. Instead, it is a historical day of remembrance. An unusual number of events happened on or near this date.

• On the ninth of *Av*, it was decreed that that generation of the Children of Israel who sinned with the golden calf after the Exodus from Egypt should not enter the Promised Land.
• The First Temple, built by Solomon, was destroyed from the seventh to the tenth of *Av* in 586 B.C.E. by the Babylonian king, Nebuchadnezzar.
• The Second Temple was destroyed in 70 C.E. by the Romans on the tenth of *Av*.
• On the ninth of *Av*, Bettar, the last stronghold of the leaders of the Bar Kochba war, was captured in 135 C.E.
• On the ninth of *Av* in 136 C.E., the Roman Emperor Hadrian established a heathen temple on the site of the Holy Temple and rebuilt

Jerusalem as a pagan city. It was renamed "Aelia Capitolina" and Jewish people were forbidden to enter it.
  • The expulsion of Jews from Spain, in 1492, is also said to have
occurred on this date.

For these reasons, the ninth of *Av*—in Hebrew, Tisha B'Av—
became a symbol for the persecutions and misfortunes of the Jewish
people. On Tisha B'Av people fast and say special prayers; many
observe customs that are associated with mourning the death of a
loved one. In Jerusalem, people also go to the Western Wall where
the book of Lamentations and other Bible passages of mourning are
recited. In the synagogue, lights are dimmed.
  It is also the belief of some that the Messiah will be born on Tisha
B'Av and thus transform it into a holiday. The month of *Av* is often
called *Menachem Av*, that is, may God "comfort" us for all our suffering this month and bring the *Moshiach* (Messiah).[2]

One week later was my thirty-first birthday, the first I had ever
spent without family. I called home and spoke with Alecia; our conversation was extremely difficult. She had very little to say, and that
worried me. My stomach knotted up. After that conversation, I decided it would hurt us both less if we did not speak, so from then on
I just sent letters and postcards. Alecia never wrote back. I wrote to
Cheryl, asking her to visit Alecia and take her places. That was all I
could do.
  My little girl was only nine years old; she tried to understand, but
could not. Three years later she told me that she had mourned that
whole day. By the time she got my call from Jerusalem, it was already
late at night back home. By then, Alecia was numb; she had been
hurting all day.
  I could relate to these days of mourning on the Jewish calendar;
the loneliness was unbearable at times. There were no familiar faces,
no family or friends. I took comfort knowing Alecia was in a warm
loving home while I was away, that she was in the best place she could

be considering the circumstances. Still, I wanted to hold her. Perhaps God had sent me to Israel in mourning that I might sympathize with Israel's time of mourning.

In addition to the loneliness, I was also broke; my money was spent on Alecia's care. I had arrived in Tel Aviv with $40 in my pocket, and I would not be receiving a paycheck from the center until the end of August. In the meantime, I survived on chicken broth, peanut butter and jelly sandwiches, and the workday communal lunches. Though it was nothing compared to Israel's experiences, my suffering taught me to lean on God; there was no one else to lean on.

Some say trouble comes in threes. Alecia's emotional state was on my mind and in my prayers constantly. The study of anti-Semitism in and outside the Church was weighing heavily on my heart as well. The photographs from World War II, the damage that 2,000 years of persecution had done, the tarnished message of the Church to the Jewish people—all these things hurt me deeply. But the problem I was about to discover would upset me for years to come.

As a Christian I had been taught to view the Bible as a whole, calling everything from Genesis to Revelation Holy Scripture. Now, I learned to break it into sections. Genesis through Deuteronomy, the Pentateuch, was called the Law of Moses because these were the only writings God gave Moses. The next section of the Jewish Bible contains prophetic books. The third section is known as the Writings, and some of the books it includes are Proverbs, Psalms, and Chronicles. In Hebrew, these three parts of the Bible are called *Torah*, *Nevi'im* and *Ketuvim*: *TNK*, the *Tanakh*. These combined writings, which are today known as the Hebrew Bible, Jesus called the Holy Scriptures.

The Protestant Old Testament contains exactly the same books as the Hebrew Bible, but the order of the books has been changed. The Catholic Old Testament includes additional books known as apocalyptic literature. These writings were not considered Holy Scripture in Judaism and therefore were not included in the Protestant Bible.

Jesus had very strong words to say about the Hebrew Bible (the Old Testament):

> Do not think that I have come to abolish the Law or the Prophets; I
> have not come to abolish them but to fulfill them. I tell you the truth,
> until heaven and earth disappear, not the smallest letter, not the least
> stroke of a pen, will by any means disappear from the Law until every-
> thing is accomplished. Anyone who breaks one of the least of these
> commandments and teaches others to do the same will be called least
> in the kingdom of heaven, but whoever practices and teaches these
> commands will be called great in the kingdom of heaven. (Matthew
> 5:17–19)

At first glance, Jesus' statement in Matthew 5:17 sounded as if he
were contradicting himself. He did not come to abolish the *Tanakh*
but rather to "fulfill" it. I thought that fulfill meant to complete or
end the Old Testament. Once again, my Jewish studies provided
answers. In the *siddur*, I learned that to fulfill a commandment means
to obey it to the best of one's ability.[3] No one can obey God perfectly,
but failing at times does not mean one should cease striving to do so.

With this new information, I understood what Jesus was saying in
Matthew. He did not come to cancel the *Tanakh*; he came to obey
(fulfill) it. As spiritual leaders, rabbis are required to fulfill the commandments as much as humanly possible. A higher level of obedience is expected of them since they serve as examples to all other
people. Jesus was a rabbi.

I discovered that Jesus was saying something more in Matthew.
Not only did he come to obey the *Tanakh*, but he stated emphatically
that it was not to be canceled by anyone. Heaven and earth still exist,
so, according to Jesus, the *Tanakh* is still valid. This means that all
the commandments are still in full force.

As if this discovery were not difficult enough for me to accept, Jesus
went even further! I thought about what happens when a Jewish
person is brought to God through the Church, about what we teach
him. We do not teach him to be zealous for the Law of Moses, as did
the elders in Acts 21:20. But if we did, Jesus would evidently be
pleased. Jesus had harsh words for those who tell Jews that God's
instructions to them are no longer valid. Jesus did not say our salva-

tion would be lost, but he did say we would be called "least in the kingdom of heaven" (Matthew 5:19).

I realized that had the Christian community maintained Jesus' view of Holy Scripture, we would carry *Tanakhs* to church today, the same Bible to which Orthodox Jews adhere. Although he instructed no one to do so, approximately thirty years after he left this earth, believers began writing down accounts of Jesus' life called Gospels. Of the many written, the Christian community chose to accept the four Gospels of Matthew, Mark, Luke, and John, as well as many letters (epistles) between leaders and congregations. These writings were added to the Holy Scriptures and became known as the New Testament.

The introduction to Luke's gospel revealed something that shocked me:

> Many have undertaken to draw up an account of the things that have been fulfilled among us, just as they were handed down to us by those who from the first were eyewitnesses and servants of the word. Therefore, since I myself have carefully investigated everything from the beginning, it seemed good also to me to write an orderly account for you, most excellent Theophilus, so that you may know the certainty of the things you have been taught. (Luke 1:1–4)

This passage revealed that Luke was not an eyewitness to the Gospel events, but rather a historian recording information handed down by others and told to him during interviews. Although this helps explain some discrepancies among the Gospel accounts, the discovery upset me. The Law of Moses had been given directly by God; prophecy was placed into the mouths of prophets by God. In contrast, each Gospel was one man's effort to record historical events. These first-century authors did not consider their writings to be infallible Holy Scripture, but rather a documentation of events.

Once I comprehended the New Testament authors' viewpoint, and Jesus' view of what qualifies as Holy Scripture, I could no longer feel comfortable calling the New Testament Holy Scripture—because the authors did not. These writings never even received Jesus' approval;

they were written long after he was gone. I finally realized there was
no heresy in reading the New Testament as its authors had written it,
but the authors' viewpoint was the opposite of that held today by the
majority of Christians. Immediately, I felt like an outsider among
Christians.

There was no single authoritative document that Jesus gave his
followers. Peter and Paul were even in dispute as to how to apply the
teachings of Jesus. Considering that Peter lived with Jesus and Paul
did not, I regard Peter's view as superior in a debate. And I have come
to believe that every New Testament writing must agree with the
*Tanakh*; if not, then Jesus' Holy Scriptures must be considered a higher
authority than New Testament letters.

Until I had sufficient time to comprehend this new view, I felt
tormented. I wanted to hang onto current Christian tradition that
teaches that the New Testament *is* Holy Scripture. I wanted to block
Luke's first chapter out of my mind, but I could not.

For many people, tradition is strong, sometimes stronger than Holy
Scripture. Tradition may be beneficial, but it changes. I need a God
that does not change. I need Holy Scriptures that I can count on to
be the same as they were 2,000 years ago, just as we found the Book
of Isaiah among the Dead Sea Scrolls. And if I were trying to understand Jesus, I had to hold firm to his foundation, the writings he called
the Holy Scriptures.

In these days of mourning on the Jewish calendar, I knew suffering. I missed Alecia terribly. I learned that to emulate Jesus, I had to
let go of traditions that conflict with the Bible. That was a painful
process because the majority of people I knew held fast to those particular traditions. Most painful was knowing that once I shared these
discoveries with my Christian friends, I might lose them.

"Can you drive?"

This was the first question that Ewa, the branch manager in the
Jerusalem office, asked me. As I discovered, in countries other than

the United States not everyone drives; some choose not to drive. A man from Holland explained that it costs $1,000 to obtain a driver's license in his country; when that cost is combined with car maintenance, insurance, and gasoline tax, many people find it too expensive to own a car. The few employees of the center who could drive were kept busy.

Yes, I could drive. There was one small problem, though. I was not able to drive the only available vehicle: a nearly new Volkswagen van. It had a manual transmission, and I only knew how to drive an automatic. Second, I was not accustomed to driving such a large vehicle and sitting at the very front. My own car had been a mid-sized Oldsmobile with an automatic transmission.

Step one was driving lessons. I had heard Jerusalem was the second worst city in the world in which to drive (Cairo is the worst). People walk out in front of moving vehicles. Vendors on foot come up to the driver's window while you are sitting in traffic. They once tried to sell us tissues this way!

A fellow employee from England, David, was a young man of great patience. He began teaching me how to drive a standard shift. Past Gethsemane and up into the heart of Jerusalem, there was a traffic light; the slight incline of that stop horrified me for days. I was petrified of sliding backward into another car. David kept his sense of humor, and soon I was driving every day.

On one occasion, Amit rode with me to the Post. Britain's previous mandate over Palestine resulted in a great deal of British influence in Israel; one was calling a post office the Post. As I rounded a turn near the Post, Amit quietly mentioned that perhaps I was not being watchful of the back end of the van. "If you're not more careful, you will get into an accident." He did not say, "you might"; he said, "you will." I became very vigilant after that remark.

Evidently, I was not vigilant enough. The following day I drove to the Post again, this time with David. As we rounded the same corner, I felt the van catch hold of something: a huge dump truck! I got out to look. I was speechless. The scratch was three feet long! I apologized to the truck driver. He assured me his truck suffered no damage. He smiled and said, "No problem!"

Right, no problem, I thought. The last thing I wanted to do was show that huge scrape to the manager, especially in light of Amit's recent warning.

To my amazement, instead of being angry with me, Ewa was mad at Shlomo (who was not in Jerusalem at the time). She had wanted to buy an older used van, but Shlomo felt it would make a bad impression on visitors.

"Everyone has an accident when they first come," Ewa reassured me. However, it cost thousands of dollars to repair that huge scratch. Nothing is cheap in Israel when it comes to vehicles. Even gas tax is 100 percent (dollar for dollar). I wanted to quit driving, but Ewa said no; they needed all the drivers they could get.

Two or three times each week, several of us would take the van up into the Galilee in northern Israel to distribute Bibles and Christian literature in Arabic. We usually left right after devotional and returned in the early evening. It would take nearly half the morning to drive up to that area. When we arrived, we would choose a village and drive into it. We drove slowly through each village distributing literature to people we met.

Several times each day someone in a village would ask us to come into their home to visit. They delighted in serving us incredibly strong Turkish coffee or syrupy sweet hot tea served in little glasses (which burned my fingers because there was no handle). They also kept cola and orange soda pop on hand at all times. A favorite treat was something that looked like huge pieces of pita bread measuring twelve to eighteen inches in diameter. Arab women baked this flatbread in outdoor ovens that appeared to be caves carved out of solid rock. Inside these caves, they built fires and placed bread dough on the cave's ceiling. When the bread was ready, they would peel it off and hand it to us, all warm and soft. It was delicious!

Whenever possible, we would have lunch in Nablus. Nablus is a large Arab town located about halfway between Jerusalem and Nazareth. This town is also known by its biblical name: Shechem. There was an excellent restaurant in Nablus; it was very clean, and we dined outdoors on a patio. The meal began with a plate stacked with four freshly baked pitas. With this, they served hummus— ground chickpeas with tahini sauce. Hummus was surrounded on the plate by vegetables. We would dip vegetables and torn pieces of pita in the hummus. It was great. But that was only the appetizer. Next they brought the meal: a quarter-chicken each, grilled and seasoned to perfection. We each had a bottle of Coca-Cola too. For all this, for four people, they charged only ten American dollars!

In the afternoons, we visited more villages. We tried to distribute Bibles and literature to as many receptive hands as we could find. Sometimes the people of the villages would tell us about their lives. A few told of unfair treatment received by Arabs in Israel. Some Arab people sent their children out of the country for college, not believing they would get a good education in Israel. But most Arab people I spoke with seemed to be content. Later, I learned why.

Between 1948 and 1967, the West Bank area of Israel had been part of Jordan, an Arab country. The Palestinians in the West Bank were poor. Neither Jordan nor any other Arab state paid much attention to the needs of these West Bank Palestinians during those years. In 1967, things changed. After the 1967 Six-Day War, Jewish settlements began, and with them came vast improvements to the area. The Jewish government began to build roads and a hospital, and the water quality improved. There was no Palestinian state, but those who lived in the West Bank saw their living conditions improve dramatically in only a few years. This situation is just part of the paradox of the Palestinian issue in Israel.

One day, late in the afternoon, when it was time to start heading back to Jerusalem, people in the village asked us to stay and have coffee. We apologized for not having enough time.

"Wait! Wait!" an older Arab man began shouting. Then he ran off. We sat in the van, wondering what would happen next. He came back with an armload of pomegranates, enough for each of us to have two. We thanked him for his generosity; he beamed with pride. We drove down the highway, our fingers stained by pomegranate juice.

Arab villages were settled long before cars existed. Smaller villages often consisted of one long, narrow road with homes crammed along both sides. Cars that were headed in opposite directions could not easily get past one another. One had to be careful to drive slowly. To leave, one had to drive all the way to the end, turn around, and drive out the way one came in. There were no side streets in small villages.

One very hot day, several weeks after the dump truck incident, we were driving in a small village. The road was quite narrow, so I became concerned there would not be adequate space at the end to turn around. If I needed to back out, I wanted to keep the distance short, so I asked two people in the van to get out and walk to the end of the road. They could tell me if there was enough room to turn the van around.

"Sure, sure, plenty of room," they reported. But one fact had not occurred to me: neither of them were drivers.

Off we went. When we got to the turn-around area, I was skeptical. After some maneuvering, I headed out. Suddenly, I heard a mournful squeaking noise. It was the van, on the same side as before, attaching itself to a large, rough, wooden pole. The opening in the road was so narrow that backing up only tightened the pole's grip. Slowly, back and forth, over and over again, I moved the van . . . unsuccessfully.

By this time, a crowd of villagers had gathered. The women covered grins with their hands; men stood around, shaking their heads; children giggled. All I could think of were the thousands of dollars it would cost to fix it . . . again. I prayed, "God, You got me into this. Please, get me out."

The only other licensed driver in the van was Charles, a man from East Germany. He only spoke German. Charles stood there before me. The pink in his cheeks was as bright as his smile. He pointed to himself and then to the van, a question mark on his face. My defeat was obvious. I gratefully climbed into the backseat.

Charles took the driver's seat and repeated the same maneuver: sliding back and forth. Then a cheer rose up from the crowd as he freed the van and slowly began to pull away. We headed down the road while the villagers applauded. What a sight. Six of us were in the van that afternoon, and everyone (except me) was yelling directions at our new driver. Some pointed the way (from the backseat). Charles just smiled that broad smile that took over his whole face whenever he felt needed. He was not bothered by what they said. He did not understand a word.

When we finally got back, I walked into Ewa's office. "I'm not driving anymore," I announced in a depressed voice.

"Oh, but you must!" she quickly responded in her heavy Swedish accent.

"Go look at the van."

Without a word, she followed me out to the street.

"Ohhh," she said softly. This time the scratch was over four feet long. A few splinters still clung to the dent. Her face held a pained expression for the longest time. Then she said, "But you must drive. We need drivers."

"No, not again." This time I was firm. I was willing to do many things. I happily washed windows, floors, and laundry. I ironed and dusted, but no more driving. I would do any office work, *ride* in the van, wrap and mail out Bibles, but no more driving!

Those weeks in Israel served as a living textbook. I had much to learn. I continued writing the ministry newsletters for people back home, but the topics were light compared to what I was learning. The gap between what I could share and what I was learning was growing each day. My questions alone sounded like heresy. I believe that God initiated my quest for truth, so I could not abandon it, but I worried that I might never fit into the world I had left behind.

Back home, most of my friends viewed Jesus as a modern-day

Christian. They saw Israel as the subject of ancient history and Judaism as having been replaced by Christianity. But God had opened my eyes to what was written in both the *Tanakh* and in the New Testament.

Now I pictured Jesus walking into the synagogue with me. Jesus stood there with his *tallit* draped over his head and shoulders, holding the Torah scroll in his arms, gazing at it with love. The Jesus I knew wore *tefillin*, the long leather straps commanded in Deuteronomy 6:8,[4] and fringes as commanded in Deuteronomy 22:12—God's reminders to all Jews to obey the 613 instructions He gave them in the Torah.

Many times, people in the New Testament touched the edge, the fringes, of Jesus' garments. To those people, the fringes were a reminder of their God of miracles. They had heard reports of God using Rabbi Jesus to heal people, so they flocked to him.

I felt a conflict of loyalty. I wanted to believe clergymen's answers about Judaism being canceled by Jesus and his disciples, but long after the ascension, Peter, who lived with Jesus for roughly three-and-one-half years, ate only kosher food. "Surely not, Lord!" Peter replied. "I have never eaten anything impure or unclean" (Acts 10:14). Even Paul, the follower whom many see as the most anti-Judaistic of the disciples, was obedient to the *Tanakh*. In Acts, chapter 21, rumors were circulating that Paul was teaching Jews not to observe Judaism. According to Acts 21:23, to prove the rumors false beyond any doubt, Paul seems to have temporarily taken on the strictest form of the Law, the Nazarite vow of Numbers, chapter 6. In Acts 22:12, Ananias, the believer who first approached Paul (Saul), was described as "a devout observer of the law and highly respected by all the Jews living there." The Law of Moses had not been canceled.

Though I had basically accepted that the Law of Moses had not been canceled, Acts 21:26 still startled me. Paul was making a sacrifice (Daniel 6:10) at the Temple after the "final sacrifice" had already been made: Jesus' death on the cross. Evidently, Paul did not think that God's commandments regarding sacrifices were canceled by Jesus. And just a few verses earlier in the same chapter of Acts, "James and all the elders" were happily telling Paul about all the Jewish followers of Jesus who were "zealous for the Law." New Testament writings such as these convinced me that James and the elders did not teach that the Law of Moses should be abandoned. They taught precisely the opposite.

This discovery made me curious about why religious Jewish people no longer make animal sacrifices as they did in the first century. I learned that after the Temple was built, sacrifices were not allowed outside Temple services. However, prayer times and services that had accompanied sacrifices were still practiced; hence, obeyed by Jews to the best of their ability. When I heard that Jewish people today pray three times each day facing Jerusalem (or the Temple Mount), I was reminded of Daniel doing the same thing.

In Christian thought, the purpose of sacrifices was to obtain forgiveness of sins. If that were true, I thought Jewish people would have feared for their souls as soon as the Temple was destroyed. But when I remembered Daniel, I knew he was not going to hell when he died just because there were no Temple sacrifices for him. And Judaism teaches that repentance and asking God for forgiveness must accompany sacrifices for sin at the Temple; without repentance, sacrifices were rendered invalid. God must have had His reasons for commanding sacrifices, but obviously sacrifices were never essential in obtaining God's forgiveness or acquiring eternal life.

That being understood, I now had a big question about forgiveness of sins. If sacrifices did not cause God to forgive sins, if He did that independently of sacrifices, then there was no need to have a "final sacrifice for sin." Paul was still making sacrifices after the ascension, so Paul must not have considered them canceled by Jesus. One Christian teaching after another came into question.

When I studied the book of Jonah, I realized that God's forgiveness must not be conditioned on one's religion. God threatened to destroy the Ninevites because of the heinous acts committed against one another, not because they did not practice Judaism. Jonah's mission to the Ninevites was successful: they repented of their awful crimes. However, they did not convert to Judaism. They were Gentiles, forgiven by God simply because they stopped treating each other horribly.

Although Jesus told his followers, "first to the Jew, then to the Gentile," apparently, Jesus was not as reluctant as Jonah to teach Gentiles about the God of Israel. Israel is to be a blessing to the nations, but it seems that few rabbis before Jesus took on that mission.

When I grasped the idea that God did not change His mind between the *Tanakh* and Jesus' coming, that He meant exactly what He said in the *Tanakh* about eternal commandments, some concepts came into clear focus. James and the elders were teaching a zealousness for the Law to Jewish people and just a few practices for the Gentile converts (Acts 21:25). Rabbi Jesus was reaching out to Gentiles as Jonah did: revealing the God of Israel, but not converting them to Judaism. From the time of Abraham, God made the Jewish people different through His eternal commandments, and Jesus said that the Law of Moses was valid "until heaven and earth disappear." I began to believe that whatever is taught in the *Tanakh* is valid today, including how God looks at Gentiles.

The entire *Tanakh* tells us what God has asked of His Jewish followers. The New Testament seems to agree on these requirements, according to Jesus' words in Matthew 5:17–19 and James and the elders in Acts 21:20–24. Of course, God loves Jews and Gentiles equally, but it is difficult to find exactly which practices Gentiles were supposed to follow when they accepted the God of Israel.

Even when I studied Jewish sources, I found it difficult to find an answer to this question because the main emphasis of both the *Tanakh* and the New Testament was the path of the Jewish people. For the most part, the New Testament was written by Jews for Jews. However in the Talmud, the Oral Law, the great Jewish sages had something to say on the subject of Gentiles following the God of Israel.

The Talmud includes instructions for Gentiles who believe in the God of Israel. The rabbis taught that believing Gentiles should follow basic principles known as the Noadic Covenant, the seven laws pertaining to the Children of Noah. They believed these laws to be essential to maintaining any society.

In Genesis, chapter 9, God makes a rather one-way covenant with Noah, an agreement not to destroy the earth by flooding it again, and the token of that covenant is the rainbow. Jewish commentary on the Noah story is given below.

Rabbinic interpretation of these verses deduced seven fundamental laws from them:

1. the establishment of courts of justice
2. the prohibition of blasphemy
3. the prohibition of idolatry
4. the prohibition of incest
5. the prohibition of bloodshed
6. the prohibition of robbery
7. the prohibition of eating flesh cut from a living animal

According to commentator J. H. Hertz:

> The Rabbis called these seven laws the "Seven Commandments given to the descendants of Noah." These constitute what we might call Natural Religion, as they are vital to the existence of human society. Whereas an Israelite was to carry out all the precepts of the Torah, obedience to these Seven Commandments alone was in ancient times required of non-Jews living among Israelites, or attaching themselves to the Jewish community.[5]

I found that James had a similar stance regarding Gentiles. Once I clearly viewed Jesus' movement as one within the larger framework of Judaism, everything began to make sense. Under James's leadership, Jewish believers were zealous for the Law. The Jewish believers' love for the Torah caused them to be concerned that the fact that Gentile followers did not convert to Judaism might influence Jews to abandon the Law of Moses. But James said that was not his concern because: "Moses has been preached in every city from the earliest times and is read in the synagogues on every Sabbath (Acts 21:20).

James felt certain the Torah would be followed by Jews until the "Last Days." Instead of adopting Judaism, James told Gentile followers of Jesus to do the following:

> It seemed good to the Holy Spirit and to us not to burden you with anything beyond the following requirements:
>
> You are to abstain from food sacrificed to idols, from blood, from the meat of strangled animals and from sexual immorality.
>
> You will do well to avoid these things. Farewell. (Acts 15:21)

When I first read the passages in Acts, chapters 15 and 21, regarding James's instructions to Gentiles, it bothered me that Christians do not avoid eating blood; rare prime rib is considered a treat. And the only way I know to obtain meat that is not from an animal that has been strangled is to buy verified kosher meat. Like the Law of Moses for the Jewish people, these instructions in Acts to the Gentiles were not a condition for salvation, but rather a way of life that God instructed.

While in Jerusalem, I realized my viewpoint had changed dramatically. When I walked to the Old City and visited the Western Wall, the only remnant of the Temple, I sat at the feet of Rabbi Jesus. I was listening to him teach the Torah as only a rabbi could. Yes, I had learned a great deal in only a couple of months. My love for Israel, and especially for Jerusalem, had grown deep. My respect for the *Tanakh*, the only Holy Scriptures Jesus knew, had grown immensely. I would never again be able to view the New Testament as my friends did (i.e., as Holy Scripture).

I had begged God to reveal the meaning of His Torah. But it would be years before I could emotionally accept what He revealed to me in Israel.

As we neared the end of the biblical calendar year of 5747, in late September, it became apparent that I would soon have to leave. When

Rosh Hashanah (head of the year) came, plans were made to return home. Two months had passed and there was not going to be enough money to bring my daughter to Israel. Alecia's birthday was fast approaching. I would be back in the United States within two weeks.

I began to say good-bye to dear, sweet Israel. There would be no more supermarkets full of kosher meats and Hebrew labels (except in New York City). I would miss the huge grapes of Israel: they actually are larger than our own. Restaurants with kosher pizza or Chinese food were rare in the United States. I dropped out of the Ulpan, the intensive Hebrew language course I had been taking for free in the evenings. In Mea Shearim I purchased books I would grow to cherish. In the midst of the holy days I would have to leave.

The ten days between Rosh Hashanah and Yom Kippur (Day of Atonement) are a time for reflection, a time to seek and grant forgiveness. At peace with our fellow man, we are able to go before God with a clean heart, a clear conscience. At Yom Kippur one approaches God in repentance and humility, seeking His forgiveness and mercy.

Yom Kippur is the holiest day on the Jewish calendar. On this day, Israel was told to "deny yourselves" (no food or water) and pray for God's mercy. Everyone whose health permits joins the fast. It is a solemn event for religious Jewish people, and I felt privileged to participate. In a very private way I felt bonded to the Jewish people and to God on Yom Kippur. This holy day is an indelible experience in Israel. The entire country shuts down: airport, businesses, and all. There are no cars or buses on the roads, at least not in Jerusalem. It is the Sabbath of Sabbaths as far as the stoppage of everyday activity. But it was much more than that.

I walked to the Great Synagogue, which was located a few blocks from where I lived. On the way, I saw many families walking arm in arm down the middle of carless streets. The unity of families, communities, and the country itself impressed me enormously.

Once inside the synagogue, I took my place in the balcony with the other women. The huge room was overflowing with worshipers dressed in white. Below, I saw a sea of men in white jackets and *kippahs*. Prayers were intense, a communal confession of sins of the heart. Sometimes, when I am feeling too self-righteous, I pray the Yom Kippur confessional in the *siddur*. These prayers remind me of how much I sin, how loving and forgiving God is, and how weak I am. They remind me how much I need God's unconditional grace.

After Yom Kippur, I made a last visit to Mea Shearim. The sidewalks were lined with Sukkot (Feast of Tabernacles) preparations. A crowd of men stood at long tables picking over the items needed to build their *sukkot*. We were also building a *sukkah* at the Center, but I would miss it; Sukkot would begin about the time I would be arriving back in the States.

On Monday night, October 5, a going-away party was held. I was leaving in the morning. In addition, Juan from California and Charles, my rescuer from East Germany, were also leaving.

Charles spoke almost no English, so few of us could communicate with him verbally. My memories are of his rosy, glowing face and his wonderful disposition. He was quiet and humble, yet filled with joyous expectancy for whatever life might bring. He had very little money, and he received a monthly newsletter from the Center. That summed up what we knew of him.

At the going-away party, each of us was given a chance to speak. Charles's speech is the only one I can recall. His was the first, and he was prepared. Sister Elsie, a member of the Center's ruling board, was visiting from Switzerland. She would act as interpreter for Charles.

Charles's speech began in general terms, but as it progressed, Sister Elsie's eyes moistened. Her words followed his after a pause and a deep breath. His home, he said, was in East Germany behind the Iron Curtain (this was in 1987). Somehow, it had not occurred to me that people from East Germany could not freely visit other parts of the world as Charles did. His East German passport did not allow him to exit his country. This trip should have been impossible.

He described his initial joy at becoming a believer in Jesus. Then came his burning desire to visit Israel, the Holy Land, the birthplace of his beloved Jesus. He "prayed and prayed and prayed," but no, the way had not been cleared for him to go. He told us how a man of God had laid hands on him and prayed. Still, there was no affirmative answer.

Much later, he returned to the pastor and asked, "Please, lay your hands on me again. Please pray that I might go to Israel." Charles received his answer; the Lord provided the way.

The East German government had a policy of distributing West German passports only to a privileged few. These people could travel anywhere they desired. Only three of these special citizens, including Charles, had been given these unique passports. What we did not know, until we saw Sister Elsie's face, was the reason for these special passports. Along with those others, Charles had a terminal illness. He was the only one of the three left alive. Upon reentry into his country, the government would take his West German passport and return his East German one. In the year he had remaining, he was allowed to make this exchange as often as he could afford travel.

Charles, however, was not in mourning. He was filled with joy because God had answered his prayers. This poor man had budgeted his money carefully during his stay and saved enough to buy not one, but two large boxes of chocolates to share with us.

When his personal story was finished (with many of us in tears), he announced that he had prepared something special. In broken English (with Sister Elsie's occasional corrections), he would relate a New Testament story he had paraphrased and memorized in English. He would continue until one of us guessed from which passage it came.

When we realized which passage it was (John 1:43–51) no one had the heart to stop his precious performance. It was obvious he had worked excruciatingly hard on it, all alone, with an English Bible he could barely comprehend. The story brought a smile to my face and joy to my heart because it was Charles's triumph and God had allowed me the privilege of witnessing it.

All the blessings—walking the streets of Jerusalem, driving through the Israeli countryside, sharing meals and smiles—these I was allowed to experience with Charles. I had seen movies and heard about godly people who knew they were about to die. Some of these people exuded a joy for living, extraordinary patience, and love for others. Never before had I witnessed this for myself.

Charles once asked what I did for a living. Frankly, I am proud to be a bookkeeper, and it has become something of a pet peeve of mine when someone assumes I am a secretary or clerk, simply because I am female and I work in an office. However, I did not know how to mime "bookkeeper," so I motioned with my fingers as though typing, and with my right hand pushed back the imaginary carriage at the sound of the bell. His face lit up immediately. He was obviously pleased to comprehend that I was a secretary.

This was just a little treasured moment in the kitchen of a big house in West Jerusalem with a saintly man from East Germany. I thank God that Charles's government had the compassion to grant him the freedom to live his dream. For one cherished moment in time, a star was allowed to emerge from behind the Iron Curtain. And shine it did.

My boss, Shlomo, had been gone almost the entire time I was in Israel. For the past few weeks, he had been traveling in Russia. He shared with us the current status of Jewish people there. He had to go underground to find and visit synagogues, and he found them with few Torah scrolls or *siddurs*. Churches fared better, but religion was still unpopular with the Communist government. Because of rampant Russian anti-Semitism, we prayed that God would get the Jewish people out quickly. (Within a year, God began to answer those prayers affirmatively.)

In the limited time we had together, Shlomo and I spoke many times. He looked over my ministry letters and offered suggestions. He said that if I wrote lighter fare, topics less threatening to traditional Christian teachings, my letters would be more popular. However, that was too much of a compromise, one I was not willing to make.

My letters told of the beauty of Jesus' biblical Judaism. Shlomo especially liked one analogy I had written:

> A young couple were recently engaged. They loved each other very much, but knew little about each other's families. One night, they were invited to a party. These were his friends and she didn't care for them very much; they ate strange foods and sang songs she didn't know. Though they were kind to her, she felt very uncomfortable and was quite relieved when it was time to go.
>
> Driving away, the young man asked, "Did you have a good time? Did you enjoy them?"
>
> "Not really. I don't seem to fit in with them. I'd rather not go there again if you don't mind."
>
> There was silence in the car for a long time. Then she noticed tears streaming down his face.
>
> "What's wrong?" she asked. "Have I done something to hurt you?"
>
> After a deep breath be replied, "The people you've rejected . . . they are my family."

The young man represents Jesus; the woman, the Christian community. The family in the story is the Jewish people. Jesus loved his family *and* those differences that God instructed.

Shlomo believed that my ministry would serve as a blessing to his people. I got the impression that as a Gentile I had the freedom to speak out in ways that Shlomo only wished he could.

Shlomo told me that a Jewish person had to reject biblical Judaism in order to join the Christian community. When Shlomo joined the Church, his Jewish wife and children suffered an identity crisis along with him, and his extended family had been shocked by his conversion. But Jewish converts are popular in Christianity; for Christians, the conversion of a Jew is verification that Judaism is wrong and Christianity is right. Shlomo and his family became completely assimilated, proving what good Christians they were.

Eventually, as Shlomo came to terms with his identity, he began to see Jesus the Jew. He realized it was biblical to practice the Judaism of his grandfather. He longed to return to his faith and yet retain his belief that Jesus was the promised Messiah.

In the synagogue they welcomed him, and he knew exactly what to do there. His son and grandson also felt at home in the synagogue. And yet the people there knew of Shlomo's belief in Jesus. Their disapproval was unspoken, but he felt it just the same. He was different. They silently hoped he would "return to his senses," return to Judaism. They had suffered too much from acts done in the name of Jesus. In their minds, Shlomo had joined the enemy.

He told me that in churches, people talked to Shlomo about "the Jews" as if he were not one. Inside he cried; outside, he smiled broadly and joked. In the Christian community, they did not consider Shlomo to be a Jew, not anymore. Only a hint of the pain would emerge when he spoke to a Jewish-Christian group. *They* should understand, he thought. But they didn't, not really, because they were assimilated Jews. Shlomo tried to be a Jewish follower of Jesus, not assimilated. Other Jewish people were Christians who happened to be born Jewish; most lived like Gentiles before converting to Christianity. For many, what they knew of Judaism was told to them by Christians or Jewish-Christians. They did not know the beauty of the Judaism that God created.

Shlomo walked a tightrope. Even the Gentile Christians with whom I lived and worked in Jerusalem showed a lack of respect for Judaism. It became evident by people at the table laughing and joking while Shlomo led prayers at the *Shabbat* table. Shlomo had two homes, two lives, two religions, belonging to neither, feeling at ease nowhere. He longed for the lifestyle of first-century Jewish believers as revealed in Acts 21:20. My heart broke for him, seeing him suspended on that tightrope. He was like a man without a country, stranded on an empty expanse of sea.

I could not help thinking how Jesus would have felt about this situation: a Jewish person having to reject the commandments God said were eternal in order to follow a Jewish Messiah. This is precisely why most Jewish people believe that Jesus could not possibly be the promised Messiah.

Shlomo hoped I could make a difference. Maybe a Gentile who accepted the Torah as valid could relay that message to the Christian community. A Jewish-Christian would only be accused of "Judaizing," but a Gentile who believes that Judaism is valid—maybe they would listen to me.

He wanted me to stay in Israel to learn and experience more, maybe to be a shoulder to cry on, but my daughter needed me more. I could stay no longer. I would have to take what I had gained and do my best at home.

To help me do that, Shlomo threw one last book my way. He probably knew I was not ready for it, but there would be no other chance to give *Has God Rejected His People?*, by Clark M. Williamson, to me. It was written by a Gentile, a theology professor at a Christian seminary in the United States. Williamson believed that Jewish people should practice Judaism. He also believed that the New Testament was not infallible Holy Scripture. That book bothered me for a long time.

Not only could I empathize with Shlomo's pain, but I was about to reenter my old world, and with all this new information, I would no longer feel comfortable there. I was about to climb onto my own tightrope. Shlomo seemed to know what God wanted me to do, and he was trying to help me. The sadness in his eyes told me he knew the price I was going to pay for standing up for the validity of the Torah; the Jews had been paying that price for thousands of years.

The next morning, a young co-worker from Switzerland drove me to the airport. He told me how much he loved America. He had visited the United States for a few months and loved everything about it. He reminded me of my father; he wore the same wire-rimmed sunglasses, rested his arm on the open window ledge of the van, and loved driving long distances. I did not talk much on the way to Tel Aviv. After a quick hug, he left me standing in front of the airport. It was the same spot where I had stood waiting the night I arrived. I watched the white Volkswagen van until it was out of sight.

I turned and entered the building. Most of the books I had collected had been mailed home, so my luggage was not heavy. There was no bag of clinking Coca-Cola bottles this time. I stood in the customs line as the officials checked everyone's luggage carefully. They did not look closely at mine. I must have looked harmless. I was leaving Israel as I had arrived . . . alone. This phase of the task God had given me was finished.

By evening, I was again in the Copenhagen airport, numb from the events of the past few months. Certain beliefs and dreams had been shattered. I still loved Israel, especially Jerusalem, but with less romanticism. My love for God and the Bible was now more mature, less emotional. I was still reeling from the answers God had given to my biblical questions.

With a twenty-two-hour layover ahead, the eight-hour sleeping room at the Copenhagen airport was a haven. That only left fourteen hours to fill. Then came another nine-hour flight. Once I got to the airport back home, no one would be able to pick me up for several hours. The trip had taken so long that I read a book called *Hind's Feet on High Places*[6] from cover to cover. The book is an allegory of the suffering that accompanies spiritual growth. It was appropriate reading, considering the trials that lay ahead, as well as the ones I had just passed through. After two days of travel and a ten-hour time change, I was exhausted.

# 12

## My Mission Revealed

My first day home, I awoke on Cheryl's couch. She and her roommate had already left for work. Life continued its motions all around me as if nothing had changed. Meanwhile, my thinking, my life had altered dramatically. But there was no time for reflection, not yet. Now it was time to take inventory, time to get on with life.

Reality was tough. I thought the price I paid for following God's will was the emotional turmoil, the separation from Alecia, and feeling separated from my Christian friends. Surely that was a high enough price. But that was not the full cost. Now I had no job, little money, no car, and no furniture. Alecia would have to stay with the pastor's family for a while longer. I had no home for her.

Calling Saul was my first order of business. Alecia had already left for school, and I asked him not to tell her I was back. After two-and-a-half months of separation, I could not say to her, "I'm back, but you can't stay with me." Her birthday was only a few days away; that did not leave much time to find a job and a home.

When I hung up the phone after talking with Saul, I called my ex-employer. I needed a job—badly. Though I had not asked him to, he had held the position open as long as he could. Unfortunately, he had hired someone a week before I returned. I put on my shoes, grabbed my purse, and took a walk. I bought a newspaper and joked with the clerk, but inside, I was scared. Putting our life together quickly was not going to be an easy task.

That week I did everything I could to find a job. If I could not have Alecia with me, I wanted to at least offer her the hope that having a job would bring. By Monday, I could not wait any longer. Her birthday was the next day. She could not be without her mother, not on her tenth birthday.

Arrangements were made for me to sleep on Saul's couch Monday night: I would wake my daughter in the morning. She could stay out of school, and we would spend a special day together. However, the plan involved too much of a wait for Genise, Saul's daughter. She had shared her bedroom with Alecia for two-and-a-half months. Genise went upstairs and asked Alecia, "Do you miss your Mom?"

A quiet "yeah" was the reply.

The teenager promptly came downstairs and relayed the conversation as though Alecia had initiated it. "She really misses you."

I couldn't stand it any longer. I rushed up the stairs and opened the bedroom door. Alecia looked so pale at that moment, as if she were in shock. Then she threw her arms around me, and we both cried. We laughed and cried and talked well into the night.

Again, God's timing was giving me an understanding of His *Tanakh*. Our time of personal rejoicing came at a special time of the biblical calendar: during Sukkot. When the week of Sukkot ends, the eighth day is called Shemini Atzeret, and the following day is known as Simchat Torah. Throughout the year, a portion of the Torah is read every Sabbath. When the year is finished, the Torah has been read all the way through, and this milestone is celebrated on Simchat Torah (rejoicing in the Torah). In synagogues all over the world, Torah scrolls are lifted high and carried around the room. In Jerusalem, processions extend out into the streets. This celebration serves as witness to the relationship between the God of Israel and the Jewish people.

The Torah created a nation, albeit a "peculiar treasure," and they in turn keep God's Torah alive by observing its instructions.

In our own way, we too were rejoicing on this day of Simchat Torah. Saturday was the first Sabbath after Simchat Torah, the Sabbath when the first Torah portion from Genesis is read aloud in synagogues. Saturday was also the beginning of our new life.

Our first two months were the most difficult, as friends offered us their floors, couches, dens, and basements so that Alecia and I could stay together. Wherever they could find space, we were welcomed. I borrowed a car to get Alecia to school and me to look for work (my car had died while I was gone). Looking for a new home was pointless; there was no money to pay for one.

After nearly two months back home, my ex-boss called. My replacement had not worked out. I could start back to work on the first of December.

Before Chanukah began, we had a home: a one-bedroom apartment just two blocks from work, buses, and stores. The neighborhood was not great, but we could afford it. Our apartment was small, but all our things fit in: air mattresses and sleeping bags for beds, a metal patio table with a hole in the middle, and a desk, dresser, and loveseat all given to us by friends. We were together in our own home, so to us the apartment was like a palace. We celebrated Chanukah as our time of deliverance that year.

We began attending both churches again, but without a car it was too difficult to keep up our previous pace. In addition, I had a lot of thinking to do; I could not handle more input at this point. All my energy was consumed just trying to assimilate the information I had already received.

How I had longed for close friends and fellowship while in Israel! Now I could attend familiar churches and recognize the faces—but my views had changed. Prayer in synagogue was directed only to God, while in church they often prayed to Jesus or to the Holy Spirit. Fellowship required conversation with like-minded people; for me, that was not possible in the Christian community.

I had grown to love the Torah; it was alive and vibrant. To my friends, though, it was old and obsolete. Only the New Testament had relevance for them. And in their eyes the Jewish people hated Jesus; Jewish people were viewed as being legalistic and ignorant of spiritual matters. My heart was torn by all this. These were only misunderstandings, but such harmful ones.

These Christians did not know Jesus the Jew. Jesus' statement in Matthew 5:17–19 meant nothing to them, and they were oblivious to passages like Acts 21:20. I prayed, "How can I teach them, God?"

One Sunday morning, during a sermon filled with such "misunderstandings," I slipped out the back door. I could not hide the tears that were streaming down my face. Life would never be the same, because I was not the same.

My prayer partner visited each week. She tried to be patient with my pro-Jewish viewpoint. In her home, I watched *Fiddler on the Roof* for the first time. Sadly, I related how the three daughters in the movie represented the three progressive stages of assimilation.

My friend confessed that she had noticed I no longer said "in Jesus' name, amen" at the close of prayers. I could not. The Messiah was not considered equal to God in the *Tanakh*; there is but One True God.

Although she was a fundamentalist Christian, she was not upset, angry, or judgmental. She responded simply, "You've crossed over to the other side."

I wanted to shout, "No, not really. I need fellowship! I need you. I need the Christian community." Instead, I sat there in silence. She was right. I no longer viewed Jesus, God, or the Bible as Christians did. When I read the New Testament, I saw a Jesus who loved the Torah. He did not consider it mere spiritual symbolism. But it had only been three years since my baptism; I was not yet willing to let go of my "family."

My ministry newsletters continued. I felt I could not leave the church even if I wanted to; God had given me a work to do there. He had opened my eyes to countless Bible passages, and it was time to share that knowledge. The Christian community was full of people who loved God. They often viewed Jesus as being against Judaism and, to a degree, anti-Jewish. I wanted to teach what I could about Jesus the Jew and the Judaism he loved. The newsletters gave me that opportunity.

Passover came in the first week of April that year, and I celebrated with our Gentile congregation. They were observing Passover for the first time, and I wanted to support their efforts. A great deal was omitted from the service, and much of Passover's meaning was lost to them, but it was a wonderful first attempt. I thanked God for every effort the Gentile congregation made to relate to Judaism.

In my mind, the importance of the newsletters was growing; I sensed that getting them out to people was now urgent. Copies were still mailed to clergy and elders for their comment, but they said nothing. My newsletters showed little evidence of the compromises Shlomo suggested; I had a message to give, and I could no longer keep quiet about it. When I kept still, I could not face God.

The following are excerpts from my January 1988 letter:

The Orthodox or "observant" Jewish person views the *Tanakh* as a vibrant source of God's revelation to man, His plan for and history of the Jewish nation (and the other nations), as well as the ultimate "how-to book" for the life of the Jew.

In contrast, we often see it as the *Old* Testament as if it is no longer valid and somehow replaced by the "new." In the past, this line of thinking caused me to concentrate my deeper studies on the New Testament. I simply skimmed the surface of the "Old."

This concept of old and new has evolved into a theology in which the eventual, logical conclusion is that God changed when Jesus came. He changed from a vengeful God to a merciful one. . . .

My faith is strengthened when I realize that our God is consistent. And rather than accepting the theology that the "old" and "new" testaments are a complete contrast to one another (which is anti-Judaism), gratefully, I can see where they agree.

That letter touched on Marcion's teachings, and it had a strong impact on its readers. It was the strongest statement I had yet made about the validity of biblical Judaism. No reader complained or appeared to disagree, but steam was building behind the scenes.

A friend informed me that "someone said" *forever* does not always mean forever in the Bible. In the newsletter I had quoted passages in which God said His covenant with Israel was everlasting. These passages stood in direct opposition to the Christian theory that God's covenant with Israel has been canceled.

My response to that comment came in the March newsletter. As gently as I could, I stood up for the validity of the *Tanakh* as written. Aware of conflicts I might be causing in readers' minds, I provided them with an "out." In retrospect, maybe I was merely inserting a disclaimer for myself:

> As I hope is also true of you, my theology has developed a great deal over the past year. Reflecting on the questions, trials, pain, and joys of the last twelve months, I realize some growth has occurred. Halleluyah!
>
> So, you may have noticed some changes in these letters since they were first begun. For the Bible to influence our thinking means we are to be in a constant state of change. That's a good thing. My faith and my comprehension of God's plan continually expand as I venture deeper into the Word of God. In this sense, you read my study travel log here.

Then came the words that got me into trouble:

> Lately, I've realized that word meanings can differ. I had to go back to the original Hebrew to answer a question brought up recently. The theory stated was that *forever* doesn't always mean forever in the Bible.
>
> Well, of course, that didn't seem right. One would have to ask then, "Did God lie?" So I checked the word *forever* in two passages: Jonah 2:6 and Exodus 31:17.
>
> In the Jonah passage, Jonah is inferring that he will remain entrapped

"forever." In Exodus 31:17, God states that the Sabbath (seventh day of rest) "will be a sign between Me and the Israelites forever." Now we know that in Jonah, he was only in the body of the whale for three days and three nights. Regarding the passage in Exodus, many people believe the Saturday Sabbath for Jewish people was canceled when Jesus came. So, the meaning of these words becomes important theologically.

My research had consisted of asking Saul, the Jewish-Christian pastor who reads Hebrew fluently, to look up both words and tell me their meanings.

Upon researching this, I found that although both have the same Hebrew word root, they are actually spelled differently in Hebrew. Consequently, they have different meanings.

In Jonah, the word we render in English as forever is a general term that can mean until a time of fulfillment. However, the word in Exodus 31:17 actually has the meaning until the universe passes away. This is a much stronger term. It should also be noted that in one passage, the word is spoken by a man from his viewpoint. The other is a direct quote from God.

It is interesting that Jesus seems to echo this thought in Matthew 5:17, when he says:

"I tell you the truth, *until heaven and earth disappear*, not the smallest letter, not the least stroke of a pen, will by any means disappear from the Law until everything is accomplished."

This means that a study is necessary of words we render as "law" in both the *Tanakh* (Old Testament) and in the New Testament. Perhaps this, too, is a purpose for these letters: to act as a catalyst, an incentive for us to look deeper into His Word (Acts 17:11).

Thank you for your comments and questions. They challenge me to dig deeper. It would be of great benefit to me to hear the results of your studies as well!

Realizing the trouble this view would cause and not wanting to force these discoveries on others, I ended my letter with the following:

There have been occasions when my discoveries were unsettling for me. This has been especially true when they posed a challenge to accepted Christian doctrines of our time. Fortunately, these times have also proved to be my greatest incentive to research the Bible for answers, and they have ultimately led to an increased faith in God.

But since these discoveries can also be unsettling for others, I want to be sure that only those people who really *want* to see these letters receive them. So, I will send future letters only to those who contact me to say they want to continue receiving them. If I don't hear from you regarding this, I will assume you are no longer interested.

As it is written, "for the sake of peace."

This letter finally caused the elders of our Gentile congregation to ask to speak with me. I was not trying to attract their attention negatively. I had been asking for their comments and guidance for nearly a year, but not one word had been offered until they called me into a meeting one Sunday afternoon.

Of the two elders present, one man was clearly angry. The other appeared to be perplexed but calm. I prayed constantly, "God, give me the answers You want me to give. They don't understand. Please keep me calm."

The angry one pointed his finger at me and said I should not write such letters.

"Why?" I asked him. "Have I said something that is not biblical? If I have, tell me and I'll correct it in the next letter."

He had no example to give. He was just angry that I did not agree with his doctrines. He was upset that such a troublemaker was in his congregation. He had no biblical argument, only an emotional one. I sympathized but I could not lie about what I had learned. I asked if I could read aloud some passages from the New Testament to explain my viewpoint.

"No," said the angry elder. "We are here to teach you. You are not here to teach us !"

"But I can't explain without reading this."

The patient one spoke up: "Let's allow her to read."

I turned to Acts 21:20 regarding the Jewish followers of Jesus who became zealous for the Law. Then, in the same chapter of Acts, the Gentile believers were taught to observe a few simple instructions, but not the Law of Moses. Next I turned to Revelation, chapter 7, where the saved people were described in the Last Days. The first group was Israel; the second, the Gentiles.

The first elder's anger was beginning to boil over. I could see a physical change in him. I silently prayed for his health as he brought up my teaching on the Sabbath. I told him I believed it was all right for Gentiles to meet on Sunday or any other day of the week, but the Sabbath command God gave the Jewish people specified Saturday. "That's the Sabbath Jesus observed," I told him.

That was more than he could take. "Jesus is dead!" he blurted out.

We all fell silent as his words echoed in the church office. We knew he did not mean them. His frustration was honest and genuine. Still, the Christian community lives a hypocrisy of following a Jewish Messiah and yet teaching that biblical commandments are invalid. Now, this elder was "forced" to hear this teaching from someone who had joined the church only three years earlier.

The patient elder said no more except to wish me well. The angry elder told me to stop writing the letters. I knew God wanted the letters to continue; I was in no position to stop. After that day, my very presence seemed to upset the elder.

Saul's help with the research was a paradox. He knew that the biblical instructions to Jewish people were to last forever, yet he "kindled a flame" (operated a car) on *Shabbat*, an act forbidden by Torah. He convincingly argued from New Testament passages that the kosher laws were still in effect, but he did not keep kosher in his home. He and Shlomo had much in common; they both encouraged *me* to share these insights, but *they* did not feel free to share them.

My March newsletter had also upset a member of the Jewish-Christian congregation. We were friends and had enjoyed exciting theological discussions with one another. He was a Gentile Christian with traditional views, but he often wore a *kippah* in service or even a *tallit*. Jewish culture was exciting to him, but when it came to believing that biblical Judaism was still valid, this was where he drew the line. After all, he was the assistant pastor of the Jewish-Christian congregation.

He disputed the meanings of the Hebrew words in the passages I had quoted. He looked them up in a well-respected Christian source. "They mean the same thing!" he insisted.

"Not according to our pastor," I responded. "Don't argue with me. Go ask Saul. He's the one who taught me."

There was not much the assistant pastor could say at this point. He held his tongue, but soon he would get his chance to speak. Though he rarely preached the Sabbath sermons, he spoke on the last Saturday of that month. His topic seemed to be a response to my newsletter.

He quoted the New Testament letter of Ephesians, chapter 2. This epistle contradicts Jesus' own words in Matthew 5:17–19 where Jesus says the Law is valid "until heaven and earth disappear." In Ephesians 2:15, it says that Jesus was "abolishing in his flesh the law with its commandments and regulations." Ephesians belittled circumcision as "done in the body by the hands of man," as though it was merely a man-made tradition. Yet, in Genesis 17:7, God said, "I will establish My covenant as an everlasting covenant." And,

> This is My covenant with you and your descendants among you, the covenant you are to keep: Every male among you shall be circumcised. You are to undergo circumcision, and it will be the sign of the covenant between Me and you. For the generations to come every male among you must be circumcised. . . .
>
> My covenant in your flesh is to be an everlasting covenant. Any uncircumcised male, who has not been circumcised in the flesh, will be cut off from his people; he has broken my covenant. (Genesis 17:10–17)

Therefore, physical circumcision is an everlasting commandment from God to the Jewish people. They were not being stubborn in their observance of it; they were being obedient. God's eternal commandments were not the cause of hostility between Jews and Gentiles. There is nothing wrong with circumcision; however, it was commanded to Jews and not to Gentiles. With his Torah, God caused differences between His peoples, and God does not make mistakes.

Jews and Gentiles were united in the first century because they came together to worship the God of Israel, the One True God. Perhaps the dividing wall of hostility that exists between Christians and religious Jews today is envy—because God chose Israel for His plan, rather than some other nation. The plan would have been the same had God chosen a different nation. But the Jewish people have had to suffer because of God's choice. I see no reason to be envious of that; on the contrary, I feel spared by God.

I do not believe Christians should be envious of and so desire to be the replacement for Israel, or as some call themselves, the "New Israel." Since those commandments pertaining to Israel are everlasting, anyone who is "Israel" would be obligated to obey them. These instructions are commanded only to Jewish people, not Gentiles. We need to learn to accept God's plan as He laid it out in the Torah.

By May of 1988, the newsletters had become a hodgepodge of all the information I could cram into two pages. Perhaps the elder's reaction or the assistant pastor's response had taken their toll on my nerves. I felt I had to hurry now. I had to share as much as I could before the opportunity to reach people in the church was lost, which I feared might happen soon because of the elders.

In additional letters I discussed New Testament passages, such as Acts 21:17–26 and Revelation, chapter 7, which show that God commanded differences between Jews and Gentiles and that these teachings were still biblically relevant. I quoted Acts 22:12 about Ananias, a follower of Jesus, who was "a devout observer of the Law and highly respected by all the Jews." This was Judaism in action: how Jesus and his followers lived.

I quoted Jewish Bible commentary about the status of God-loving Gentiles (Exodus 12:19).

> *Sojourner. Heb. ger. The resident alien.* "He was not directed or compelled to resume a religious duty of Israel, but he was prevented from interfering with the religious practices of Israel" (Sulzberger). In later Hebrew law, the resident alien is either a *ger tzedek*, a righteous proselyte who has been received into the covenant of Abraham, and thereby enjoys the same privileges and obligations as the born Israelite; or *ger toshab* or *sha'ar,* the "stranger at the gate," the alien squatter who remains outside the religious life of Israel, but who has undertaken to adhere to the seven Noachic laws.[1]

In newsletters, I shared that this Jewish commentary had helped me understand how we who were "far off" could come near and join Israel in worship of the God of Israel without becoming Israel (proselytes). Now I understood why Jesus told his followers to obey the rabbis, the teachers of the law (Matthew 2:2–3).

The newsletters related how God had instructed His people to build the Temple to include a special place for Gentiles. The Court of the Gentiles was by far the largest courtyard in the Temple because His Temple was to be a "house of prayer for all nations" (Isaiah 56:7).

I closed one of the final letters with the following:

> We know that the laws, any laws, were not able to save souls. Only the grace of God has the power to save us. We are all sinners in need of His mercy, forgiveness, salvation, and instruction. We have no righteousness of our own. This is a fundamental doctrine of both Christianity and Judaism.
>
> Lord knows how far I am from having all the answers. I remain foggy about so many things, but my study continues. How patient you are with me. How merciful is our God with all of us!

I finished that letter with a listing of books from which I had learned a great deal; I sensed that the doors to this part of my life were beginning to close. If the letters came to an end, I wanted to be certain that open-minded people knew of books that would help them continue their studies.

Although I no longer believed as many of my friends, I still cared for them. Alecia and I were grateful to everyone for all they had done for us, and we looked for ways to thank them. At the end of May, Saul and his wife took a trip to Israel. Alecia and I stayed at their home and I took care of their two teenagers. It was not a big favor, but they appreciated the help. I was grateful that God had given me a chance to say "thank you."

By the ninth of *Av* that year, in late July, the last ministry letter was written. I was loosely involved in both congregations, and my prayer partner still came over regularly. To avoid conflict, I seldom volunteered my point of view. Alecia and I observed some practices of Judaism, not because I had converted but because I loved the Sabbath and the prayers of the *siddur*. The Hebrew language had become music to my ears. Yet once again, the ninth of *Av* was a sad time.

The lack of freedom in conversation and close fellowship made me feel lonely; my friends and I would never be as close as we once were. What I had loved most in my first year with the Christian community was the open communication. We could question and speak our minds, and we usually agreed. They could no longer agree with my views; voicing them just made people feel uncomfortable, and I could no longer tolerate the safe and meaningless conversations we were left with.

Consequently I began searching for fellowship with people whose beliefs more closely resembled mine. That summer I contacted several Bible scholars. One was the Christian author of a pro-Judaism book. One was a pro-Jesus, non-Christian Jewish professor. The third was an Orthodox rabbi. These were experts on the Bible. If anyone knew the answers, they would. I received little response. Maybe they thought I was asking the wrong questions. Perhaps they worried that I could not handle their answers emotionally or intellectually. Regardless, I was disappointed. Months passed with no answers and little fellowship.

We had not attended either church for months by the time I heard a knock at the door one Saturday morning. It was the pastor of a Jewish-Christian congregation in Portland whom I had met on several previous occasions. He had a great sense of humor, and I had always enjoyed his company. This time, however, he came to ask why I stopped attending Jewish-Christian services. We spent many hours talking; he seemed to understand how I felt.

He was born to Jewish parents in New York City; his parents were not observant, but his grandparents were. Recently he had begun adopting more practices of Judaism into his life. He had spent countless hours teaching himself Hebrew. Many Christian practices had become foreign to him, as they had to me. He too prayed only to God, not to Jesus or the Holy Spirit. How wonderful this new fellowship felt!

It was a long-distance relationship, but we felt close immediately. Usually he was a lot of fun, something my life was seriously lacking. After a few weeks, he asked me to marry him.

I thought I had finally found someone who believed as I did. The loneliness was gone; I had a partner in life. And now I had an excuse for converting to Judaism, something I had secretly wanted to do for a long time. Also, he had been to Israel twice and loved it as much as I did. We both longed to live there. It seemed perfect!

In the Torah it is taught that Jews and Gentiles cannot intermarry; it is forbidden by God. My faith in the Bible meant that in order to marry a Jewish man, regardless of his beliefs, I would need to become a proselyte. Also, we both had to be Jewish to immigrate to Israel.

A few months earlier, I had called the local rabbi with a question about the Noadic Covenant. Now I had an appointment to ask him to help me convert to Judaism.

"Ah, you must be Kim, and how are you? Come in, come in." The rabbi's accent reminded me of New Yorkers I had heard in the movies. As it turned out, he and his wife were both raised in New York City. As I walked into the house, I noticed that off to the right was a room filled with teenage chasidic boys. All eyes were fixed on me.

"This way, follow me." We walked down the hall and into his office. I sat down and he closed the door.

Before I had only *wanted* to convert to Judaism; now I had to convert if I was to get married. I was so nervous!

The rabbi was friendly but suspicious: few Gentiles come to Orthodox rabbis for conversion. The biblical way of life is not an easy one. The rabbi wanted to be certain I had counted the cost of converting. "Why not go to a Reform rabbi?" he asked.

I shocked myself with the swiftness and clarity of my answer: "If I didn't want to take the Bible literally, I would go back to the church."

"What about your daughter? Is she converting too?" From our earlier conversation the rabbi knew of my Christian background. He was well aware of the Christian view of salvation.

"No, she doesn't need to."

"No?"

I brought up Deuteronomy 4:12–20 and told the rabbi this passage led me to believe Alecia was okay with God without converting to Judaism or Christianity. He seemed surprised that I was aware of the passage and of this interpretation.

He was also convinced I was serious about converting to Orthodox Judaism. However, he did not personally handle conversions. Instead, he sent me to another Orthodox rabbi, who was not chasidic, to begin the process. My local rabbi said that I could attend synagogue and join a women's class his wife was teaching, if I wished.

I loved Judaism; attending a synagogue and observing Judaism was a dream come true. But my few remaining Christian friends had difficulty understanding my new choice of lifestyle. Judaism was still a rejection of Christianity. However, the Jewish-Christian man I was about to marry was a pastor in a church, so even if I practiced Judaism, I would still be "acceptable" in the eyes of my Christian friends. That smoothed out a few ruffled feathers.

Upon the announcement of our engagement and my conversion plans to his parents, they offered to pay our way to Israel! Evidently this was a dream come true for everyone. There was one problem though—although I wanted a nice Orthodox Jewish lifestyle like those I had witnessed, my fiancé did not. I was to convert, he said, just enough to satisfy the Israeli authorities that I was now Jewish. I was not to expect him to live an Orthodox lifestyle.

I had already begun attending synagogue on Saturdays. The rabbi was kind and knowledgeable. He had a large, happy family, and his wife was an intelligent, vibrant woman. It was a small synagogue with few women in regular attendance on Shabbat, so I quickly became friends with Beth, the only other woman who attended Saturday services regularly.

As I continued attending synagogue, each service became more enjoyable than the last. Not being Jewish, I felt a little out of place, as if I had no right to be there, but the rabbi tried to make me feel welcome. Best of all, they prayed to the One True God, not to or through anyone else, and the worship brought me closer to God. Discussions after services were fascinating. This was a chasidic synagogue, ultra-Orthodox, yet women took equal part in discussions. I felt more at home in the synagogue than I could ever again feel in a church.

Though I was happy at the synagogue, my fiancé insisted my heart was in error because I had left the Church. He did not want there to be a barrier between me and the Christian community. I thought he was just trying to keep me from burning my bridges, which sounded reasonable.

Purim came in March that year. Both the synagogue and the Jewish-Christian church planned festivities. On the day before Purim, religious Jewish people fast from sunrise to sundown as they did in Esther 4:16. All the Jewish people in Esther's kingdom were to be murdered. Purim celebrates the deliverance of the people in Esther's day, as well as any time God delivers the Jewish people from the hands of oppressors.

The Purim celebration includes reading aloud the Book of Esther, putting on plays based on the book of Esther, and giving gifts. The Jewish-Christian church decided to perform a play on the weekend near Purim, and I was asked to take part. I agreed to give an introduction. I spoke of persecutions of the Jewish people, the celebration of God's deliverance, and of His punishing oppressors. It was a serious message to a Christian audience. (Well, they enjoyed the play.)

When I walked into the synagogue on the evening of Purim, I was surprised to see whole families there because on the Sabbath, women and children usually remained at home. Many people were dressed in costume. Little girls were dressed like Queen Esther, boys like Mordecai or Haman. People were crowded into the small room, but they were loud and happy.

The rabbi began to read aloud the Book of Esther. Each time he read the name of Esther or Mordecai, everyone in the audience would shout, "Yeah!" Each time Haman's name came up, everyone would yell, stamp their feet, and generally try to drown out his name. Once I loosened up a little, it was great fun.

After the reading and a short sermon, the rabbi announced that festive food and drink were available in the large room behind him: soda, chips, and cookies called *hamentashen*, which are shaped like little Haman hats. I relaxed and began to enjoy myself. Everyone was friendly and kind.

Just then, a young man from the Jewish-Christian congregation entered the room. He was Jewish and I was glad he was there, but at the same time, I was afraid he might say something I did not want my Orthodox friends to hear. I did not believe in Christianity anymore, but I wanted to have a positive influence in the Church. I felt like a hypocrite. I left as soon as possible.

Shortly thereafter, my fiancé and I had a revealing discussion. I was answering his questions about my beliefs, and he suddenly became angry. "What makes you think you know more than . . ." (he listed off the names of some of the Jewish-Christian pastors and leaders we both knew).

Now the truth was coming out. He felt the same way they did; it was all right for Jewish people to practice as much Judaism as they wished, so long as it was clearly understood that because of Jesus, God no longer required *anyone* to practice biblical Judaism. According to him, that was purely the business of hard-core, self-promoting rabbis. He sounded as anti-Judaism as any member of the church—maybe more so!

Problems were mounting. In church, I had to keep my opinions to myself. In synagogue, I felt deceitful because everyone except the rabbi thought I was Jewish. My daughter was supportive, but she was not converting, and it was difficult to keep a kosher home while living with someone who did not practice Judaism. Alecia understood that she was okay with God as she was, but for a child, not following the faith of the parent is confusing. I felt pressure from every side.

Most important, God had given me a "mission," and finally that mission was clear: to teach the Christian community about anti-Semitism in the church. Also, I had a message about anti-Judaism for the church: that God created Judaism and He made no mistake in His creation of it. With so much racism, poverty, and inhumanity in this world, God's people need to unite. Instead, we fight each other. But lately I had done no work that would help deliver these messages.

I was concerned that if I converted to Judaism, I would become just another Jewish voice against Christianity. I was afraid I might be cutting off the possibility of having a voice in the Christian community. I could not face God if I allowed that to happen.

At work, I began to feel the pressure that society creates for the observant Jew. My new boss was a Christian and a very kind man. I had to tell him I was converting to Judaism, as I needed to take some time off in April for Pesach (Passover). He did not understand, but allowed the time off.

The observances of Passover include a commandment to remove all leaven from one's possession for the day of Passover and for the following week; hence, its name, the Feast of Unleavened Bread. This required a thorough cleaning of my home. Thankfully, the apartment was small, and we had few possessions from which to remove bread crumbs and flour.

Beth stopped by unexpectedly the night before Passover and caught me in worn jeans, a scarf on my head, and a dirty rag in my hand. She laughed and confessed that she too was cleaning like crazy at the last minute. She had come by to invite Alecia and me to enjoy the first Passover *seder* (meal) in her home.

Alecia and I walked to Beth's house the next evening and found a group of twenty people busy with last-minute preparations. We sat down and each person was handed a *Haggadah*, a book that details the Pesach ceremony. The ritual portion of the meal came first. After most of the ceremony was complete, we ate the regular festive meal and then completed the ceremony. It was an extraordinary experience filled with laughter and joy, and by the time it was finished, I too felt connected to the Israelites who had left Egypt so long ago. As Alecia and I left that night and walked home, I was filled with love for the holy days God commanded and I felt in awe of Jewish people who faithfully practiced His precepts.

On the second night of Pesach, everyone was invited to the synagogue for the second *seder*. I wanted to go. I had taken the days off work, but Alecia was not Jewish; she would be attending school the next day. The *seder* would run late, and I was not able to find a babysitter.

I felt all the conflicts and confusion of the past few months come crashing down around me, along with the guilt of not fulfilling my mission from God. I loved Judaism; it was the most God-centered, Bible-based lifestyle I had ever known. I loved the *siddur*, the rituals, Hebrew, the people, everything. I longed for like-minded fellowship. And I finally admitted to myself that the relationship with my fiancé was not going to work either. He believed Jesus was the Messiah; I did not. He thought belief in Jesus and the New Testament got one into Heaven; I thought they taught idolatry. I was alone again. I felt utterly defeated. Instead of attending the second *seder*, Alecia and I got in the car that afternoon and took a long drive.

In the morning I admitted to myself that I could not do the work God wanted me to do if I converted to Judaism. As a Gentile, my impact on the Christian community would be greater than if I were Jewish. I was not a pro-Jewish or pro-Judaism Jew. I was a Gentile who knew God and who believed in the validity of the Torah . . . today. There would be no conversion, no marriage, no Israel. It was time to accept the work God had given me to do.

# 13

## COMING TO TERMS

I spent a year in seclusion from religious matters. It was time to regroup with my daughter, my working life, life outside the chaos I had been living in.

I told my local rabbi I would not be converting. He invited me to attend services anytime I wished and suggested I might enjoy their Sunday morning breakfasts at the synagogue. Their newsletter came informing me of topics to be covered in upcoming Sunday talks. But I kept my distance.

One day my daughter gave me the news that she had volunteered me as a speaker for her sixth-grade history class. They had been studying the Middle East and were now ready to learn about the current century. Perhaps I was grateful Alecia was showing signs that she was proud of me instead of my past fear that she resented my trips to Israel without her. Maybe I just longed to break the silence—a chance to be open about my current beliefs.

Fearful of not doing justice to the topic, I spent many hours preparing the speech. I reread portions of *O Jerusalem* and typed a synopsis of the history of the State of Israel, including a number of dramatic episodes in 1947, 1948, and the Six-Day War in 1967. Just before beginning the speech, I handed to each of the children copies not only of the speech but also of a chronological progression of anti-Semitic events in history and the Hebrew alphabet.

As I spoke to those intense little faces, I nervously paced the front of the room. They felt the excitement of each event, visualized the faces and streets of Jerusalem under fire. One little boy in particular stared intently and hung on my every word. I related our Fourth of July to Israel's rebirth, spoke of racism in general, and discussed the Holocaust and how it led to the events of 1947. I finished by saying, "With anti-Semitism on the rise today in the United States and in Europe, the Jewish state remains an important refuge. We can take pride in (the United States policy of) supporting that refuge called Israel."

The teacher cringed in the corner of the room. But Alecia was grinning. I asked if anyone had questions. Now, an adult audience may have challenged my political views or asked for the sources I quoted; I readied myself. Instead, they asked if people in Israel had television sets. I laughed and amazed them with the news that Israel also had videocassette recorders and dishwashers, a great public transit system, movie theaters, and so on. Modern Israel was now a reality for them. After applause for an "exciting" speech, I left with warm satisfaction. That night Alecia told me the boy who had been staring usually ran around the room whenever a speaker came. "And by the way," she added, "he's Jewish. He doesn't eat kosher or anything, but his parents are both Jewish." This was the first insight I had that Jewish people might be interested in what I had to say, even if Christian people did not want to hear it.

By this time I had begun to write. I wrote a book for Christians about Judaism, somewhat of a soapbox treatment of anti-Semitism in Church doctrines. My local rabbi read the manuscript and evidently shared it with his colleague. When I arrived for a Sunday morning breakfast at the synagogue I was approached by a rabbi I had never met; he loved the book and chatted with me for a time. The rabbis I knew greeted me warmly. I saw Beth again, married now, smiling broadly, a scarf on her head. She hugged me and quickly told me she did not feel betrayed at all when she found out that I was not Jewish and seemed even more pleased that I was not converting. I no longer felt like a hypocrite; I could be myself and still feel welcomed in the synagogue.

That morning the rabbi introduced me to Doug and Kal Taylor, a Gentile couple. They too had come to hear the talk. They were on the same path as I was. This was the first time I had met other self-professing Noachides. Until that day, I thought I was absolutely alone in my beliefs (among Gentiles, that is). Doug told me about other Noachide groups and the annual Noachide conference held in Athens, Tennessee, each year. Eventually, I met other ex-Christian Gentiles both locally and later at the conference in Tennessee. A connection was made that day that gave me a great deal of strength.

Soon, several of us began meeting with rabbis at a local Jewish high school. We began to learn about the Thirteen Articles of Faith, how the Talmud affects Gentiles, and lessons from great sages like Maimonides. We had a place to ask questions openly, combat false teachings we had received in church, and receive encouragement to question and study. Each visit was revitalizing.

The first manuscript was abandoned in favor of the one you have in your hands. This is a wiser way of teaching Gentiles than the first manuscript could ever be.

Three years after standing before the sixth-graders, I was invited to speak at the local Jewish high school. This time it was my story, my reformation. Eyes were intent; humor was present this time. The timing was ironic—Christmas Eve. I spoke of not celebrating the holiday and how that, among many other things, had dramatically changed my life. Alecia sat nearby, a wartime child of the events of the past seven years. She was not certain of how she stood religiously and shared this openly that day with her Jewish peers. Gratefully, they did not judge her for the confusion, but seemed to sympathize. I found myself explaining why it is so difficult for a Christian to let go of beliefs that seem absurd to a religious Jewish group. In the end, they had developed an understanding.

I was reminded of the title of a little booklet I had received in Jerusalem in 1987 entitled *Building or Breaking*. I realized the bridge of understanding must be built from both directions, and perhaps as a Noachide I could be instrumental in constructing that bridge.

Like hundreds, perhaps thousands of Gentiles, I meet with other Gentiles of like mind whenever possible. Our local group is fortunate enough to have an Orthodox rabbi teaching and guiding our studies. I receive newsletters and study tapes from Tennessee, North Carolina, and Israel. I met J. David Davis and his wife, Sandra, wonderful Gentile leaders of the Noachide movement. I called David several times for advice while writing my book and discussing the book he is writing about his own life on the front lines of the movement; he used to be a Baptist preacher. He and Sandra have been a great source of information and strength. We each do what we can along this path.

Now I have the courage to speak openly, yet gently, to Christian friends on whatever level they can handle. I speak of my beliefs, as well as Christian misconceptions regarding Judaism and the Jewish people. If they ask, I share what I have learned about the Bible versus what we Gentiles have been taught in churches. Recognizing how painful my own journey has been, I am careful not to give them more than they can assimilate at any given time. For each individual, it is a difficult process. When speaking to others, I try to remind myself that it took ten years to progress from a Christian baptism to studying Torah and Talmud. I have learned to have patience with myself and with others.

Recently, I spoke with my niece who escorted me to the church where I was baptized. Several years ago she became disenchanted with Christian teachings. After asking me a number of questions regarding what I believed and why, she asked the crucial question from a Christian's point of view, "But how can I know that I will enter Heaven? If Jesus is not the way, and now I'm not certain, how do I know if I'm living the way God wants me to?"

I do not remember all the words that passed between us. But I left her with these thoughts: "Be certain you are on the path. Read the

Bible. Ask questions. Think about it and read it again. God wrote the Bible for all of us, and the only way to live as He wants is to read what He gave us."

"But I don't understand it; I get so confused by everything I hear."

She wants to understand. Every person who loves God wants to be able to sort out the truth. But we need teachers and information and a sense that we are not alone in our search. We need encouragement.

Before leaving, I told her a story I once read. A *tzaddik* once asked God, "If there is anyone who prays better than I do, send me to him, that I might learn." He walked many miles out into the countryside and found a shabbily dressed man praying in a field. The man did not know the Hebrew language, did not have a prayer book, and could not recite any Hebrew prayers. He knew a few Hebrew letters, though. With a full heart, he lifted his eyes and continually repeated those letters. This was the man to whom God sent the *tzaddik*.

My niece understood and said she would begin reading her Bible again.

My religiously confused daughter recently moved out of my home. Many of her things are still stored here, and she came by one day to pick up more items she wanted to take with her. I noticed that among books she left behind were some Bibles. A little fearful of nagging, I asked, "Do you want to take a Bible with you?"

"Mom, I have a Bible, already. I always keep a Bible with me."

Today, I plant seeds as I can. If they grow, I am often amazed. People know I am a source they can turn to when they have a question. I have learned from my rabbi and through experience that people must be ready to question before they can benefit from an answer. Some search more diligently than others. Some are afraid to question their beliefs. I empathize. But I have chosen a different path.

I long for the day when I will have more like-minded fellowship, at the same time realizing that day will not come soon. I also long for the coming of the Messiah, but for many reasons (many people) I hope that day will not come too soon.

# Epilogue

Many years have gone by, and much has been learned. My beliefs continue to evolve as I delve deeper into Torah with the help of the rabbis and Noachide leaders.

I no longer have a voice in the church. Part II of this book was originally written to help ex-Christians and new Noachides make sense of this path they are taking and to feel that they are not alone and not stupid. Perhaps a Christian may read it and learn, perhaps not.

Many of the beliefs expressed in this book, even those near the end of Part II, are no longer my beliefs. Those were the beliefs I held at the time of those experiences. I do not write this to apologize, but only to be certain that my narrative is understood as a path toward Torah, not as correct Torah teaching.

My journey was a painful and difficult one, but not a unique one. Thousands of ex-Christians have and do and will experience such confusion and pain. I applaud all those who stay on the path. The price being paid is worth the end result: a clearer understanding of the One True God and knowledge of how He wants each of us to live. Giving up on religion or going back to pagan faiths never satisfies. Living the Torah-based life God designed for us is the only way to inner peace. Only the Creator could design a lifestyle that would totally satisfy His creation.

For the Jewish reader who has not yet become involved in the Noachide movement, *Turning to Torah* is a window for you to look in, to see what God is doing among the Gentiles as part of His plan. I did not share these experiences with you to make you feel sorry for the Noachides or even to tell you that you must become involved. But perhaps this book will add to your understanding. Perhaps you can now feel reassured that these Gentiles are not interested in converting Jewish people to Christianity, nor are they in the process of converting to Judaism. We do need learned Jewish people to teach us, and perhaps you can offer emotional support to those rabbis who are performing this *mitzvah*.

The Torah is kept alive by those who observe it; that is all God asks of any of us, Jew or Gentile. Of course, world peace would be nice; but that will not happen until each of us loves God with all our hearts, with all our souls, and with all our might. That is a pretty high expectation, but then again, so is world peace.

# Notes

## Introduction

1. *Tanakh, The Holy Scriptures* (New York: Jewish Publication Society, 1985).

2. "Tennessee Baptists Turn to Judaism for New Inspiration," *Wall Street Journal*, 20 March 1991.

3. *Tanakh, The Holy Scriptures*.

## Chapter 8—The Holy Land

1. c.e. is a term used by non-Christians meaning the Common Era. It is synonymous with a.d. b.c.e. (Before the Common Era) is synonymous with b.c., or before Christ.

2. *The NIV Study Bible* (Grand Rapids, MI: Zondervan, 1985), p. 82.

3. David Bridger, ed., *The New Jewish Encyclopedia* (New York: Behrman House, 1976), p. 40.

4. Rivka Gonen, *Biblical Holy Places* (New York: Macmillan, 1987), p. 149.

5. Deuteronomy 16:16.

6. Shep referred to Proverbs 20:27 in Hebrew.

7. *The NIV Study Bible*, p. 1530.

8. "And there was evening, and there was morning—the first day" (Genesis 1:5). The Day of Atonement (Yom Kippur) is also observed from evening to evening (Leviticus 23:32). This is the biblical basis for the Jewish reckoning of the day as beginning the evening before.

9. A *mikveh* is a ritual bath, an immersion tank akin to a baptismal.

10. Maimonides is considered the greatest of the famous Jewish sages; he lived in the twelfth century.

11. Clark M. Williamson, *Has God Rejected His People?* (Nashville: Abingdon, 1982), p. 45.

12. *Biblical Holy Places*, p. 78.

13. Biblically fit, meaning "allowed in the Bible."

14. Contact with a dead body renders a priest "unclean," meaning temporarily unable to serve as priest.

15. *Biblical Holy Places*, pp. 151–152.

### Chapter 9—The Jewish Connection

1. J. H. Hertz, ed., *Pentateuch and Haftorahs* (London: Soncino Press, 1987), p. 20.

2. Stephen D. Eckstein, *From Sinai to Calvary* (Kansas City, MO, 1967).

3. Adolph Hitler, *Mein Kampf* (New York: Houghton Mifflin, 1930).

4. David Pawson, *Israel the Nation* (audiotape) (Covina, CA: The Hope of Israel, 1980).

5. *Encyclopaedia Britannica*, 1990, s.v. "Holocaust."

6. This conference held in Evian, France is referenced in *The Memoirs of Cordell Hull*, Vol. 2 (New York: Macmillan, 1948), p. 578; Arno J. Mayer, *Why Did the Heavens Not Darken? The Final Solution in History* (New York: Pantheon Books, 1990), pp. 165–66; Martin Gilbert, *The Holocaust—A History of the Jews of Europe during the Second World War* (New York: Henry Holt, 1985), pp. 64–65; *The Liberation of the Nazi Concentration Camps 1945— Eyewitness Accounts of the Liberators* (Washington, DC: U.S. Government Printing Office, 1987), pp. 158, 162.

7. *Encyclopaedia Britannica* (1990), s.v. "Rites and Ceremonies."

8. William Sansome, *A Book of Christmas* (New York: McGraw-Hill, 1968), p. 29.

9. Alexander Hislop, *The Two Babylons* (Neptune, NJ: Loizeaux Brothers, 1916), p. 103; T. Alton Bryant, ed., *The New Compact Bible Dictionary* (Grand Rapids, MI: Zondervan, 1967), p. 59.

10. *The Two Babylons*, p. 105.

11. Ibid., 109.

## CHAPTER 10—TRUST AND OBEY

1. *Fortune*, January 1966, as quoted in Lee Amber, *Chosen* (Santa Ana, CA: Vision House, 1966), p. 58.

2. A *siddur* is a Jewish prayer book; it contains all the standard prayers recited in synagogue and in the home.

3. Dr. Goran Larsson, *The Jews! Your Majesty* (Jerusalem: Center for Biblical Studies and Research, 1987).

4. *Encyclopaedia Britannica* (1990), s.v. "Biblical Literature," "Christianity."

5. Ibid., s.v. "Marcionite."

6. The *Shema* begins, "Hear O Israel, the Lord our God, the Lord is One," from Deuteronomy 6:4–9.

## CHAPTER 11—ISRAEL

1. *Jewish Art Calendar 5747* (Seattle: Central Organization for Jewish Education, 1987).

2. Ibid.

3. Rabbi Nissen Mangel, ed., *Siddur Tehillat Hashem* (Brooklyn: Merkos L'Inyonei Chinuch, 1987), p. 12.

4. *Tefillin* are called phylacteries in the New Testament (Matthew 23:5).

5. J. H. Hertz, ed., *Pentateuch and Haftorahs* (London: Soncino Press, 1987), p. 33.

6. Hannah Hurnard, *Hind's Feet on High Places* (Wheaton, IL: Tyndale House, 1975).

## CHAPTER 12—MY MISSION REVEALED

1. J. H. Hertz, ed., *Pentateuch and Haftorahs* (London: Soncino Press, 1987), p. 257.

# Suggested Reading

## Scriptures, Commentary, and Prayer

Hertz, J. H., ed. *Pentateuch and Haftorahs*. London: Soncino Press, 1987. Contains rabbinic commentary.

Mangel, Rabbi Nissen. *Siddur Tehillat Hashem*. Brooklyn: Merkos, L'Inyonei Chinuch, 1987. Prayer book.

*TANAKH, The Holy Scriptures*. New York: Jewish Publication Society, 1985. The Hebrew Bible.

## Anti-Semitism

Chaikin, Miriam. *A Nightmare in History—The Holocaust 1933–1945*. New York: Ticknor & Fields, 1987.

Hersey, John. *The Wall*. New York: Random House, 1988.

Hizak, Shlomo. *Building or Breaking*. 3rd ed. Jerusalem: Center for Biblical Studies and Research, 1986.

Larsson, Goran. *The Jews! Your Majesty*. Jerusalem: Center for Biblical Studies and Research, 1987.

*The Liberation of the Nazi Concentration Camps, 1945: Eyewitness Accounts of the Liberators*. Washington, DC: U.S. Government Printing Office, 1987.

Shirer, William L. *The Rise and Fall of Adolph Hitler*. New York: Scholastic, 1961.

Williamson, Clark M. *Has God Rejected His People?* Nashville: Abingdon Press, 1982. This is written from a Christian point of view; the author is a professor of theology.

## Jewish History

Collins, Larry, and LaPierre, Dominique. *O Jerusalem*. New York: Simon & Schuster, 1972.

Potok, Chaim. *Wanderings: Chaim Potok's History of the Jews*. New York: Fawcett Crest, 1978.

## Noachide Books

Clorfene, Chaim, and Rogalsky, Yakov. *The Path of the Righteous Gentile: An Introduction to the Seven Laws of the Children of Noah*. Southfield, MI: Targum Press, 1987.

Gallin, Aryeh. *The Root and Branch Noahide Guide/5742*. Jerusalem: The Root and Branch Association, 1991.

Lichtenstein, Aaron. *The Seven Laws of Noah*. Brooklyn, NY: Z. Berman Books, 1981.

Novak, David. *The Image of the Non-Jew in Judaism*. Lewiston, NY: Edwin Mellen Press, 1983.

Palliere, Aime. *The Unknown Sanctuary: A Pilgrimage from Rome to Israel*. New York: Bloch Publishing, 1971.

## Other Books of Interest

Bridger, David. *The New Jewish Encyclopedia*. New York: Behrman House, 1976. A single-volume encyclopedia.

Donin, Rabbi Hayim Halevy. *To Pray as a Jew*. New York: Basic Books, 1980.

Eckstein, Yechiel. *What Christians Should Know about Jews and Judaism*. Waco, TX: WORD, 1984.

*Encyclopaedia Judaica*. Jerusalem: Keter Publishing House, 1972.

*Facts About Israel*. Jerusalem: Ministry of Foreign Affairs, 1979.

Greenberg, Blu. *How to Run a Traditional Jewish Household*. New York: Simon & Schuster, 1983.

Hislop, Reverend Alexander. *The Two Babylons*. 2nd ed. Neptune, NJ: Loizeaux Brothers, 1959.

# Index

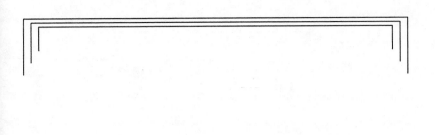

## About the Author

Kimberly E. Hanke has been involved in the Noachide movement since 1988. She currently resides in Washington State with her daughter.